PUT THE VERMONTERS AHEAD

The First Vermont Brigade in the Civil War

George W. Parsons

 WHITE MANE PUBLISHING COMPANY, INC.

This White Mane Publishing Company, Inc. publication was printed by Beidel Printing House, Inc.
63 West Burd Street
Shippensburg, PA 17257 USA

In respect for the scholarship contained herein, the acid-free paper used in this book meets the guidelines for permanence and durability of the Committee on Production Guidelines for Book Longevity of the Council on Library Resources.

For a complete list of available publications please write
White Mane Publishing Company, Inc.
P.O. Box 152
Shippensburg, PA 17257 USA

Library of Congress Cataloging-in-Publication Data

Parsons, George W., 1927-
    Put the Vermonters ahead : the First Vermont Brigade in the Civil War / George W. Parsons.
        p.   cm.
    Includes bibliographical references (p.   ) and index.
    ISBN 0-942597-97-4 (alk. paper)
    1. United States. Army. Vermont Brigade. 2. Vermont--History-
-Civil War, 1861-1865--Regimental histories. 3. United States-
-History--Civil War, 1861-1865--Regimental histories. I. Title.
E533.4.P37 1996
973.7'443--dc20   96-2060
                                                            CIP

PRINTED IN THE UNITED STATES OF AMERICA

"I ACCORDINGLY DIRECTED THE OFFICERS TO FORM THEIR MEN OUTSIDE THE WORKS AND OPEN FIRE, AND THEN RODE BACK OVER THE FIELD TO BRING FORWARD THE VERMONTERS IN THE FOURTH LINE, BUT THEY HAD ALREADY MINGLED IN THE CONTEST AND WERE FIGHTING WITH A HEROISM WHICH HAS EVER CHARACTERIZED THAT ELITE BRIGADE."

COLONEL EMORY UPTON,
OFFICIAL RECORDS, MAY 10, 1864.

DEDICATED TO CAROL

TABLE OF CONTENTS

PHOTOGRAPHS

MAP KEY

▼ .... VERMONT BRIGADE

▬ .... UNION TROOPS

▬ .... CONFEDERATE TROOPS

▬ .... ROADS

▦ .... RAILROADS

〰 .... CREEKS AND RIVERS

〰 .... WOODLAND AND FOREST

⚏ .... ARTILLERY

MAPS

BY KELLEY DYMEK

BY KATE KENNY

ACKNOWLEDGEMENTS

Throughout the many years of searching for information, I have met many fine, knowledgeable people. They not only helped make the researching easier, but also gave me encouragement. The assistance and time given are greatly appreciated and not easily repaid. Thank you, each and everyone.

I want to thank those librarians in the many small towns in Vermont who assisted me and who at times literally opened their doors to me.

Thanks to the people working at the Vermont Historical Society who allowed me access to information.

Thanks you to the many dedicated town clerks who eagerly assisted me in obtaining such things as rosters, muster rolls, and who also directed me to others for help.

Particularly, I want to extend my gratitude to the following: Joseph Covais, founder of the Society of the Greek Cross, for his interest, photographs and letters.

To Kate Kenney, honor graduate of the University of Vermont and Civil War enthusiast, sincere thanks for all the help you gave me when I was researching at the University of Vermont archives and library. Thank you also for the time, dedication and talent in obtaining rosters of the Vermont Brigade, and for the maps you worked so hard to get for me.

Thanks and appreciation to Robert Titterton, author and historian and A. D. (Nancy) Slade, author and fellow member, S.O.G.C., as well as others for their encouragement and interest.

Thank you, Jeffry Wert, noted Civil War author, who gave me much needed advice and direction, and Nick Picerno, noted historian and collector of Civil War memorabilia, for his suggestions and kindness.

Thank you and sincere gratitude to Colonel Bruce Lawlor, Commander of the 86th Armor Brigade, Vermont National Guard, who wrote the postscript for the book and has been very helpful.

Mac Wyckkoff, historian and guide at Fredericksburg National Military Park; Wendall Lang, noted Civil War historian and collector; Jerry Sullivan, in charge of Lindenwood Cemetery, Stoneham, Mass. and member of V.F.W.; and J. R. (Bob) Powell, Sr., author and historian. Jim Enos, for his help in getting me photographs of officers of the Vermont Brigade. Thanks to you all.

Thank you, Robert Austin, and also his uncle Perry Austin for opening their home to me and giving me information about their relative, Orlo Austin, 11th VT. James Hanson, fellow Civil War "buff", who has given me support and friendship. Irene Guidette, and her sister Ivis Miller who gave me so much of the information about Gardner Hawkins.

Thank you to my publisher, Martin and Diane Gordon, for accepting my book and for suggestions and corrections of the manuscript.

I extend my sincere thanks and gratitude to the following family members: Gail and James Doherty, Steven and Laura Parsons, and Philip and Mary Parsons. They not only helped with my research, but also gave me the encouragement, love and understanding needed to complete my work. Thank you to my loving and understanding wife, Carol, for her patience and her support. She not only typed the whole manuscript, but also helped me edit the work. Her patience and determination helped me to finish my book. It was her suggestion that I write this book.

INTRODUCTION

The American Civil War produced many great fighting units, both in the North and South. There were over two hundred brigades in just the Union armies.

The 1st Vermont Brigade had a fantastic record. They stood firm on the field of battle and always held the line when ordered to do so, and never lost their flags to the enemy.[1] They marched over two thousand miles in their many campaigns. The brigade had the greatest loss of life of all the brigades in the Union army.[2]

In the four long years of war, the Vermont Brigade held the line at Savage Station, White Oak Swamp, Banks's Ford, Funkstown, and Charlestown. In the fierce fighting during General Ulysses S. Grant's Overland Campaign, that heroic unit took some of their heaviest losses and then went on to win some of their greatest victories.

In 1864 the Vermont Brigade helped save the nation's capital. They were then sent on to the Shenandoah Valley, aiding in the destruction of the Confederate army. That great fighting unit was the first to break the lines of the South's forces at Petersburg[3] and went on to join in the pursuit of General Robert E. Lee's dying army.

President Abraham Lincoln had knowledge of them. Generals requested their service often and praised their actions.

Those achievements are only part of the great record of that indomitable unit, "The First Vermont Brigade".

CHAPTER I

The Beginning

It was a fine June morning in Burlington, Vermont, in 1861. The quietness of the hour was broken by the sound of a military band. A regiment was on the march: the 2nd Vermont Volunteers. They were a magnificent body of men, both in spirit and physique. The ten companies forming that unit were specifically picked out of sixty by an adjutant general and inspector, called Baxter.[1] Those men represented almost all the counties in the state. It was the first of the three-year regiments to answer the call to the colors, and every man was truly a volunteer.[2]

Leading the regiment and carrying the colors was Color Sergeant Ephraim Harrington. He was the tallest man in the regiment, well over six feet, four inches.[3] In the next two years, in more than a dozen battles and conflicts, he carried the colors, earning a battlefield commission and advancing to rank of brevet major. By the close of the war he was a captain. Harrington was awarded the Medal of Honor for his bravery in action at Fredericksburg, Virginia, on May 3, 1863.[4]

The uniforms the men wore had been made in the town of Reading, Vermont.[5] They were gray with green piping. The piping was the way regiments distinguished themselves from one other. Early in the war the Vermonters discarded those uniforms and adopted the regulation dark blue of the Federal forces.

It was a stirring sight to see those fine young men marching off to answer the call from President Abraham Lincoln. There were tears

1

in the eyes of many who watched them; their loved ones marching to do battle in this country's most terrible war. As they passed by, the spectators could see a sprig of evergreen sticking out from the brim of their hats, the symbol of their state.

The 2nd Vermont regiment was mustered into Federal service on June 20, 1861, by Lieutenant Colonel Gabriel J. Rains of the regular army. He told the men they looked like a fine regiment and said, "I know you will fight. The South will also fight and blood will flow!"[6] That statement would prove to be all too true as it was played out in all parts of the country.

Lieutenant Colonel Rains was from North Carolina. A few months after he spoke to the Vermonters, he resigned his commission in the United States Army and became a brigadier general in the Provisional Confederate Army.[7]

A large train with twenty-four cars transported the 2nd Vermont regiment to Troy, New York. Large crowds greeted the men from the "Green Mountain" state. A group of men calling themselves "The Sons of Vermont" took charge. The regiment was then reviewed. The Vermont men again boarded the train and went on to New York City where a beautiful regimental standard was presented to them. That flag and many like it were later carried in twenty-eight official battles and thirty-seven other engagements, totaling fifty-three days of fighting. Not one of those flags fell to the enemy.[8]

The train rolled on into Philadelphia, where the men were warmly received. This city would always be remembered by the "Green Mountain Men" as a very friendly place. They received a good meal and lodging while they were there. Later in the war a fine hospital was set up there where the Vermonters received good treatment and care. Although the Philadelphians were friendly, the people of Baltimore were not. The men had to march through the streets with loaded muskets. They encountered little trouble though, finally reaching Washington, D.C., and camped just east of the capital.

In Washington the Federals were building their army, and fourteen new regiments were there with the 2nd Vermont. The new army was to be under the command of Brigadier General Irvin McDowell, soon to replace Brevet Major General Winfield Scott, commander of the United States Army, who was too old to take to the field of battle.[9] However, Scott's plan to surround the Southern states and cut off supplies, was ultimately adopted and was a major factor in the downfall of the South.[10]

The city of Washington was in turmoil. Confusion was everywhere. Things needed to be organized, and with great speed, because the one thing the North was sure of was that Confederate General Pierre Gustave Toutant Beauregard had an army of twenty thousand, which was growing every day. It was feared they would march on the city, and the capital would fall to the Rebels. All would be lost!

Under McDowell's direction, the Federals marched across the Potomac River. The movement took two weeks, from July 1 to 15, 1861. They set up camp near Alexandria, Virginia. The 2nd Vermont regiment came in on July 10, 1861. They were brigaded with the 3rd, 4th and 5th Maine regiments, under command of Colonel Oliver Otis Howard.[11] Colonel Howard's brigade was assigned to Brigadier General Samuel Peter Heintzelman's division as the 3rd Brigade. The total force of that army was twenty-eight thousand men and guns.[12]

On July 16, marching in a westerly direction by several routes, Howard's brigade brought up the rear. Colonel Henry Whiting and the rest of the officers of the 2nd Vermont marched on foot as there were no horses. It was midnight before the men fell out exhausted by the side of the road. The next day they reached Sangster Station which had been vacated by an Alabama regiment. The boys helped themselves to the supplies left behind as they were hungry and had used up all that they had been issued. They were new to making war.

Up to that time McDowell had led his troops well and was ahead of General Beauregard. He lost the advantage, though, when the Federals went into Fairfax Courthouse, Virginia, and camped for two days. The loss of those days allowed Beauregard to be reinforced by General Joseph E. Johnston who was with the Army of the Shenandoah. His forces arrived in the middle of the battle of Bull Run, adding ten thousand men and thirty more guns.[13] That caused disaster to the Federal army.

Colonel Howard had been ordered to halt his brigade at the crossroads. McDowell had feared that the Confederates would attack down the turnpike and cut him off in the rear. Howard waited more than four hours, listening to the sound of the battle from across Bull Run. The Confederates were pushed back over a mile behind the turnpike. The battle was going well for the North, with some Southern troops throwing down their arms and in full retreat toward Manassas, until Johnston's men entered the battle. Their entry caused panic among the inexperienced Union regiments. Heintzelman sent for Howard's brigade to strengthen his hard-pressed troops.

The brigade marched by way of Sudley Ford, the long route. Men fell by the side of the road from heat exhaustion. On the way they began meeting Union troops in retreat. It was not an encouraging sight, especially for the men going into battle for the first time.

The battle of First Bull Run or Manassas, as the South called it, was fought mainly around the property owned by a Mrs. Henry. That area became the focal point where Howard's brigade started their fighting. Captain James B. Ricketts' Union battery was holding that position on the hill. Twice the battery was lost to the South, and twice regained. In the end though, the guns had to be abandoned, and were taken by the Confederates.[14]

When Howard's brigade rushed onto the field they found no friendly troops. In fact, they were the only Union troops in the area. Later in his report on the battle, Colonel Whiting said, "I saw no organized troops at all!"[15] The 2nd Vermont led the brigade up the slope and over the crest of the hill, where the enemy's guns began to take a toll on them. Corporal Russell H. Benjamin of Company C was killed by one of the very first shells. He was the first man from the Vermont Brigade to be killed in action.[16] Sergeant Urban A. Woodbury's arm was severed and eight other men were wounded. Those men were among Vermont's first casualties. Woodbury was taken prisoner and later exchanged; and he re-enlisted as a captain in the 11th Vermont.[17]

Moving into a hollow that provided better cover, Colonel Whiting ordered the Vermonters to fire. In the meantime Colonel Howard was trying to get the brigade together. Confusion was everywhere, due not only to the artillery fire but also due to the lack of experience of the men and officers. The Vermonters formed the first line out in front. The 4th Maine was a little to the rear of them. The second line was made up of the 3rd Maine and the remnants of the 5th. Most of the men of the 5th Maine had scattered under the heavy artillery fire of the Confederates.

The 2nd Vermont found themselves alone on the ridge. They were only three hundred yards from the Confederate troops led by Brigadier General Thomas J. Jackson. It was during that battle he received his nickname, "Stonewall". Brigadier General Bernard E. Bee was credited as having said, "Look at Jackson, standing there like a stone wall."[18] Jackson would carry this nickname for the rest of his life. His brigade came to be known as the "Stonewall Brigade".

When the command to open fire was given by Whiting, the 2nd Vermont fired ten to fifteen rounds per man. That made most of Jackson's brigade fall back into the protection of the woods. Captain James H. Walbridge, commander of Company A, asked Whiting if he could move his men to the flank, as the Northern forces were starting to press the attack from that point. The request was granted and Company A began the move. They were armed with the Springfield musket, a smooth bore weapon that could do a lot of damage, especially at close range; which was just over two hundred yards.

Lieutenant Colonel George Jerrison Stannard, 2nd Vermont, saw Captain Walbridge move off to the flank. He knew it was not a good move and asked Walbridge to return his men to the lines; but because the move was okayed by Colonel Whiting, he let the company of men stay where they were. The 2nd Vermont held their position for over a half hour. Those soldiers were the most advanced of any of Howard's regiments. Realizing they were receiving heavy fire from Jackson's brigade, Colonel Howard tried to bring up other regiments of his brigade. The 3rd Maine had tried to support the Vermonters in the first rush of battle, but, having come under heavy fire from the enemy artillery, they had retired back over the hill. Quickly Howard settled his regiment down and brought them back over the hill to the welcome support of the hard-firing Vermonters. The men from Maine started firing over the heads of the Vermonters. That help gave Whiting the opportunity to give the order to the Vermonters to retire. Due to the heavy and devastating artillery fire, only some of the men heard the order. The remaining men retired only after all their ammunition was gone.

Company A though was still fighting. They had joined with a battalion of United States regulars, under command of Major George Sykes. As a veteran of the Mexican War, and also having fought Indians in the West, he had the experience to lead. When Sykes and his regulars started their retreat, they were the only men that kept order and did not panic.[19] When the retreat of the Union forces began, Walbridge detached Company A from those regulars and retired them with the rest of the retreating "mob" of the Union army.

The 2nd Vermont fell back by company and squads. When they reached the shelter at the brow of the hill, the regiment was reformed. It was the only regiment of Howard's brigade that retired as a unit. When they returned to the turnpike, they found everything in total chaos. Men, artillery, wagons and equipment from all units were scattered everywhere. Whiting thought that the colors of the regiment were lost. He had been told that the captain of the color company had been hit and had not retired from the field. The truth of the matter was that Captain Edward A. Todd of the color guard was helped from the field by his men and Lieutenant Colonel Stannard placed him on a stray horse. Later that night he reached the camp of the Vermonters. It wasn't reported who brought the colors off the field, but they were safe.[20]

With disorder everywhere and the regiment broken up, it was everyone for himself. The men finally retreated to their former camp grounds at Centerville, where the 2nd Vermont was finally reorganized. Only one in twenty men had lost their rifles.

In the first battle of Manassas, two men were killed and thirty-four wounded. Thirty men were missing, thirty-one captured. Of the captured, twenty were badly wounded, and three of those men died of their wounds a few days later in Richmond.[21]

The 2nd Vermont regiment survived its baptism of fire there at Bull Run, and those men would be used as the foundation for the 1st Vermont Brigade, which was to go on to become one of the best units in the Union army.

USAMHI

Major General William F. Smith

After the Union's devastating defeat at Bull Run, the men from Vermont were very downhearted. That was mostly due to their leadership, which would eventually change. Those soldiers had "seen the elephant", a term that evolved during the Civil War, meaning the soldiers had gone through their first battle.

Because of the poor morale, Whiting started stricter discipline. Better equipment and new Enfield rifles were issued. By the 6th of August the men of the 2nd Vermont, again in top form, were reviewed by General McDowell. He commented that the troops were in good condition.

During the first week of September, 1861 the 2nd Vermont was brigaded with the 3rd Vermont and the 33rd New York. Along with an artillery battery, under command of Brigadier General William F. Smith, they moved to a position across Chain Bridge and helped build fortifications that would encircle Washington.

CHAPTER II

The Brigade

In the fall of 1861, Brigadier General William F. Smith suggested to Major General George B. McClellan that he should form a brigade of Vermont troops as other states were doing. McClellan was already forming the Army of the Potomac and so, on October 15, the Vermont Brigade was formed.[1]

Smith, nicknamed "Baldy", was born in St. Albans, Vermont. He graduated from West Point in 1845 as an engineer officer. At the start of the Civil War he was promoted to the rank of colonel, leading the 3rd Vermont regiment. After being appointed to the staff of General McDowell, he was promoted to brigadier general in August 1861.[2] Smith was a very controversial man, crossing swords with many of his counterparts. Some generals praised him though, Ulysses S. Grant, William T. Sherman, and George Thomas among them; and Smith did a fine job for the Union armies throughout the war. Probably one of his greatest achievements was initiating the formation of the Vermont Brigade.

The five regiments of the Vermont Brigade were brought together at Camp Griffin, and those units would stay together throughout the whole terrible war.[3] Even though the men's enlistments would expire in 1864, most of the men would sign over until the end of the war. They would eventually be known as some of the best fighters and would have the highest loss of life among more than two hundred brigades in the Federal army.[4]

7

8

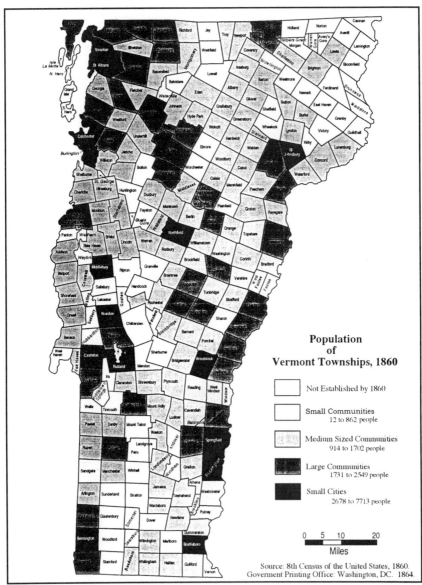

Population
of
Vermont Townships, 1860

Not Established by 1860

Small Communities
12 to 862 people

Medium Sized Communities
914 to 1702 people

Large Communities
1731 to 2549 people

Small Cities
2678 to 7713 people

0   5   10   20
Miles

Source: 8th Census of the United States, 1860.
Goverment Printing Office: Washington, DC. 1864.

Kate Kenny

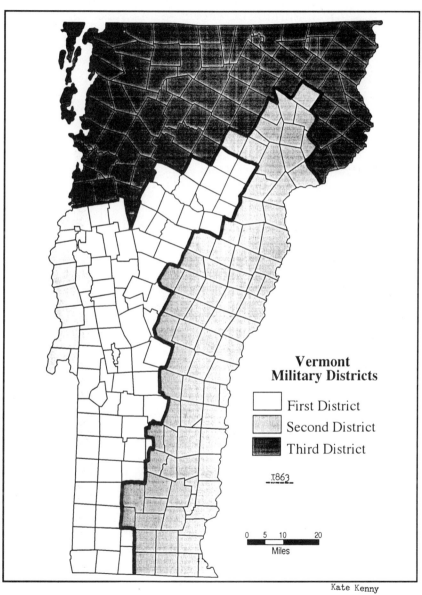

**Vermont
Military Districts**

First District

Second District

Third District

1863

0 5 10   20
Miles

Kate Kenny

Each regiment had its own characteristics and most of the commissioned and non-commissioned officers were known to the men in the ranks as they came from the same area in Vermont.

The 2nd Vermont, the senior regiment, was mustered in on June 20, 1861, in Burlington. Known as a fighting regiment, they had been engaged at First Manassas, one of twenty-eight battles listed to them.[5] They would uphold the honor of the state of Vermont. That was proved time and again by their excellent record in the ensuing four long years of war.

The 3rd Vermont was mustered in on July 16, 1861, in St. Johnsbury. Most of the men came from eastern, central and northern towns. They were recruited from the following areas: Company A from Springfield; Company B from the little town of Coventry; and Company C from Wells River. Members of Company D were from Charleston, Company E from Johnson and Company F from Hartford. Company G's men came from St. Johnsbury and Company H from the only town in the western part of the state, St. Albans. Company I came from Guidhall and Company K from the East Montpelier and Calais areas.[6] Most of those men were large in stature for those times, averaging over five feet ten inches in height and weighing over one hundred sixty pounds. They were led by Lieutenant Colonel Thomas O. Seaver, a gallant officer. Hard fighting lay ahead for them in the battles of the Wilderness, Spotsylvania, and Cold Harbor in 1864. One hundred and four men, along with Colonel Seaver, Lieutenant Colonel Samuel E. Pingree and Major Thomas Nelson would be discharged from the service after their enlistment was up. The regiment was then made into a battalion of six companies, under the command of Major Horace W. Floyd, who led the men through the last year of the war and brought them home July 1865.[7]

In Brattleboro, the 4th Vermont was mustered in. The men came from the southeast part of the state. Company A came from Bennington; Companies C, E, and K from Windsor County; Company B from Orange County and Company D from Orleans County. Company F and Company I were men from Windham County. Companies G and H were formed in Washington and Caledonia Counties.[8] It was September 21, 1861, and that regiment would be the first Vermont regiment to be issued the dark blue uniforms of the Federal army. The unit would take the brunt of the heavy skirmishing at the first battle of Fredericksburg, when they were placed as the advance skirmish line of the VI Corps. After losing one hundred and forty-one officers and men at the battle of Weldon Railroad, they would go on to take part in the great victories at Cedar Creek and Petersburg.

The 5th Vermont was mustered into service on September 23, 1861, in St. Albans. Most of those men came from both large and small towns in the west and north. St. Albans produced Company A, Middlebury Company B; Swanton provided the men of Company C and Hyde Park Company D. Most of the recruits for Company E came from Manchester and those of Company F from Conwall. Rutland claimed credit for Company G and Brandon for Company H. Company I came from the large town of Burlington and Company K from Richmond, Vermont.[9] They were ordered to Washington, D.C., as soon as they took the oath, but due to a lack of uniforms and rifles, they were delayed a few days. Colonel Henry A. Smalley led the regiment for a short time. From September 1862 on the regiment was led by Lieutenant Colonel Lewis A. Grant. He would later command the Vermont Brigade and lead it to some of its greatest victories. The 5th would do some hard fighting at Savage Station, the Wilderness, Spotsylvania, and Petersburg. There the flag of the 5th Vermont would be the first to fly over the captured positions of the Confederates.[10]

When their three-year term was up, the regiment lost, due to discharge, one hundred and seven men, including officers. That left no field officers and therefore the regiment was formed into a battalion, under the command of Captain Addison Brown, Jr. Transferring from the 4th Vermont, he was promoted to lieutenant colonel. However, he served only a short time, and was mustered out because of a disability. The 5th was then taken over by Lieutenant Colonel Ronald A. Kennedy, another courageous officer from the 3rd Vermont.[11] Lieutenant Eugene O. Cole from the 2nd Vermont was promoted to major and transferred into the 5th. The 5th Vermont produced excellent examples of leaders rising from the ranks. When mustered out of service in June 1865, of the twenty-four officers, everyone had enlisted as a private.[12]

The 15th of October 1861, the 6th Vermont was mustered into service at Montpelier. Those men came from many areas of the state. Company A came from the area near the town of Monkton; Company B from the Bradford area; Company C from the Woodstock area; and Company D from the Troy and Coventry areas. Danville claimed Company E and the Burlington area Company F. Company G came from both the Moretown and Warren areas, while Company H came from Waitsfield. Company I came from Essex and Company K came from the Sheldon, St. Albans area.[13] On the 26th of October they joined the other Vermont regiments at Camp Griffin, making the brigade complete. There was a great deal of sickness in the brigade's ranks and more than fifty men died in the 6th Vermont alone before the men went into active service.[14] Under the leadership of Colonel Elisha L. Barney they would excel on many battlefields. A colonel of the 7th Louisiana would surrender his sword to Colonel Barney. At Petersburg, one of the final battles of the war, the 6th's flag was one of the first to fly over the captured positions. October 1864 would end the three-year terms for the officers and men of that courageous regiment. When they were mustered out, the regiment had only three hundred and twenty officers and men. Those were the ones who had re-enlisted and were still on the rolls. They were split into six companies and made into a battalion.[15] At the close of the war, Lieutenant Colonel Sumner H. Lincoln would bring the 6th Vermont regiment home.

Good leadership was a keynote in all of the Vermont regiments. Over the course of four years of war, the Vermont Brigade would have only fourteen officers dismissed or cashiered from the service.[16] That was a small number when compared to the two hundred and seventy officers who served and led their men. The first commander of the brigade was Brigadier General William T. H. Brooks.

A West Point graduate, Brooks was sent to Florida during the 1840's where he took part in the war against the Seminole Indians. After that he fought in the War with Mexico. For his leadership in that war he won temporary commissions of captain and major.

Brooks was a firm, brave leader and many times he led his men right up in the front lines. He was wounded twice, at Savage Station and later in the battle of Antietam. There he was wounded in the mouth, but he never left the field until the battle was over. General Brooks was a tough old professional, who trained the men of the Vermont Brigade well and led them in battle the first year and a half of the war.[17] The Vermonters were very fortunate to have had such a leader at the start of the war, because

USAMHI

**Brigadier General
William T. H. Brooks**

there were few well trained officers to lead those citizen soldiers. Brooks was one, and another was General "Baldy" Smith.

At Camp Griffin the Vermont Brigade was organized and trained. The camp would be remembered by the young soldiers for two reasons. One, it was the camp they stayed at the longest and the other reason was the great amount of sickness in the ranks while there. Conditions were so bad that the governor of Vermont sent the noted Dr. E. E. Phillips to find the cause. Five other physicians were sent to help him. Over two hundred men, in the 5th Vermont alone, were on the sick list. The 6th Vermont had over a third of their men ill.[18] Disease was rampant and the tragic fact was that many of those men died of typhoid fever and other deadly illness before they ever got to the firing lines. The decision was made to move the men from the polluted area. Clean water supplies and new clothes were issued. Better housing was also provided, and the health of the Vermonters greatly improved.

From December until March 1862, the brigade drilled many hours. The men learned how to picket the advanced lines, guarding the lines and preventing the army from being surprised. Performed in all kinds of weather and night and day, picketing was not only tiring and boring, but dangerous. During training, a soldier, while on picket duty, was shot in the chest by an enemy sniper. Private George M. Lampher was lucky, though. He always carried a small Bible in his chest pocket. The bullet penetrated the Bible and stopped at the gospel of St. Luke. That saved his life and the only injury was two broken ribs.[19]

The men had some fun while training, though. On Washington's birthday, they celebrated with a field day. Races were held between units. They chased a greased pig and had a rough and tumble football game. They enjoyed their games after they listened to Washington's farewell address while standing in the mud so deep it covered their shoes.

When the men from Vermont first signed up to fight for the Union, very little thought was given to the question of slavery. As the war continued they realized they had another cause to fight for: the freedom of the enslaved Blacks. Vermonters understood the desire for freedom. While on picket duty, they would allow escaped slaves or as they were called, contrabands, to pass through their lines on their way north. On one cold night, twenty-four of them were taken into camp and fed. They were given warm clothing and then sent on to freedom.

The Vermont Brigade was assigned to the 2nd Division of the IV Corps. They were indeed in good company. It was a crack division, commanded by General "Baldy" Smith. It was said that that division was the best in the army, probably due to the brigade commanders it had. Brigadier General Winfield S. Hancock, Brigadier General John W. Davidson, and Brigadier General Brooks were three of those commanders.[20] With great fighting regiments and those leaders, it was easy to see why the 2nd Division was rated so high. By March 1862 the IV Corps and the Vermont Brigade were ready for the hardships and terror of the battlefield.

CHAPTER III

The Brigade's First Battle

On the morning of March 9, 1862, in the pouring rain, the Vermont Brigade, along with the 2nd Division, marched to Alexandria, Virginia. General McClellan was planning a new campaign. The plan was to get his army to Fortress Monroe and then march up the peninsula. His goal was to capture Richmond.[1] At that time many of the generals and men were amateurs at war; very few were veterans of the 1861 campaigns.

The march to Alexandria was not well planned and was done under harsh conditions. The men remained in camp there for two weeks before they boarded steamships for their voyage to Fortress Monroe. Bands played, flags waved and much cheering was heard. It was quite a sight to see all those ships carrying the IV Corps. Starting their expedition, they sailed only a short distance and anchored just off shore of historic Mount Vernon, home of the country's first president. The next day the fleet sailed down the Potomac River to Chesapeake Bay and then on to Fortress Monroe.[2] Upon arrival, the men saw the famous ship, *Monitor* lying at anchor. It was just after the battle against the Confederate ram, *Merrimac.*

On April 2, as the Vermonters disembarked, perhaps they realized that they were going to be a great part of the history of their country, as their forefathers, the "Green Mountain Boys", had been during the American Revolution. The men were eager to help defeat the forces that were trying to break up the Union.

14

As the brigade marched past the charred ruins of the village of Hampton, they got their first look at what warfare could do to the country. The village was the oldest and once the most beautiful in the area. Camp was made in a large field near the James River.

After a good rest the troops marched up the peninsula. April 4 was a clear, warm day, and the men marched ten miles, reaching Youngs Mill. No opposing forces were seen.[3] The march was resumed the next day, but they only covered three miles because of severe thunderstorms. On April 6 they arrived at the Warwick River. The Vermont Brigade led the advance of General Smith's division and were the first units to reach the river, which ran north to south across the peninsula.[4] The Confederates, under the command of Brigadier General John B. Magruder, had built dams at different places along the river and turned these areas into forts or rebouts.[5] They had also dug rifle pits along the shore and mounted artillery on the slopes above. General Magruder had only five thousand men to man those defenses.[6]

The Vermont Brigade approached one of the river crossings called Lee's Mills. The brigade should have attacked immediately, but instead, they spent two days in a swampy and wooded area, with only the pickets exchanging shots and artillery fire with the enemy. They then were pulled out and camped on Garrow's farm. If McClellan had ordered an attack at that time instead of holding back, the North would have had a five to one advantage in manpower. That was to be the first of that commander's typical hesitations. General Magruder didn't understand either, and acknowledged that in a report.

About a month went by while General McClellan brought up his siege trains. The delay allowed the South to strengthen their positions. Throughout the delay President Abraham Lincoln was urging McClellan to attack.[7] When they finally did attack, it was the first one on entrenched positions made by the Army of the Potomac.[8] The Vermont Brigade was the first unit into battle, and was to be their first real test, except for those men of the 2nd Vermont who had fought at First Bull Run. Most of the fighting was done on the Garrow farm. On the morning of April 16, Federals moved into assault positions. When McClellan gave the order to attack, he qualified the command by saying he didn't want a general engagement at that time.[9]

The Confederates mounted guard while their band played the tune "Rosa Lee". Captain Thaddeus P. Mott's 1st New York Light Artillery Battery began firing on the Confederate positions.[10] Although that was supposed to soften up the enemy entrenchments, it only made them dig in closer along the river bank. They suffered little loss from the cannon fire. The 3rd Vermont moved to the river's edge while the 5th Vermont brought up hand-picked marksmen to shoot Confederate gunners. They succeeded and most of the artillery was silenced. At that point the engagement should have ended; the objective accomplished, but it did not. General McClellan was riding up accompanied by the Count DeParis, Prince DeJoinville and other royalty who were on his staff. As they approached, he overheard the report of Lieutenant Edwin M. Noyes, 3rd Vermont, who had just come back from scouting the river. He reported it would be easy to cross the river and that the Confederates were retiring from their positions. McClellan ordered Smith to engage in an assault. As before, he ordered him to attack but not to bring on a major engagement. Companies D, E, F, and K of the 3rd Vermont made the first attack. Captain Pingree, in place of the sick Captain Fernando C. Harrington, led the men.[11]

One hundred ninety-two men charged across the river, wading waist high, carrying their rifles and ammunition high over their heads. Heavy fire overwhelmed the men as they struggled in the water. Many were hit. One of the first to go down was Private William Scott, Company K, 3rd Vermont. As he lay dying, on the banks of the Warwick River, he praised the president and said he was not afraid to die for his country. It had only been a few months before, that same young man had been sentenced to death for sleeping at his post. At the very last moment President Lincoln had pardoned him.[12] Today, on a quiet roadside in Vermont, a small monument honors the brave lad.

It had been planned that Corporal Alonzo Hutchinson of Company D wave a handkerchief to let remaining forces know they had crossed over the river. That would have signaled more troops to be brought up. He never got the chance as he fell mortally wounded, by the side of the rifle pits. Before his death he relinquished the handkerchief to a fellow soldier and said that he was sorry he wouldn't get the chance to wave the men on.[13]

The men of the 15th North Carolina who had been guarding the rifle pits were driven out by the Vermonters, but they soon counter-attacked under the leadership of Colonel Robert M. McKinney.[14] That was quickly broken up by rifle fire from the Vermonters. Many soldiers on both sides died, among them Colonel McKinney. The Union forces were just holding their ground. Before the fighting was over, six more Southern regiments had to be put into the fight. There was much confusion especially within two of the Georgia regiments, but once they settled down, they started to counter-attack. The "Green Mountain Men" continued to fight, at-

Vermont Historical Society

William Scott
Company K, 3rd Vermont
The Sleeping Sentinel
K.I.A., April 16, 1862

IN MEMORY OF
WILLIAM SCOTT
THE SLEEPING SENTINEL
PARDONED BY
ABRAHAM LINCOLN
SEPT. 9TH 1861. BORN ON
THIS FARM APR 9TH, 1839.
ENL IN Co. K. 3RD. VT. VOL.
JULY 10TH, 1861. DIED
OF WOUNDS AT LEES
MILLS APR. 16TH, 1862.
ERECTED BY
THE WILLIAM SCOTT
MEMORIAL ASSOCIATION
OF GROTON, VT.

Author's Collection

Monument of the Sleeping
Sentinel, West Groton, Vermont

tracting heavy rifle fire from the front and both flanks. They expected support from the other side of the river, but received none. Captain Pingree, although wounded, sent two successive messengers asking for help. No reinforcements came. Instead came a message from Colonel Breed N. Hyde of the 3rd Vermont telling Pingree to retire his men, which he did, under heavy gun fire from North Carolina, Georgia and Louisiana regiments.[15] The Vermont soldiers, stumbling and floundering, retreated back across the river.

After the fighting, Captain Harrington took complete credit for leading that charge. He filed a report to that effect and also stated that he had saved the colors when they were dropped in the middle of the river. A few weeks later, it was proved he hadn't done any of those acts and Harrington was dismissed from the service.[16] The dismissal order was revoked in 1870.[17]

Some of the highest acts of heroism were carried out during that retirement. Corporal James Fletcher, Company E, 3rd Vermont, sick with fever, wading back from the fighting, saw many men wounded and left behind. He went back across the river and helped to save many of those soldiers. Julian Scott, a sixteen-year-old drummer boy, crossed twice to rescue the wounded. Later, he was awarded the Medal of Honor.[18] After the war ended, he became

**Lieutenant Colonel
Samuel E. Pingree
3rd Vermont Infantry**

a noted artist, painting many of the battles, such as Cedar Creek. That particular scene, a large mural, hangs in the statehouse in Montpelier, Vermont.

The 6th Vermont had made a crossing further down river. Five companies participated. Colonel Nathan Lord Jr. had been ordered to put only four companies into battle, but realizing the opposition's positions were heavily protected, he put the fifth company into combat.

Heavy losses by the 3rd and 6th regiments were taken during the recalls from forward positions. They no sooner arrived at the battle when they were called back. As they waded across the river, they were easy targets. The 4th regiment covered the retreat. They originally had been ordered to support the other regiments, but due to the strict orders from McClellan to Smith, they were held back. Ninety soldiers were lost from the 3rd Vermont, wounded or killed. The 6th lost twenty-three killed and fifty-seven wounded. The 4th had two men killed and ten wounded.[19]

More acts of heroism occurred within the 6th Vermont as the soldiers were retiring. Those deeds were noted. Mentioned for good service and conduct were Colonel Lord, surgeons Charles M. Chandler and Lyman M. Tuttle, Captains Edwin F. Reynolds and David D. Davenport, Company H; Captain Edwin R. Kinney, Company I, and Second Lieutenant Charles F. Bailey, Company D. The enlisted men mentioned for extreme bravery were: Sergeants Edward A. Holton,

Company I; Porter Crane Jr., Company H; Corporal Warren B. Dunshee, and Corporals Augustus T. Cox, and Patrick M. Duggan, both of Company A.[20]

Captain Davenport of Company H was wounded. His son Henry, a drummer boy of eleven, helped his father out of the water and to the rear. Going back to the river for a cup of water for his father, he had the cup shot right out of his hand. Unfortunately, although the captain was saved that time, he died later in the campaign of disease and exhaustion.

As Sergeant Rubuf L. Bellows of the 6th fell mortally wounded, Sergeant Holton picked up the fallen colors and called on his men to rally round them.

In his report about Lee's Mills, General Smith reflected that those acts of heroism were common with the Vermont troops. The Medal of Honor was awarded to Captain Pingree twenty-nine years later for great leadership. Sergeant Holton received a battlefield commission and also was awarded his medal thirty years later, both honors well deserved.[21]

In the aftermath of the battle, the Confederate commanders made many wild claims about the fighting at the Warwick River. Magruder claimed the Federals had been forced back at the point of the bayonet; when in truth, they retreated because of no support and heavy rifle fire. The Union General McClellan tried to keep a low profile about the outcome of that engagement. He and his fellow officers were well aware of the consequences of a poor showing. Brigadier General Charles P. Stone, after the battle of Balls Bluff in 1861, had been arrested and imprisoned without charges, due to a disastrous outcome of battle.[22]

The battle at Lee's Mills would probably have been a victory for the North if McClellan had not been such a weak leader and if he had supported his troops. Instead, it was a complete failure and some of his officers, trying to find a scapegoat, told stories about General Smith. They said that he was drunk all the time. Smith demanded a court of inquiry. Those officers finally signed a statement that the allegations were false and charges were dismissed.[23]

After the battle of Lee's Mills, the Vermonters won high praise from the officers of the Union army. Northern newspapers praised them. A New York paper wrote of their bravery and said that they had covered their state with glory. Even though that battle had not been successful, it was the start of the great record of the Vermont Brigade, and the first of many battles that they took part in as a unit.

When the Confederates left their fortified positions along the Warwick River, Smith's division, including the Vermont Brigade,

Battles and Leaders

Battle at Lee's Mills, April 16, 1862
Sketch by Julian Scott, 3rd Vt.

crossed the river and proceeded to Williamsburg. Brigadier General Joseph Hooker's division marched along the other side of the river toward Williamsburg by a shorter route. Hancock, leading Smith's division, came upon a bridge across a branch of the Warwick River. It had just been burned by the Confederates as they were retreating to Williamsburg. Hancock ordered four companies of the 2nd Vermont to drive off the retiring Southern soldiers and to secure the bridge. They accomplished their task but the bridge was too damaged to be used. Brigadier General Edwin V. Sumner, commanding general of all forces, ordered Smith's division to go back, cross the Warwick River again, and proceed to Williamsburg on the other side. With the Vermont Brigade in the lead, Smith's division came to an intersection before Hooker's division, so Smith was ordered to take the lead. At that time the Vermont men began to build the reputation as being great marchers. The men moved along so fast they were three miles beyond a placed called Halfway House before the orders to halt reached them. Brigadier General Erasmus D. Keyes, corps commander, after hearing how much ground had been covered, said to one of his orderlies, "If your horse has bottom enough to catch up with that Vermont Brigade, I want you to overtake them and order a halt. Tell them we are not going to Richmond today."[24]

The battle of Williamsburg was fought with little planning and poor communications. The Union army lost over two thousand men.[25] Brigades were ordered from one place to another, among them the Vermont Brigade. Incompetence and indecision led to the success of the Confederates as they finally reached Richmond, virtually unopposed. So many Union men were lost because of poor decisions. Had the Vermonters been sent in pursuit earlier, perhaps the Confederates wouldn't have reached Richmond and been able to regroup. That battle was typical of McClellan's campaigns, and was part of the reason the Army of the Potomac's record was forged in blood and blunders.

After allowing the Confederates to escape at the Battle of Williamsburg, it could be considered only a limited victory. One outstanding part of that battle for the Union was Hancock's great leadership. He led his re-enforced brigade, defeated the Confederate forces in his front and forced them to retire.[26]

The Vermont Brigade began a long and arduous march up the peninsula, stopping at New Kent Courthouse and Cumberland Landing. They then proceeded to Whitehouse. That camp was to become the Army of the Potomac's major supply base. There, while the Vermonters rested, General McClellan organized the new Army of the Potomac.

CHAPTER IV

War on the Peninsula

On May 18, 1862, Major General George B. McClellan formed the VI Corps. McClellan's job was to build the Army of the Potomac, a task he was well fitted to perform. The VI Corps was one that survived, fighting right up to the end of the war. The corps also would be very successful and victorious in many of its battles. No other unit in the Army of the Potomac or any other army would meet the enemy as many times.[1]

McClellan planned to take Richmond with an army consisting of more than 100,000 men. Two divisions made up the VI Corps. Brigadier General Henry W. Slocum, commanded the 1st Division. The 1st New Jersey Brigade, one of three brigades, included the 1st, 2nd, 3rd, and 4th New Jersey regiments, under the command of Brigadier General George W. Taylor. The 2nd Brigade, commanded by Colonel Joseph J. Bartlett, included the 5th Maine, 16th and 27th New York, and the 96th Pennsylvania. The 3rd Brigade, commanded by Brigadier General John Newton, had the 18th, 31st, and 32nd New York, and the 95th Pennsylvania.[2]

The 2nd Division, which had never been routed from the field, had been transferred from the IV Corps. It was under the command of Brigadier General William F. "Baldy" Smith. Brigadier General Winfield S. Hancock commanded the 1st Brigade. The brigade included the 6th Maine, 43rd New York, 49th Pennsylvania, and the 5th Wisconsin. The 2nd Brigade, better known as the Vermont Brigade, was commanded by Brigadier General William T. H. Brooks.

At that time, the 2nd 3rd, 4th, 5th, and 6th Vermont regiments made up this famous unit. The 3rd Brigade, commanded by Brigadier General John W. Davidson, was comprised of the 7th Maine, 20th, 33rd, 49th, and 77th New York regiments. Seven artillery batteries and two cavalry brigades were also part of the VI Corps at that time.[3]

McClellan put his plan into operation by May 22. The Peninsula Campaign, or Seven Days Battles as it was sometimes called, was about to begin. The VI Corps, under command of Brigadier General William B. Franklin, was holding the right side of the Union line on a ridge near Gaines Mill. They were only eight miles from Richmond. In that particular area, many of the fine Southern homes and farms were actually guarded by Union troops, but that protection ended as total war broke out.

The Vermont Brigade moved forward three quarters of a mile from the banks of the Chickahominy River. The only cannon fire that could be heard was that from another battle at Fair Oaks or Seven Pines. The men of the brigade heard the artillery fire all day.

Meanwhile, the III and IV Corps were moved across the river within six miles of Richmond. About that same time General Robert E. Lee took over as leader of the Army of Northern Virginia, replacing the wounded Joseph E. Johnston.

In the opening battle, the Federals put up a good and bloody fight, driving the Confederates back toward Richmond. The Vermont Brigade crossed the river by way of a grapevine bridge.

The grapevine bridge was built by the 5th New Hampshire regiment and would be finished on May 29.[4] It began to rain well into the night and the river became a rushing torrent. Other bridges were washed away, but not the grapevine bridge. It had been built with logs, laid on posts and tree stumps, then interlaced with grapevine. There were no nails, spikes or wooden pins used to hold it together. That sturdy structure was built with the help of men from the 64th New York and the Irish Brigade; about a thousand men working chest high in water. General Sumner had asked Colonel Edward E. Cross if anything was needed to help get the job done. The colonel said that a barrel of whiskey would do the trick. The bridge was finished in two days. It would help save the Union from defeat, allowing supplies and artillery to get across, as well as the men of Sumner's division. Had they not been able to cross, the battle of Fair Oaks would have been lost.

The Vermonters marched up the right side of the river to Golding's Farm. They kept strong picket lines out and were constantly under artillery fire. It was three o'clock on June 25 when they reached the farm, and it appeared that the enemy was ready to attack. Colonel George T. Anderson's Georgia Brigade attacked Hancock's men and the 4th Vermont was sent to help. Hancock placed the Vermont fighters with the 5th Wisconsin and the 43rd New York. The "Green Mountain Men" were in good company. Heavy Union fire halted the attack. Then the 6th Vermont added their rifle fire to end the enemy advance. It was dark by the time the Georgia regiments were driven back, having taken heavy losses, over two hundred men from two regiments alone.[5] That was twice the loss of the Union troops. The battle honor was officially given to the Vermont Brigade, and they bore it on their colors as "Golding's Farm".

The main part of McClellan's army was on the north side of White Oak swamp, on their way to Savage Station.

Vermonters were part of a force that was to hold Magruder's men at Savage Station, so that McClellan's men could continue to march out of the area. The Federals marched toward White Oak Swamp, and long lines of wagons, guns, and men filled the road to Savage Station. Any supplies that couldn't be taken were destroyed. Large, brilliant fires lit up the area. As the Vermont Brigade marched to Savage Station they were under constant heavy artillery fire from across the river. The men of the Vermont Brigade exchanged rifle fire with the enemy. The dead and wounded lay along the way. Long lines of railroad cars, filled with gun powder and other ammunition, were deliberately set on fire by Union engineers. The cars were set loose and plummeted down a grade to a bridge where they exploded in one great fire ball, fragments of shells and cars going in all directions. That was a sight the Vermont soldiers would never forget. Destruction caused by fires and gunfire made the men's spirits sink to a new low.

Most history books pass over the battle of Savage Station with little notice. If the battle had been lost and the Union army cut in two, it would have been disastrous. Untold numbers would have been captured and supplies confiscated. The units of the rear guard saved that day and allowed McClellan's men to fight another day. Ironically, that rear guard action was supposed to be fought by both Sumner's corps and Major General Samuel P. Heintzelman's corps. However, Heintzelman did not remain on the field, marching on to White Oak Swamp, leaving Sumner to fight alone.[6]

General Franklin, riding with General Smith, arrived at Savage Station, but it was lightly guarded. Smith ordered his men to hold until relieved by General Sumner's corps. Only then did Smith continue on to White Oak Swamp. He was two miles east of the station when Sumner requested that he return immediately to support him. At double quick time and in the burning noonday sun, Smith and his troops returned. The Vermont Brigade was assigned

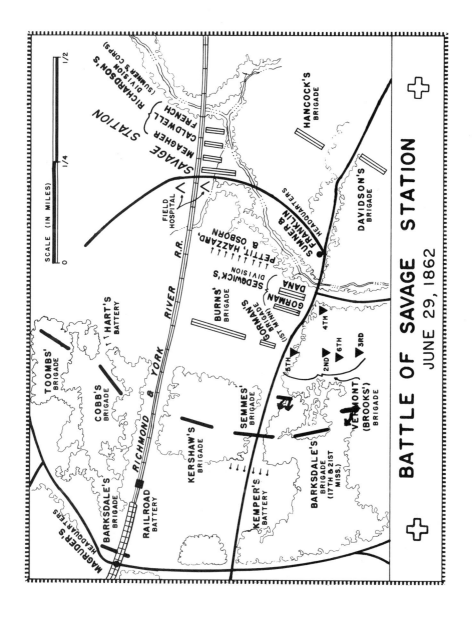

BATTLE OF SAVAGE STATION
JUNE 29, 1862

to Sumner's left flank, and the only fighting done by Smith's division at Savage Station, was that done by the Vermont Brigade.[7]

Magruder's forces consisted not only of his division and those of Brigadier General David R. Jones and Major General Lafayette McLaws, but a very impressive railroad gun, a 32 lb. rifled cannon. It was covered with iron plate for protection. The gun was called "the Railroad Merrimac". When the battle started, it was late afternoon. Artillery fire came from both sides. The Vermonters, after marching all day, the last few miles at double quick time, advanced on the left side of Williamsburg Road into the woods. Their orders were to stop the Confederate advance. Brigadier General John Sedgwick's division was already fighting on the right side of the road. They had engaged Brigadier General Joseph B. Kershaw's South Carolina regiments who were starting to overlap Sedgwick's left flank. The 1st Minnesota was fighting a desperate battle to hold on. Brigadier General William T. H. Brooks stationed two regiments abreast, the 5th Vermont to the right, the 6th on the left, the 2nd and 3rd Vermont in support, and the 4th in reserve. The 5th started the advance of the brigade. Twilight was coming on as they moved through the heavy woods. The thickness of those woods and the darkness and shadows from the night caused each regiment to fight its own individual battle.

Charging on through, the men of the 5th ran right over a New York regiment. The men of that New York regiment had refused to advance and were lying on the ground. The soldiers from Vermont cursed them out, calling them cowards. The enemy's batteries constantly shelled the woods, shredding bushes and trees, causing few casualties.

Finally coming out into a large, rolling field, the 5th Vermont was face to face with Brigadier General Paul J. Semmes' brigade. That unit consisted of the 10th and 53rd Georgia, 5th and 10th Louisiana, with the 15th and 32nd Virginia regiments held in reserve. There was also supporting artillery. The Confederate troops were in a gully and the 5th Vermont drove them out. Mingling with a few soldiers of the 1st Minnesota, Colonel Lewis A. Grant ordered a bayonet charge. The enemy fell back into the woods with the Vermonters firing into their ranks. All hell broke loose. Captain Del Kemper's battery cut the ranks of the 5th Vermont to pieces.[8] Over half the regiment was down, dead or wounded. Yet, through all of that, those courageous Vermont men held their ground, returning fire; even using the rifles belonging to their fallen comrades. Their rifles became too hot to fire. Those men of the 5th Vermont held that position for several more hours, withdrawing only when ordered to do so!

If it had been later on in the war, Colonel Grant would probably not have ordered that charge. He would have silenced the guns first; but that early in the war, Grant carried out the orders given him without question.

Out of four hundred men taken into battle, the 5th Vermont lost two hundred six men dead or wounded. It was a grim record and was the highest amount of casualties ever in the Vermont Brigade's regiments in one battle.[9]

Company E was hit the hardest. In its ranks were five brothers by the name of Cummings, who had come from Manchester, Vermont. There was also a cousin, William, and a brother-in-law named H. Clayton. Of the seven members of that family, six were killed and the other wounded severely. What a price was paid for the Union![10]

Other Vermont regiments didn't suffer as much. The 6th Vermont advanced to the left of the 5th and drifted toward the left flank of the line. In the darkness, a Confederate regiment came on their left flank without notice. A fatal volley was fired by them, and immediately, the Confederates retired. Sixty men from the 6th were cut down. The 6th Vermont held their position, retiring only when told to.

USAMHI

**Colonel James H. Walbridge,
2nd Vermont Infantry**

The 2nd Vermont was trying to move by columns through the thick woods with heavy artillery in front of them. Colonel Whiting ordered a halt and was about to order a bayonet charge, but in such close quarters that was impossible. Instead he ordered his men to start to yell and cheer. The forest rang out with their loud cheers as they forged ahead with the front rank firing on the enemy lines. After a successful engagement, Whiting said that it had been one of the best orders he ever gave. It bolstered the men's spirits and gave them initiative to keep fighting.

The 3rd Vermont supporting the 6th and advancing, suddenly heard a challenge from the darkness. They were asked who they were. A Vermonter replied that they were the 3rd Vermont. In answer to him came a volley of shots. The men returned the fire and remained in position for a good hour. Company C was hardest hit with half of its men going down.

Throughout there was much confusion. It was hard for anyone to know where the enemy was. General Brooks, a tough old soldier, rode on the left flank and, while trying to find the end of his lines, he and Major Walbridge of the 2nd Vermont heard movement to their left. He called out to ask who was there and the answer was the same question. Next he heard an order to ready. Walbridge turned and rode quickly back to his own lines. The gunfire missed him, but Brooks was wounded, though not too seriously.[11] That volley of fire, the last at the battle of Savage Station, probably came from the 17th or 21st Mississippi. Those regiments were on the extreme right of the Confederate lines.

In the rear guard action at Savage Station the Vermont Brigade lost one hundred and seven men killed, two hundred and seven wounded, and another seventeen missing. It must be noted, though, that of that seventeen missing, fourteen men stayed behind to care for the wounded. Even with the losses, the Vermonters helped stop the enemy's advance and were instrumental in saving a large part of McClellan's army.[12]

An observer at Savage Station, Count DeParis, reported that the battle was a great success for McClellan, when in reality, the only success he had was that most of his army and a large part of the artillery were able to escape the area and fight another day. Leaving thousands of wounded and sick men behind to be captured, destroying tons of supplies and equipment, did not make that battle a success. The Confederates suffered huge losses as well. The 10th Georgia probably took the most. Generals reported losses well over four and five hundred men in each of four regiments, twice the losses reported by Confederate brigade commander Semmes.[13]

At the close of the war it was found that the Union prisoners who had been left behind at Savage Station had very little care. Many wounded died. The Confederates, having taken such heavy losses as well, took care of their own troops first, leaving the Yankee soldiers to be cared for by their own men who had light wounds, as well as the few men left behind to help.[14]

After the battle, Smith ordered his troops to retire. After holding their position for hours, Brooks and his men finally started their movement to White Oak Swamp about ten o'clock in the evening. The dead were left on the battlefield. The wounded were placed in the hands of two surgeons and their attendants. A heavy rain was falling, so the wounded were laid on pineboughs to help make them comfortable. The rest of the division marched toward the bridge at White Oak Swamp. Many of the slightly wounded and sick hobbled along the line of march, causing confusion in the darkness. The units, many mixed up, reached the bridge by break of day on June 30. After men, wagons and guns crossed over, the bridge was destroyed, and the batteries led by Captains Romeyn B. Ayres, Thaddeus P. Mott and Charles C. Wheeler were positioned on either side of the bridge to stop any attempt made by the opposition to cross. The Vermonters tramped into a field littered with wagons and guns. They threw themselves on the ground and fell asleep, exhausted.

In the meantime, Stonewall Jackson marched his men in close pursuit of the retiring Federal troops. At the destroyed bridge he moved twenty-eight guns into position out of sight of the Union troops.[15] At two o'clock in the afternoon they opened up a heavy barrage of artillery fire on the unsuspecting Federals. Complete confusion reigned in the Federal camp. Some ran in blind panic, others hid. Officers wandered, looking for their units. Generals Smith and Davidson were sleeping in a small wooden house when it was hit by shellfire. They ran out just in time. The owner of the place was not so lucky; he was cut in half by a cannon ball. Smith left so fast that he left a very expensive watch and never did go back to find it. Most of the brigade took shelter from the attack over the crest of the hill at the edge of the field. General Brooks rode among them to calm them. A mounted officer, Captain Scrymer, sent by Smith, seeing the color bearers of one group, ordered them to uncase their colors and take positions one hundred yards apart. Then he told the men to rally around their colors.[16] Confusion still persisted as the men found it hard to recognize their colors. Realizing that, Scrymer shouted to the men that they all belonged to the state of Vermont and directed them to fall in with the colors nearest them and advance. They advanced, firing on the Confederate skirmishers. That battle was fought primarily by artillery. When Jackson opened fire, the Union batteries were put out of action, and were ordered from the field.

The mules used to pull the wagons stampeded in the confusion, and the valuable pontoons were left to be captured by the enemy. Captain James Duane of the engineer corps suggested to General Franklin that the pontoons be rescued. At first the idea was denied as it would be too dangerous to do so with the heavy gun fire. After some persuasion, Franklin finally agreed. Captain Martin T. McMahon volunteered to do the job. He asked General Brooks for volunteers from the Vermont Brigade. Colonel Grant's 5th Vermont was detailed for that dangerous task. Under heavy fire from Jackson's batteries it was impossible for the Vermonters to get the job done. They tried to pull the pontoons out, but couldn't. Finally, Captain McMahon made his way to the pontoons and set them on fire, destroying them. He was able to save one wagon with the much needed engineering tools. McMahon was awarded the Medal of Honor twenty-nine years later for that deed.[17] Later, when Sedgwick took command of the VI Corps, he made McMahon his chief of staff.

Jackson recalled his skirmishers and called off his infantry attack when he saw the advance and the strong artillery action. He received criticism for that. That decision was one of five times that Jackson failed to deliver in that campaign, a complete reversal from his Valley campaigns.

The men of Vermont were proud to fight side by side with the gallant men of the 1st New York Light Artillery, commanded be Captain Romeyn B. Ayres. Later promoted to command of the 2nd Division, V Corps, he and his men would fight in just about every battle of the Army of the Potomac.

During part of the campaign, the Vermont Brigade was flanked on the left by a large fine looking regiment, the 20th New York, which was a two-year regiment. It was made up of men of German descent, many of whom had served in German armies. McClellan used that unit as a show-piece. It had a good band and good looking uniforms. Unfortunately, it also had poor leadership and when the firing started those men were hard to find. As the shells began ripping through the trees and plowing up the fields, the regiment broke and ran.[18] Other units witnessed the retreat and Major Thomas W. Hyde of the 7th Maine said that all you could see were their large black hats racing to the rear. The Vermonters were highly praised by Major Hyde, who called them the magnificent Vermont Brigade, worthy successors of Ethan Allen and his "Green Mountain Boys".

The Peninsula campaign proved costly for the South. Jackson not forging across at the bridge prevented him from reinforcing Major General Daniel H. Hill and Major General James Longstreet at the battle of Glendale[19] The Vermonters had held fast and only retired when given the order to.

In the darkness of night, General Smith ordered his division out of line and quietly marched them along with the VI Corps, down a little used road that ran parallel with Quaker Road. Marching all night, they arrived at Malvern Hill. The men sank to the ground and slept for three hours. The spirits of the men were at an all time low. They had performed all that was asked of them and then some; yet, they had experienced no victories. It was clear to the men there was little or no leadership in the Army of the Potomac. During the long week of retirement or fighting retreat, McClellan's army had fought battle after battle. The soldiers had marched to new positions and prepared to fight. Most of the moving was done at night. Out of rations, they became weak and many had fallen out. Many were broke in health and had malaria. The ones who did survive those seven days and nights eventually went on to become the foundation of the Army of the Potomac.

The VI Corps wasn't needed at Malvern Hill because the infantry and artillery were able to stop the valiant but unsuccessful attack of Lee's tired army.[20] The Army of the Potomac was in a safe position at last, but General McClellan didn't think so. The river was not wide enough at that point, so he moved the men seven miles south to Harrison's Landing.

Smith's division of VI Corps was again the rear guard in that last withdrawal. Smith chose the Vermont Brigade to do that.[21] The 3rd Vermont brought up the rear. Their orders were to hold for two hours and then to withdraw, picking up stragglers and destroying arms found along the way. That march was to be the worst the Vermonters would endure. Heavy rain made the road a sea of mud. It was as if they were walking in glue. Men fell from complete exhaustion by the hundreds. They finally staggered into fields, cutting hay to sleep on. Some died on the roadside, some never recovered their health. After a couple of hours sleep they marched two more miles north of Harrison's Landing.

Lee took heavy losses and was frustrated at not being able to crush the Federal army. Some of his own generals had let him down by not carrying out his orders. His biggest failure in the campaign was General Stonewall Jackson. Jackson had become both physically and mentally fatigued due to lack of sleep and stress of battle. That made him an insufficient commander, and McClellan benefited by blunders made by Lee's generals.[22]

The Union army was in terrible shape. The men were spent. From a camp on a farm owned by a man named Ruffins, more than six thousand sick and injured were shipped out to hospitals in the North. Another twelve thousand were put on the sick rolls and marked unfit for duty. Many contracted scurvy. General McClellan saw his army melting away in front of his eyes. He requested more troops, fifty thousand the first time. Washington sent only five thousand. Many men, sick and broken in spirit, were discharged and sent home. If it had not been for the hard fighting and long marches of the brave soldiers, the Army of the Potomac would not have been saved. McClellan boasted that he saved the army and had lost only one gun, when in fact Lee had captured over forty guns.

General McClellan reviewed the troops July 4, and on the 8th, President Lincoln came to the camps specifically to see the condition of McClellan's army, and he reviewed the troops also. The men of Vermont waited for hours as they were the last unit to be addressed. When the president finally got to them, the men gave him three great cheers, saluting him.

Receiving orders from Washington, McClellan withdrew his troops from the Peninsula, and marched to Fortress Monroe. On

August 16, 1862, the VI Corps got off to a late start, because of a twenty-five mile long wagon train that was sent first. Again the corps formed the rear guard. The temperature was in the eighties, the sun beating on the men. The heat caused many to fall by the wayside but they would catch up in time to get on the transports. On the third day they reached Williamsburg. Three months earlier those same soldiers had come through there on the way to battle. In August they were headed north. The brigade marched to Yorktown, and then on to the village of Hampton. While waiting for transportation, the men went to the beach and dug for clams. Union gunboats mistook them for the enemy and fired upon them. Luckily, no one was hurt. They finally embarked on to the steamers with the rest of the men and sailed for Alexandria, Virginia. The short sea voyage helped many back on the road to better health. Better rations and rest aided them in lifting their spirits.

One bright spot in the Peninsula Campaign was the behavior of a fourteen-year-old drummer boy of the 3rd Vermont, Willie Johnson from Salem, Vermont. He was the only drummer to hold and keep his drum through the seven days of battle and the seven nights of retreat. He was the only one who could drum for the review of the troops. On the recommendation of General Smith, Willie was sent to Washington to receive the Medal of Honor for his fidelity and bravery. He was the youngest recipient at age 13.[23] He set a fine example for the men of 2nd Division and helped lift their spirits.

That campaign had been long and tiring. McClellan called the action a change of base when in reality it was a retreat. The retreats that were made were exhausting to the men. It had been a hard fought and disappointing venture for the Vermont Brigade. Many of the regiments were down to a few hundred men. The brigade had been tested in battle and they had not been broken. The Vermont Brigade was willing to march and fight for the Union again.

Years later it was noted that of the thousands of men shipped north to hospitals, over two hundred men from the Vermont Brigade died. Hundreds of others, being disabled, were discharged.

CHAPTER V

On with the War

In September of 1862, the war was not going well for the Union. In Mississippi Vicksburg was withstanding a siege by the Union, and the South was mounting campaigns in Kentucky and Tennessee. McClellan's attempt to take Richmond had failed. Leaders in Washington, having lost faith in McClellan, replaced him with Major General John Pope. McClellan was given a smaller force to defend Washington.

The two generals disliked each other intensely. Pope was not an easy person to like. A West Point graduate, he had connections in high places and had married into the family of Mary Todd Lincoln.[1] He was a braggart, loud and boastful; so much so that Generals Lee and Jackson made plans to end his bragging. That plan would start after the battle of Cedar Mountain.

Jackson joined Lee's forces, making the Confederate force a large army to contend with. The strategy was to attack, destroying Pope's army before it could be reinforced by McClellan's men. Finally, after the battles at the Fords of the Rappahannock and Gainesville and the second battle of Bull Run, the Southern generals would finally put an end to Pope's career and any other high command for him during the Civil War.

VI Corps was not involved in any of that fighting, held back, for whatever reason and by whom was never explained. Perhaps it had something to do with a remark that was made by McClellan to Lincoln. He said that they should let General Pope get out of the scrape he was in by himself. Shortly after a disastrous campaign, McClellan was given back the top command post with six corps of infantry, VI Corps being one of them.

Lee planned to take the war out of Virginia and gain support and supplies for the Southern cause. He marched through Maryland. In a field near Frederick City, a copy of Lee's war plans was accidentally found by a Union soldier belonging to the 27th Indiana. The plans were passed up the chain of command to McClellan. They revealed that Lee had sent General Jackson and Major General Lafayette McLaws with four divisions to capture the Union garrison along with supplies at Harpers Ferry. McClellan sent General Franklin, with VI Corps, over South Mountain at Crampton's Gap, with the intention of cutting off McLaws before he reached Harpers Ferry.

McClellan's plan was a good one but unfortunately it didn't work due to Franklin's slowness. General McClellan should have ordered Franklin to start the march immediately, but he didn't, and the march did not start until the next morning. The delay allowed McLaws and his Confederate units to reach Crampton's Gap first. Brigadier General Howell Cobb and the Georgia Brigade, along with General Semmes' and Brigadier General William Mahone's brigades, were ordered to hold the gap at all cost in order to allow Jackson and McLaws to get their men through and on to Harpers Ferry.

It was September 14th when Franklin started the march to Harpers Ferry, which began the Maryland campaign. He did that with a largely reorganized army.[2] VI Corps was under Franklin, but the 1st Division, IV Corps (under command of Major General Darius N. Couch), was attached to them. Almost a third of the army was made up of new regiments just mustered in a few weeks before. They had no training whatsoever. The 125th, 130th, and 132nd Pennsylvania were all nine-month regiments. The 13th New Jersey, 14th Connecticut, and the 107th and 122nd New York consisted of newly joined men, and the next battle would be their first. The veteran 2nd Division of VI Corps had only one regiment added to them — the 137th Pennsylvania. Having new regiments was not an asset, because many of those men, when they received the first volley of fire, broke and dissolved; others fired into their own units. The Vermont Brigade was fortunate in being in a veteran division.

Franklin and the VI Corps reached the gap just before noon on September 14. He took his time, studying the enemy's positions, and somewhat like McClellan, was slow to attack. 1st Division commander, Major General Henry W. Slocum, sent his first brigade in, led by Brigadier General Joseph J. Bartlett. It was three o'clock in the afternoon by that time, and Slocum had urged Franklin to attack finally.

Maneuvering through the fields to the right of the town of Burkittsville, they charged the small Virginia Brigade of Colonel William Parkman. They were at the base of the mountain, at the start of the gap. Parkman's brigade was composed of the 6th, 12th, and 16th Virginia regiments and Colonel Thomas T. Munford's cavalry.[3] They were posted behind a long stone wall that ran beside the field. In the first charge, Bartlett's brigade was stopped cold and took heavy casualties. Realizing that Bartlett was in trouble, Slocum sent Brigadier General John Newton's brigade and Brigadier General Alfred T. A. Torbert's 1st New Jersey Brigade to drive the Confederate forces back. The Federal forces outnumbered the Confederate troops by a four to one ratio.

Meanwhile, on the left flank, the Vermont Brigade was rushed through the town amid the cheers and yells of the townspeople, most of them women and children. Confederate artillery fire was falling in the fields and on the homes in the town. From the left side of town, Brooks, leading the Vermonters, sent the 2nd and 4th Vermont charging, holding the 3rd, 5th and 6th in reserve. The 4th

USAMHI

Brevet Lieutenant Colonel George W. Hooker, 4th Vermont Infantry

charged over the stone wall, capturing a number of Confederates who were posted there, and continued up the mountain, followed closely by the 2nd Vermont. They moved quickly to attack the battery that had been shelling the town. They moved so fast that they cut off Major Francis D. Holliday of the 16th Virginia and one hundred and fifteen of his men who had been tricked into surrendering.

1st Lieutenant George W. Hooker of the 4th Vermont earned the Medal of Honor for his part in the capture of the Virginia regiment. He had ridden in advance of his regiment and, realizing he had cut off the Virginia troops, took them prisoner, even before his own regiment had come up.[4] Lieutenant Colonel Charles B. Stoughton, with the rest of the 4th Vermont, went after the battery; but it was too late. The battery had limbered up and retired.

The 2nd Vermont, at the same time, advanced over the crest of the mountain and took prisoners during the advance. Most of them were wounded. Reaching the base of the mountain, they came upon a twelve pound howitzer abandoned by the Confederates. The horses were still tied to the gun. The Vermonters brought the gun back into their own lines.[5]

There were few casualties in the Vermont units because of their ability to advance so quickly. Very little credit was given those men in the successful attack on Crampton's Gap. Most of the credit was given to Slocum's division which had attacked on the right side of the gap. The Vermont Brigade took one hundred and forty prisoners in their attack. All four brigades fought with the utmost gallantry and bravery.

The victory at Crampton's Gap was an empty one. Harpers Ferry fell to the enemy, one of their most fruitful victories, due mostly to the slowness of Franklin. The full story of the Union victory at Crampton's Gap was that Newton's and Bartlett's brigades had taken part in the charge that drove the Confederates from the pass and had done a lot of fighting. The 16th New York had even taken a stand of colors in the wild fight on the mountain side. In the attack on the left, the Vermont regiments not only took prisoners, but had driven a battery off and captured the colors of the 16th Virginia. The 1st New Jersey's charge had taken them to the top of the gap. The fighting was heavy and caused a slight halt to their advance. That allowed the enemy to retire.

The next day, September 15, instead of attacking at break of day with his superior force, Franklin did just about nothing. He did send part of the 4th Vermont and the 6th Maine to hold Brownsville Gap, but that was only a small skirmish. On that same day Major General Darius N. Couch's division was attached to Franklin's VI Corps. He sent them off to Harpers Ferry. Next he sent his 1st and 2nd Divisions on the march to Sharpsburg, Maryland. From Pleasant Valley the Vermonters marched to the battlefield along Antietam Creek, six miles away. Smith's division was the first to reach the battlefield. They hurried across a creek to help Sumner's men. Major General John Sedgwick's division, II Corps, had been torn to pieces with losses of more than two thousand men.[6] Stonewall Jackson was ready to launch an attack on the exposed flank of the Union forces when Smith's men came to their rescue. Hancock's brigade stopped Jackson's attack and held the ground they took. Brooks' brigade came onto the field of battle next, and was sent to the aid of Major General William H. French's division. That filled the gap where

Author's Collection

The only monument, of the many battlefields that the brigade fought on, is at Antietam.

Generals McLaws and Early and their men had broken through and cut up Sedgwick's division.

During the battle of Antietam, McClellan had a two to one advantage in man power and yet committed less than half his forces to battle.[7] Lee, on the other hand, used all his forces to stop McClellan's piece-meal attacks. General Smith would later complain that he had not been ordered to use his other two brigades, and instead was ordered to support French's troops, thus losing an important part of the battle. He remarked that at two other battles, the same thing had happened and the enemy had benefited because of the blunders. Smith, who was very outspoken, was later pushed out of the war by General Ulysses S. Grant and the politics played by Major General Benjamin F. Butler. Smith was a fine general but had crossed swords with too many people in high places.[8]

The Vermont Brigade made a quick advance over the cornfield which was covered with the dead and wounded of both armies. They had advanced so fast they took only a few casualties. That allowed them to take the field and hold it for the rest of the battle. The Vermonters took position on the right flank of General French's men, taking cover wherever they could. It was at that time Lee's line was being broken in the middle and the 7th Maine was ordered to drive the sharpshooters out of nearby Piper Farm. The 7th was a small regiment, only one hundred and eighty men, and they weren't able to hold the farm and were driven back. Only sixty men came back with their colors. As they passed the Vermont Brigade, the Vermonters cheered that gallant Maine regiment led by Major Thomas W. Hyde.[9] Hyde's orders were given by Colonel William Irwin who was in command of the 3rd Brigade of Smith's division. He had been drinking when he ordered the advance and really had no authority to do so. Smith was unaware of that order and when he realized what was going on, ordered the men to retire. If Smith hadn't done so, the regiment would have been completely destroyed. Irwin left the service in October 1863. Twenty-nine years later, Major Hyde was awarded the Medal of Honor for his bravery.[10]

General Lee was being attacked by Major General Ambrose E. Burnside and the IX Corps on Lee's right flank. Darkness was coming on though, and the battle slowed and then stopped. Vermonters stayed at their positions all night. They could hear the groaning and the cries for help from the wounded and dying soldiers. They gave what help they could, but there were so many wounded it was almost an impossible task. The next morning Lee asked for a flag of truce to be able to take care of the wounded and bury the dead. That request was granted. It was not a good move on McClellan's part as it allowed Lee and his army to slip away to continue the war with many costly battles to follow.[11]

The Vermont Brigade marched from the battlefield after the battle through the town. The dead and dying were everywhere. Those sights they would never forget. They marched to Williamsport and later on to Hagerstown, Maryland, where they camped for a month. General Brooks was made military governor and the Vermont men drew duty as provost guards.

Lee wondered why the Army of the Potomac was still in Maryland. While thinking about it, he sent Major General James E. B. "Jeb" Stuart and fifteen hundred troopers on a raid that took them completely around the Union army. They destroyed government property and took shoes, clothing, and horses to outfit his army. The

2nd and 5th Vermont were rushed in railroad cars to Chambersburg, Pennsylvania, to stop the raids; but when they arrived, there were no signs of the raiders. They returned to their unit.

The brigade received two hundred and fifty recruits from Vermont, a welcome addition. The 26th New Jersey was also temporarily added to their ranks. That was a nine-month regiment and the men were as green as grass. The Jersey men were mostly bounty men and not a congenial group, but did look up to the Vermonters, knowing they were veterans and had built a fine reputation. Around that same time the men from Vermont noticed they were losing meat from their larder. It was pretty clear that the New Jersey men were taking it. The Vermonters took a large Newfoundland dog, owned by Colonel Andrew J. Morrison, a New Jersey officer. They killed, dressed it and hung the carcass in the meat larder. Sure enough, the meat was taken that very night. The news spread quickly and every time a Vermont soldier greeted a New Jersey soldier they would give him a friendly "bow-wow".[12] It was hard to beat the men from Vermont. Later in May 1864, when the 11th Vermont was added to their ranks, it enhanced the Vermonters' record, not distracting from it.

Changes were taking place within the Army of the Potomac. General Brooks was advanced to command the 1st Division of VI Corps. While in command of the Vermont Brigade he had come to have great respect for them and had great trust in them. Brooks had instilled iron in the brigade.[13] As he was leaving, the officers wanted to give him a gift. A solid silver tea set was chosen, and one of the officers stood up and asked who would be brave enough to give it to him. When he received it, there were tears in his eyes.

Some of the changes in command were not liked. Colonel Henry Whiting took over command of the Vermont Brigade. Many believed that Colonel Whiting was timid in battle, and he was not a Vermonter. He had been criticized for his actions at First Bull Run.

Another change came at the top of command. McClellan was replaced by General

USAMHI

**Colonel Henry Whiting
2nd Vermont Infantry**

Ambrose Burnside. On October 16 at New Baltimore, the VI Corps gave General McClellan a farewell review while the guns fired salutes and the bands played. He said good-bye to the Army of the Potomac, an army he built but could not lead.

The army was then divided into three grand divisions, a total of one hundred and twenty thousand men. Franklin commanded the left grand division which was made up of I and VI Corps. Smith was in command of the VI Corps. Major General Albion P. Howe led the 2nd Division and Colonel Whiting remained in command of the Vermont Brigade.[14]

During the previous campaign, the Vermont Brigade had sustained relatively few battle losses. Only one man was killed, and there were eighteen wounded at Crampton's Gap. Five were killed and fifteen wounded at Antietam. A sad part of that Maryland Campaign was the loss of men due to disease and the hardships of the march. More than fifty men died. Most of those men are buried in the national cemeteries at Antietam, Maryland, Arlington and Fredericksburg, Virginia.[15]

CHAPTER VI

Cold Mud and Battle

In November 1862 the VI Corps was on the march, stopping to camp just outside Stafford Courthouse, Virginia. There they stayed for eight days awaiting the pontoon bridges that would take them across the Rappahannock River. The delay was a costly one. Major General Henry W. Halleck took full blame for the mixup in orders that caused the delay, but it was the men in the ranks that ultimately would pay the price.[1] Eventually, five bridges were put across.

The area where Burnside's men would cross had been well scouted, and reports confirmed that it would be an easy crossing at the lower fords. Much to the surprise of his commanders, Burnside directed the troops to cross the river opposite the center of the city, right under the guns of Lee's artillery. Weather conditions began to deteriorate. Men became sick and were frostbitten. Some froze to death in the bitter cold. It was impossible to get fire started with snow falling.

During the delay by the Union troops, Lee was able to strengthen his positions around Fredericksburg, moving more troops into the area. When the fighting started, the Army of the Potomac paid a high price for the delays and slowness of their commanders.

December 11, the Union guns began bombarding the town of Fredericksburg from the north side of the river, on the heights, with little effect on the troops, but causing much damage to the town. The Vermonters had left their camps five miles from the banks of the Rappahannock, and marched to a position from which they

could cross the river when ordered to do so. Bitter cold made the
marching difficult, and the men could see little of the town or the
position of the enemy troops, as fog and smoke lay heavy on the
river, obscuring their view. That night the men camped on the frozen ground and the next morning crossed the river on a pontoon
bridge. They advanced one half mile to the Richmond Stage Road.

The ensuing battle would last five grueling days, marching,
maneuvering and fighting. On December 12 General Franklin didn't
commit the VI Corps to the main assaults on Marye's Heights, nor
was it in the attacks of the left or right flanks of the Union. Still the
Vermont Brigade had losses in that battle when they were placed on
the center of the line. Confederate artillery fire was heavy as they
moved into positions as advance skirmishers for the 2nd Division of
the VI Corps. All Vermont regiments were engaged in fighting during the next two days except the 6th regiment.[2]

The 2nd Vermont went forward to the front of the skirmish line
and drove the Confederates from their forward positions. The Southerners counter-attacked, trying to regain the lost ground. Again the
Vermont men stopped the attack, capturing several prisoners, many
of whom were part of Brigadier General William D. Pender's brigade, a good fighting unit. On Saturday afternoon, a strong attack
was made against Brigadier General Albion P. Howe's line. The 3rd
Vermont took the brunt of that fighting. Alabama and North Carolina brigades, led by Brigadier General Evander M. Law, fought hard.
To the right of the Vermonters was Brigadier General Alfred Torbert's
1st New Jersey Brigade. A deep ravine separated the two. The 4th
New Jersey was sent up the ravine to drive the enemy back. The
15th and 23rd New Jersey were sent to support the action. Through
a mixup in orders the two supporting regiments were withdrawn
and the 4th New Jersey was driven back after heavy losses. The
fighting became heavy, and the 3rd Vermont, under Colonel Seaver,
advanced up the ravine.

The 3rd was almost at the railroad when the attack started.
Seaver had placed his men well. The enemy did not catch sight of
them until it was too late. The Confederates were caught in a heavy
flanking fire and soon broke and retired with heavy losses in their
ranks. It was later reported that General Law lost two hundred and
fourteen men, killed or wounded. The 16th North Carolina lost fifty-
four officers and men, as prisoners.[3] During that battle Colonel Hyde's
lack of leadership became obvious. He did not command the 3rd
Vermont in that advance and shortly after he was asked to resign.[4]
It was in the Vermont Brigade's favor that he did so. Colonel Thomas O. Seaver then took command of the regiment.

The 4th Vermont was in support of Major General John Gibbon's division. They distinguished themselves by their steadiness and efficiency under fire and took the most casualties.[5] The 5th Vermont was engaged Saturday and Sunday on the skirmish line and gave good service in holding the line for the Union.

The night of December 13, 1862, was a night of horror for the men of the Army of the Potomac. By that date they had lost hundreds, even thousands of men. The dead and dying were everywhere; their cries and calls for help could be heard all through the night. That scene

USAMHI

**Colonel Breed N. Hyde,
3rd Vermont**

would be played out many more times on the battlefields of the Civil War. The Vermonters, as one of the units that did not take part in the previous foolhardy charges were able to carry the wounded off and bury their dead. Even with so many men lost, General Burnside still wanted to make another charge with the IX Corps upon Marye's Heights but was finally talked out of it by other corps commanders. That fighting had been a disaster for the Union.

In a cold, driving rain the Vermont Brigade marched back to their camp at White Oak Church. Later the weather improved, and so did the health of the soldiers with rest and food. The roster at that time showed 2,760 men present for duty. Twenty-four men had been killed and one hundred and twenty-seven wounded at the battle of Fredericksburg.[6] The Vermont warriors considered that battle only heavy skirmishing.

The 2nd Vermont was detached and sent to Belle Plain Landing to help unload supplies and build roads, which they did for the next three weeks. Belle Plain was the main supply depot for the North. The rest of the men went into a usual routine of inspections and drills, and even had a couple of brigade reviews.

On January 19, 1863, marching orders were received and the men from the green mountains started out with three days' rations. Four miles out they halted and were ordered to cross the Rappahannock River at Banks Ford. They were to attack the Confederates at Salem Heights. It began to rain. The roads turned into a sea of heavy, sticky mud. Everything became chaotic. Wagons, ammunition, and ambulances got bogged down. The pontoons used to cross the river presented the most problem. Even with hundreds of men and dozens of horses, those heavy floats could only be moved a few hundred feet. The troops began corduroying the road, cutting wood as they went. That march had become a disaster, men falling in the thick mud, swearing as they did so and wondering what madman had ordered the march. Burnside himself rode through the ranks and saw what a mess everything was. He ordered his units back to camp, thus ending the "Mud March". That was also the last straw concerning Burnside's leadership of the Army of the Potomac.

President Lincoln, after receiving complaints from the corps commanders, accepted Burnside's resignation. Before that Burnside had submitted a list of generals that he wanted removed. Burnside was allowed to return to command the IX Corps, and Lincoln appointed General Joseph Hooker to command the Army of the Potomac.

Hooker made improvements. He supplied the men with fresh bread and meat, revamped the hospitals and improved the care of the sick and wounded. When he bettered the ambulance service, it became a model for all armies. He also instituted the wearing of corps badges. Hooker had exhibited good fighting abilities at the battles of Glendale, Malvern Hill, and Antietam. His personal habits were another story. Women and whiskey were always in and around his headquarters.[7] The term "hooker" has been associated with the women who ply their trade in the streets of our cities, the type of women who visited his quarters.

In the winter of 1863 General John Sedgwick took over the VI Corps. He was a fighting general. Previously he had been wounded at Glendale and had led a division at the battle of Antietam, where he was wounded three different times.[8] Sedgwick was well liked by the men and, in turn, he liked their fighting abilities. As time went on he would

Joseph Covais, Private Collection

Major General John Sedgwick
Commander VI Corps

put the Vermonters into the heaviest fighting, and they never let him down.

Colonel Whiting resigned his commission as commander of the 2nd Vermont on February 6, 1863. He had also been leader of the Vermont Brigade, being senior colonel. He had helped make the 2nd Vermont into one of the best units in the Union army and the brigade one of the finest. In spite of those achievements, he was passed over for promotion many times. Speculation said that was because he wasn't a Vermonter and some thought he wasn't aggressive enough. Other officers called him an out-right coward. After writing his resignation explaining to his superiors that he had been bypassed, he went home to Michigan. In a way he was another casualty of the war.

The command of the Vermont Brigade went to Colonel Lewis A. Grant from the 5th Vermont. Originally a lawyer from Bellows Falls, he had very little military training, but through hard work and courageous leadership he mastered the trade of the soldier. He continued to command through some of the hardest fighting of the war. In the months that followed, he led his men at Banks Ford and took three battle flags. He would also take the Heights of Fredericksburg, thought to be impenetrable, and for those feats a grateful nation awarded him the Medal of Honor.[9] He

USAMHI

Colonel, later Brevet Major General Lewis A. Grant, Vermont Brigade

was wounded twice, but fortunately only slightly. Those were only a few of the many battles he would lead and receive high praise for.

The regimental commanders of the brigade changed. Colonel James H. Walbridge led the 2nd Vermont. The 3rd was led by Colonel Seaver. The 4th was led by Colonel Charles B. Stoughton. Lieutenant Colonel John R. Lewis commanded the 5th and Colonel Elisha Barney the 6th.[10]

The winter of 1863 took its toll on the men while they were camped at White Oak Church. Many of the sick were sent north to Philadelphia where there was better care. Sickness claimed more lives than bullets did. The spirits of the men began to improve as spring approached. In the winter they enjoyed snowball fights, especially against regiments they didn't get along with. The 26th New Jersey, a large nine-month group, considered themselves the best. They challenged the 3rd and 4th Vermont to an old fashioned snowball fight. It took place on February 25, and many came to watch. Both sides lined up in battle order, the New Jersey regiment outnumbering the Vermonters. The officers, mounted, gave the command to start. Back and forth went the fighting. Both sides gave it their all. It ended when the Vermonters captured the colonel adjutant and the chief quartermaster of the 26th New Jersey. The "Green Mountain Men" had not gotten off lightly, though. They had bloody noses, bruises, and black eyes to show for it. That mock battle helped release some of the tensions and petty quarrels that were prevalent among the regiments.

Snowball battles did not belong to the Northerners alone. The South had theirs between whole divisions and brigades. The first large one had four to five thousand men on each side. Officers rode their horses just as they would do in real battle. One particular battle occurred when Brigadier General Micah Jenkins' South Carolina Brigade was surprised by Law's Brigade. They had a large supply of frozen snowballs. Jenkins' men were victorious. To add insult to injury, the men from South Carolina ate the breakfast that Law's men were preparing when they were attacked. Lee's headquarters was right in the middle of that light-hearted skirmish. Upon hearing the noise, he came out to investigate. He was hit several times with snowballs. That was one of the few times Lee had to retreat.[11]

In preparation for another large campaign, there was another grand inspection. On April 3, 1863, the Vermont Brigade, along with the rest of the VI Corps were lined up and reviewed by General Hooker and his staff. That was just a warm-up for the next review on April 8 when President Lincoln and many other top brass reviewed the VI Corps. That was a busy time for the president as he also reviewed the III and V Corps the same day. The men realized that the spring campaign was not far off.

CHAPTER VII

Storming the Heights and Holding the Line

New orders were issued to the corps regarding what officers and men could take on the line of march. They were given eight days' rations, some to be carried in their haversack. The larger supplies would be carried in their knapsacks. With all the rest of the gear they carried, that would be a heavy load. The officers' supplies were carried by a mule instead of wagons. When wagons were used on the march, they stretched for miles and were more of a hindrance than help sometimes.

At the start of the spring campaign, or the battle of Chancellorsville, as it became known, the Vermont Brigade had over two thousand eight hundred men fit for duty.[1] The weather, again, played a role, delaying the march for two weeks. On April 27, General Hooker put his army on the march. The Chancellorsville campaign was about to start.

Hooker's plan was to send three corps to Fredericksburg as a diversionary measure. He wanted to draw General Lee and his army away while Hooker's troops attacked on the flank. That part of his plan went well. With more than fifty thousand men, he marched to the crossroads at Chancellorsville, Virginia. He was right in the center and rear of Lee's lines, but because of his indecision, and a surprise flank attack by Stonewall Jackson's men, the situation looked desperate for the Union cause. Hooker recalled two of the three corps

47

he had sent as diversion, leaving only Sedgwick and his VI Corps. The recall order was received after the I and VI Corps had already crossed the river at Pollock's Mill and Franklin's Crossing.

Saturday, May 2, 1863 the 1st, 2nd and 3rd Divisions of the VI Corps, under Generals Brooks, Howe, and Newton, crossed the river and were on the south shore on the Fredericksburg side. They moved into position the next day, ready to attack the Heights of Fredericksburg. General Sedgwick, having learned of Jackson's flank attack at Chancellorsville, realized Hooker was in trouble. He attacked with two divisions. Brooks' division was held in reserve. General Gibbon's men, part of the II Corps, were being held up in the town. For that reason, Sedgwick was forced to attack the positions on Marye's Heights.

General Howe formed his division into three lines of attack. Brigadier General Thomas H. Neill led the first line, including the 7th Maine, 77th and 33rd New York and five companies of the 21st New Jersey. The second line, under Colonel L. A. Grant, had the 2nd and 6th Vermont, along with the 26th New Jersey. The third line, under Colonel Seaver, included the 3rd and 4th Vermont and five companies of the 21st New Jersey. To the right of Seaver's columns, just across a stream called Hazel Run, Brigadier General John Newton formed his columns.[2]

In the attack, the Vermonters didn't have to worry about their right flank, as it was well protected by Colonel Hiram Burnham's famous Light Division, VI Corps.

Sunday morning, May 3, was a beautiful day. The weather was growing warm, though, and knowing the attack would literally be uphill, the men took off all equipment and clothing that had any weight to it. Knapsacks, cooking gear, and sleeping rolls all were piled along the roadside.

Orders were to take the heights at point of bayonet. At the signal to charge, the Union troops crossed a quarter mile of open ground to the heights

Joseph Covais, Private Collection

Sergeant Ephraim W. Harrington, later captain Company G, 2nd Vermont brevet major, April 2, 1865. Awarded the Medal of Honor for his actions at the Battle of Marye's Heights, May 3, 1863.

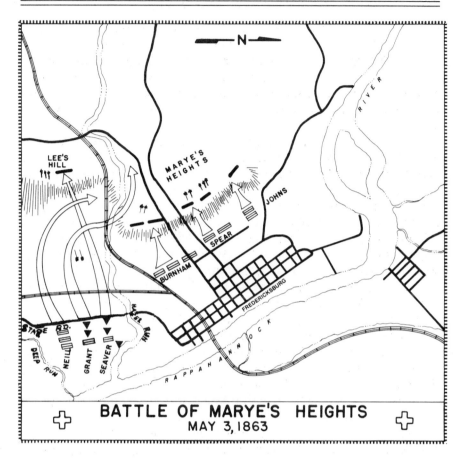

BATTLE OF MARYE'S HEIGHTS
MAY 3, 1863

above. Those who witnessed that gallant attack said they would never forget the sight of the VI Corps soldiers on that charge. The Confederates opened heavy fire on the attacking troops. The Vermonters moved so fast they took fewer casualties. They drove the opposing riflemen from their pits on the railroad embankment, then moved to the right, splashing across Hazel Run, and started the climb to the heights above. The 26th New Jersey of L. A. Grant's line held back. That caused the lines to become mixed up.[3] The 2nd and 6th Vermont were first in the advance. The Confederate gunfire was overpowering and the attack started to falter. During the attack on Marye's Heights, Colonel Grant disengaged the 2nd Vermont from the New Jersey men because they were mixing up the lines and not attacking. After straightening the lines, Grant led the 2nd Vermont and several companies of the 26th New Jersey and 33rd New York up the hill to the heights. There, Sergeant Ephraim

Harrington, 2nd Vermont, carried the national colors to the top, never wavering. That eventually won him the Medal of Honor.[4]

To the left was Lee's Hill where heavy cannon fire was coming. That position had to be taken. The 3rd Vermont took on the job. They faced Brigadier General Cadmus M. Wilcox's brigade, and three Mississippi regiments from Brigadier General William Barksdale's brigade.

Captain Martin's Battery F, 5th U.S. Artillery, moved along with the men from Vermont. They shelled their opponents, thus aiding the foot soldier in the charge. Cowan's 1st New York battery also helped.

Colonel Seaver, in the meantime, led the column that made the attack to the left of Lee's Hill. The 3rd Vermont first entered the rifle pits at the crest of the hill, closely followed by the 4th and 5th regiments.[5] A short hand to hand fight drove Barksdale's Mississippi regiments from their positions.

Howe's attack was made so fast that Early could not support Barksdale. He lost eight guns, five of them taken by the Green Mountain men. The Confederates lost over six hundred men, three hundred of whom were taken prisoners.[6]

As they retired, Early moved his men to new positions away from Lee's forces. That left only Wilcox and his brigade to retire up the Plank Road toward Chancellorsville.

Some historians believe that Sedgwick should have rushed the VI Corps to pursue Wilcox's forces, but his men were in great need of rest and rations. One hour after the capture of Marye's Heights and Lee's Hill, the Vermonters were relieved by regiments of Brooks' division. They stumbled back down to the lower road, where they had left their haversacks and rations. After a short rest and nourishment they marched with Howe in pursuit of Wilcox's retiring troops. They had lost one hundred and thirty men in storming Marye's Heights, one hundred and five from the 2nd Vermont at the charge on the second crest.[7] The storming of the Heights added another gallant battle honor to the brigade's history as well as to the VI Corps'.

After hearing that the Heights had been taken by the VI Corps, and that Early's men had fallen back, Lee sent General McLaws' division and a brigade of Anderson's to reinforce Wilcox's lone brigade. He then took the rest of Major General Richard H. Anderson's division to march against and destroy the VI Corps.

The battle of Salem Church was fought on May 3, 1863, late in the afternoon. Brooks' division attacked Wilcox. Brooks was stopped and his troops were driven back, saved only by the Union artillery.

Brooks took heavy losses; well over fifteen hundred soldiers fell on that battlefield. In a quiet statement to his aide, Brooks said that his military career came to an end at Salem Church. A few weeks later, Brooks was transferred to the Department of Pittsburgh.[8]

Lee knew he was facing the VI Corps, but he also thought that the I Corps and Gibbon's 2nd division of the II Corps were with them. He didn't know that after the storming of the Heights, Gibbon's men retired back across the river. Thinking there was a large Union force, Lee put as many units as he could against Sedgwick's force. He wanted to crush them. Sedgwick, recognizing the trap, placed his three divisions into a U-shape, with the river at their back. He had already secured the crossings at Banks's and Scott's Fords where Brigadier General Henry W. Benham with his engineers had built two bridges. The enemy gunfire didn't stop all day, not even when it got dark. The noise of troops moving into positions for the next day's attack was heard all through the night. The Union divisions were moved into position early the next morning. Newton's men had their right flank at Banks's Ford, their line running south in a large curve extending to the Plank Road. Brooks' division ran east along the Plank Road connecting with Howe's two brigade division which continued for two miles north to the river. The Vermont Brigade was at the angle connecting to General Neill's brigade, whose lines went down to the river bank, slightly in advance of the Vermont Brigade.[9]

Also, on May 4, Lee was placing his troops, making ready for an attack. It took almost all day to do that. When the fighting began, the Confederates carried the fight to the enemy with a very strong attack. After fighting and marching in an overpowering heat the two days previously, they still charged with great force.

General Howe had only two brigades to hold the two mile line, with some artillery. Most of the fighting was being done by Neill's and L. A. Grant's infantry.[10] Lee hit the northern lines with three tough fighting units, brigades of Brigadier Generals Robert F. Hoke, Harry T. Hays and John B. Gordon. At five o'clock in the afternoon the fighting commenced. Heavy artillery fire hit the Union lines. Howe's lines were moved, making two lines. Brigadier General Thomas H. Neill's brigade made up the first line with the addition of the 5th Vermont. The second line consisted of the rest of the Vermont Brigade and the 26th New Jersey.

The Louisiana Brigade, commanded by Hays, led the enemy's fighting. That tough unit was nicknamed the "Louisiana Tigers".

Neill's brigade, after firing several volleys, began to fall apart, attacked by overpowering numbers. Neill had sent his men forward

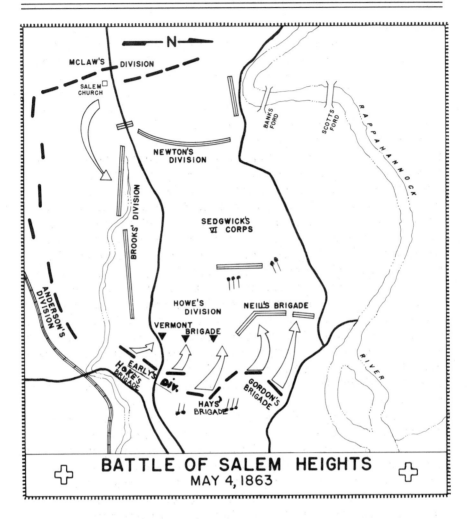

BATTLE OF SALEM HEIGHTS
MAY 4, 1863

to meet the enemy instead of standing fast, and his brigade was being torn apart.[11] Men were fleeing to the rear in sheer panic. During that savage attack, the 5th Vermont poured heavy fire into the flank of the charging "tigers", and then withdrew by way of a gully, to the rear of the 3rd Vermont and safety. Howe later stated that his troops had been attacked with a violence he had never seen before.[12]

Because of the action of the Vermonters and Lieutenant Frank G. Butterfield's leadership of the 6th, he would later earn the Medal of Honor for having presence of mind to retire his men to a safe position.[13] As Neill's troops fell to the rear, Howe ordered them to rally to the rear of the 3rd Vermont. Colonel L. A. Grant made changes in his regiment's positions. He placed the 26th New Jersey on the right of the line in order to have the Vermont regiments take the brunt of the next attack. Hoke's charging North Carolina troops, driving the retreating men before them, advanced on the 26th New Jersey. They fired back in a hasty volley that slowed the "Tar Heels", but only for a moment, and then broke and ran to the rear.[14] Giving the Rebel yell, the North Carolinians continued the charge, expecting to overwhelm the rest of the Union line.

The men of the 2nd Vermont were lying on the ground in the path of the advancing enemy. Waiting until the opposing troops were only a few yards in front; and on command, they stood up and fired a devastating volley into the Confederate lines. When the 26th had gotten clear of the line of fire, the 3rd Vermont was then able to add more fire to that volley. The Vermonters had recently been issued new water-proof cartridges that allowed them to use more ammunition.[15] Hoke's men broke and fell back under the deadly firepower. Hoke and his officers tried to rally their men, but their hitting power was gone.

Hays' Louisiana regiments charged the position held by the 4th Vermont. It was there that 1st Lieutenant Daniel Wheeler of the 4th won the Medal of Honor. Even after his horse was shot from beneath him and being wounded, he was able to hold his position and help stop the Rebel advance.[16] The regiment fired in quick volleys, clearing the slope to their front, leaving the hillside covered with dead and wounded. Over half the attacking Louisiana soldiers were down. As they ran to the rear, the Vermonters continued to fire.

Sergeant Robert J. Coffey, 4th Vermont, distinguished himself during the battle with the Louisiana Brigade. Later he too was awarded the Medal of Honor. He moved out from the advance line and singlehandedly captured two officers and five soldiers of the 8th Louisiana.[17]

The 6th Vermont, under Colonel Barney, came under heavy assault by another regiment. Keeping his men low, Barney waited until the men of the 9th Louisiana were almost upon them. At his command, the men rose up and fired one heavy volley and then charged with bayonet, driving the Southern troops back down the slope. The advance was stopped. Lieutenant Colonel Leroy A. Stafford and eighteen other southern officers were among the two hundred and thirty-seven men who were captured.[18] Because of the great losses, Early and Lee couldn't mount another charge; and night was coming on.

Up to that time in the war, prisoners were exchanged almost immediately. Thus with a few short weeks those officers and men were back in the fighting against the Union.

It must be noted that the 26th New Jersey, after a disastrous start, and after seeing the Vermonters firing in rapid volleys, came forward again and joined in the charge that broke Hays' brigade. In fact, Sergeant Major Amos Cummings of the 26th New Jersey won the Medal of Honor. He helped save a Union battery which was in an exposed position.[19]

General Neill's brigade was in disarray. After severe and almost devastating fighting, some of his regiments had been driven to the rear. Sedgwick sent two infantry regiments to help hold the line on Neill's front. L. A. Grant moved the 4th Vermont back to cover the left flank. The two regiments sent were the 62nd New York and the 98th Pennsylvania, along with the 2nd U.S. artillery battery, G. Those units were from Newton's division.

The Confederates mounted one more attack. It began in semi-darkness, early in the evening. That was a mistake because the lighting allowed the artillery men to see the enemy very clearly. They made good targets. The artillery took the heart out of the charge before it ever got started. By the time the moon came up on May 4, the fighting had stopped and the moonlight revealed many dead and dying Confederate soldiers. That exchange was the last conflict of the Chancellorsville campaign for the VI Corps. The Vermont Brigade had helped save the VI Corps and won one of its greatest battle honors, although Lewis A. Grant did not receive his Medal of Honor until thirty years later![20]

After waiting for orders that never came, Sedgwick started to withdraw his troops back across the river at Banks's Ford and Scotts Ford. He realized that he was in a precarious position, and with a lull in the fighting he had to move his corps out of the trap. He carried out that maneuver in the dark. He left Howe's division as the rear guard, and the Vermont Brigade was the last unit to retire across the Rappahannock River. The 2nd, 3rd, and 6th held the rear at two fords. Companies A, D, and I of the 6th Vermont were the rear skirmishers of that rear guard.[21] When they reached the river they found the bridge down, cut loose on the southern side. Because a fog had set in, Major Charles P. Dudley's Vermonters were able to cross in abandoned boats. Others marched farther down river and crossed at Scott's Ford.

Other units have claimed they were the last units to cross during that retreat, but the record shows that the Vermont Brigade was the one that did. After they crossed, the men staggered over a hill and into a large field where they slept in total exhaustion, ignoring the stray shells that sometimes would fall among them. After the battle the men wore their Greek Cross with even more pride. The men of Vermont felt strongly that the Chancellorsville campaign was not the defeat others thought it was. They had held their line and saved the VI Corps from being crushed by the Army of Northern Virginia. They had stormed and taken the heights at Fredericksburg. During the fighting, fifteen pieces of artillery had been taken, five regimental flags captured and fourteen hundred prisoners taken.[22] The numbers taken prisoner would have been higher if there had been enough men to guard them. As it was, many of the captured men just walked away and returned to their respective units. As a matter of record General Sedgwick, in his report of that Chancellorsville campaign, said that with no disparagement to other regiments, the steadiness and valor of the 5th Wisconsin, 6th Maine, 7th Massachusetts and the Vermont Brigade could not be excelled.[23]

The Vermonters suffered forty-six killed and two hundred thirty-two wounded. Colonel L. A. Grant came near the truth when he stated that his men had inflicted four times those losses on the enemy.

On the 5th of May the soldiers were on the march to Falmouth, but before they got there, they were ordered to fall out at the side of the road. For two days they watched as the rest of the Army of the Potomac returned to their camps, and then they marched to White Oak Church and their old campsites. At Belle Plain they built one of the best and most comfortable camps. The weather was good. Passes were issued to the men and they visited with their loved ones. They had fresh meat and vegetables, and they had built a bakery and had fresh baked bread. They held dances and had parties. They enjoyed that time and would remember that it was the best of their service. The health of the men was good, which would hold them in good standing for the next campaign.

CHAPTER VIII

The Gettysburg Campaign

While still at White Oak Church, Colonel L. A. Grant surprised his brigade with an inspection. The next day Major General John Sedgwick, the VI Corps commander, reviewed the Vermont Brigade and issued a fine report about them and their leader. It was no secret that Grant was working his way up to become a general. Constant drilling and picket duty were the orders of the day.

General Joseph Hooker was still commander of the Army of the Potomac. He ordered the VI Corps to go on the march, and the men were not too unhappy, as they were tired of drills. Hooker didn't know what General Robert E. Lee was planning. He asked for more men, as there had been many losses during the last campaign and some of the nine-month regiments had completed their time. He had only eighty-five thousand men left in his army and feared that was not enough manpower. That fear, in the weeks to come, would cause Hooker's downfall.

Hooker blamed Sedgwick for the disaster at Chancellorsville. There was no love lost between the two men, and Hooker ordered Sedgwick and the VI Corps to recross the river and find out what Lee was up to. Hooker's decision validated the opinion of their opponents. The Confederates used to call across the river to the Union men yelling that no Yankee soldiers would ever be able to get back across the river again, except those fellows who had taken the Heights at Fredericksburg and the soldiers that battled them at Banks's Ford. They of course meant the VI Corps.[1]

As the Vermonters trudged past White Oak Church, they stopped, but held services outside as it was sadly in need of repair. The men regretted leaving the comfort of their camp. They marched on toward the Rappahannock River with a strong determination to get the job done. Their orders were to force a crossing and find out if Major General Ambrose P. Hill's newly formed III Corps was still in the area, and what its strength was.[2] The new corps, or the "Light Division" as it was nicknamed, was the largest in Lee's army.

General Lee had started his campaign to carry the war into the Northern states, and his army was on the march. He left the III Corps behind to keep General Hooker guessing as to where the Army of Northern Virginia had gone.

Howe's 2nd Division was selected to make the crossing. Approaching Franklin's Crossing, they came under Confederate firepower. Realizing that the engineers couldn't put a bridge across under that severe gunfire, Howe sent four batteries of light artillery to the brow of the embankment. For over a half hour the artillery, including the 1st Massachusetts Light Artillery, shelled the Confederate side of the river. Heavy clouds of dust and dirt covered the rifle pits, making it almost impossible for their soldiers to see the on-coming attack by the North. The 5th Vermont and 26th New Jersey made the assault crossing, but again there was trouble in the New Jersey ranks.[3] A few of them refused to cross, saying that their time of service was up and they weren't going to fight, and were going home. Most of the New Jersey soldiers obeyed, though, and with the 5th Vermont, rushed to the river. With the engineers' help they launched the pontoon boats and made their way to the other side, under rifle fire. Two boats carrying the men from New Jersey reached the shore first, where they dug in.

The Vermonters reached shore and immediately charged up the embankment and right into the enemy rifle pits. Major Dudley of the 5th Vermont and his men, were first to jump the positions held by the 8th Florida. A very quick fight ensued and the Vermonters captured between one and two hundred men.[4] Then the 2nd and 3rd Vermont crossed the river in boats that made the bridgehead secure. A pontoon bridge was put in place across the river. The 4th and 6th Vermont rushed across and advanced another half mile inland. That secured their position even more. The 5th Vermont had only seven men wounded. It was a successful operation and a job well done.

That night in the forward positions held by the 4th Vermont, thirty-six officers and men of the 19th Mississippi walked in to the Union lines. They said that they had enough of the war and they surrendered.[5]

The next morning was a different story. A strong attack battered the 6th Vermont as they held the left flank of their line. The gunfire was so heavy that ammunition became scarce and had to be rushed up to them. They held the line and the enemy was unable to advance. The 6th lost four men with thirteen wounded. Through that savage attack they did not give up one foot of ground, in spite of being outnumbered two to one.[6]

The Vermont Brigade was the only Union force on the south side of the river. General Howe realized that a full corps of Confederate infantry was at his front, so he rushed more troops across to strengthen the bridgehead. The 3rd Brigade of the 2nd Division, under command of Colonel Daniel D. Bidwell, was sent. Bidwell had replaced General Neill who was on sick leave. The 1st New Jersey Brigade of the first division relieved the Vermont Brigade. They were under the impression that there had been no opposition to the crossing.

The Vermont Brigade marched back across the river Sunday night. They made camp on the Stafford Hills. Monday night some of the Vermont regiments moved down river for picket duty. Conversations began among the men from both sides. Newspapers were exchanged and the North Carolina soldiers said that they had heard of the Vermont Brigade. Needless to say, all talk stopped quickly when officers came into view.

The VI Corps went on the march again on June 13, 1863. It was night when they headed north. Previously, the brigade had marched eight days and had fought gallantly throughout. They were tired and to make matters worse, the weather became stormy. Heavy rain fell, and the road turned to a thick gray mud. The area was thickly wooded and the trees hung over the road making the night even darker. They slipped in the mud, cursing and grumbling as they proceeded. At times they tried to cheer themselves by breaking into song. At two o'clock in the morning the order to fall out came. While the men got as comfortable as possible, the supply wagons rolled forward to the next camp. The next day the sun came out, and the temperature climbed. With so many troops on the road, marching was a nightmare. Thick clouds of dust rose up, choking the weary soldiers. Many fell by the wayside from sheer exhaustion. Others fell from sunstroke. The number that died by the road was never recorded. A letter sent home by Private Wilbur Fisk of the 2nd Vermont told of the "killing march". He also said that the road was like a burning furnace, seven times heated. He said that his corps lost forty-six men from heatstroke. Other corps lost up to one hundred each. He said that seeing the numbers of dead proved that their marching strength had been pretty well tested.[7]

After a short rest, the march continued on through the night. The next day was a little cooler and marching a little easier. It was nine o'clock in the evening when the brigade went into camp at Fairfax Station after a twenty-five mile march.

Although they were not sure where Lee's army was going, the Union commanders did know that his advanced units had crossed the Blue Ridge Mountains and were approaching the Winchester area. Hooker had a good plan for once. He wanted the Army of the Potomac to turn and attack Hill's III Corps while the rest of Lee's army was strung out. He knew his army could be victorious and with that large corps out of action Lee's army would be much smaller and easier to handle. The high command and President Lincoln didn't agree with the plan. If the truth be known, they all feared an attack on Washington. That fear persisted all through the war. Heavy fortifications had been built around the capital, and heavy artillery regiments were stationed in the forts. Even that didn't stop the anxiety.

While at Fairfax Station the Vermont Brigade was ordered drawn up in a hollow square. They had to watch while punishment of forty men of the 26th New Jersey was issued. Those were the men that had refused to cross the river. They were drummed out of the corps to the tune of the "Rogues March".[8] That was a depressing sight. On June 18, the 26th New Jersey was mustered out of the service, and the Vermont Brigade was comprised of Vermont men only.

After General Hooker had asked for more men to bolster his ranks, from troops at Harpers Ferry, and was refused, he asked to be relieved from duty. In his place, Major General George G. Meade took over. He would hold that command until the end of the war, even though he was not the first choice.

The Vermonters continued on to Bristoe's Station. They stayed there three days. Gunfire could be heard in the distance in the areas of Snicker's and Ashby's Gaps. They continued to Centerville where they met for a second time the 2nd Vermont Brigade and together they marched into Maryland. Crossing the Potomac River, they went into camp at Edward's Ferry. From there, they marched twenty miles a day, and finally camped at Manchester, Maryland. A town called Gettysburg, Pennsylvania, was just thirty miles northwest of camp.

Many Civil War historians have argued about which troops were the best marchers. The facts show that few units could match the record of the Vermont Brigade. As a matter of record, the brigade marched well over two thousand miles, sometimes without shoes, through all kinds of weather.[9] In the next two months the brigade would march hundreds of miles. They would fight several battles and then be rushed north to help keep the peace in the draft riots of New York and New Jersey. The endurance of the men was really to be tested.

On July 1, 1863, the Vermont Brigade and the rest of the VI Corps were camped at Manchester, unaware that the biggest battle of the war had already begun. By early evening though, they received orders to march toward Gettysburg as quickly as possible. Howe's division was one of the first to start. Marching in darkness and with much confusion, they marched four miles in the wrong direction. Changing direction and quickening their pace, they reached the turnpike.

At that time General Sedgwick issued a now famous order. He ordered his adjutant, Colonel Martin T. McMahon to "put the Vermonters up ahead and keep the column well closed up".[10] The brigade entered the state of Pennsylvania about 11 A.M. They could see the smoke of battle in the distance. Resting briefly, they stepped out on the march again and as they approached Littleton, the men began to see many wounded. Wagons and carts filled with the most severely wounded passed by. The less wounded walked at the rear of the wagons. As they passed, some of the wounded men yelled to the Vermonters telling them that they were going to "catch it", when they reached the battlefield. That apparently didn't shake the men as they quickened their pace.

High temperatures, along with carrying heavy gear and five days' rations, added to the difficulties of the march. In addition, the men were given moonshine to drink along the way. The townspeople had made it and thought they were being kind. However, mixture of liquor and heat affected the men and some couldn't keep up. They dropped behind, and were lucky they were still in friendly territory. They were picked up by their own cavalry.

The men from Vermont realized that a great battle was being fought and that they were badly needed. By the time they reached Gettysburg, General Meade had committed all existing troops and had none in reserve. The I and XI Corps had been just about used up and the III Corps was fighting to stay alive after being attacked by General Longstreet's units. Two brigades of the V Corps were deep in fighting to save the "Round Tops", two hills that figured greatly in winning the battle. They were on the left flank of the Union lines. More than two thousand men of Meade's army had been lost already.

Inside a small house used as a headquarters, Meade's officers looking out toward the Baltimore Turnpike saw clouds of dust rising. They couldn't be sure if the troops making the dust were friend or foe. One officer exclaimed they had to be infantry because he could see the flash of their bayonets, and the troops appeared to be in long lines. Then they saw the flag of the VI Corps. Cheer after cheer was shouted for that gallant corps of men who had marched so many miles to aid in the Union cause.[11]

It was a most inspiring sight to see those men, who had marched thirty-four long and grueling miles, immediately get into position for battle. The Vermont Brigade was not the first unit to reach the battlefield at Gettysburg though. Due to a confusing start and the leapfrogging of the divisions, the 3rd Brigade, 3rd Division, commanded by Brigadier General Frank Wheaton, and led by the 98th Pennsylvania, was the first to reach Gettysburg. That brigade was primarily a Pennsylvania unit which included the 62nd New York, 93rd, 102nd and 139th Pennsylvania. The 93rd Pennsylvania was rushed onto the battlefield and was the first regiment of the VI Corps to engage in battle.[12]

Howe's division was split up. Neill's brigade was sent to the right flank in support of General Slocum and his XII Corps. L. A. Grant and the Vermont Brigade were sent another mile and a half to the left flank near the Round Tops. Their orders were to hold the position and stop any attacks the enemy might try. Dividing the VI Corps in that manner was a blunder because a concentrated attack by them would have yielded better results.

The next day while still holding the line, the Vermont Brigade could only hear gunfire and could feel the ground trembling under their feet. It was July 3, late in the afternoon, and the 1st Vermont Cavalry made a charge on the enemy's lines. The fight was close to the Vermont Brigade. Some of the Vermont troopers got trapped within the enemy positions. A few escaped by riding around the base of the Big Round Top and right through the skirmish line of the 4th Vermont. The Vermonters helped by stopping any pursuit of the cavalry. That was the only action the Vermont Brigade saw in the battle of Gettysburg, except for the following day when while advancing they were involved in a light action against Rebel pickets. One man was wounded. After the battle was over, Private Luther Hulburt of the 5th Vermont was listed as a deserter; but later was found to have been killed in the last skirmish. He was the only man from the 1st Vermont Brigade to be killed at Gettysburg.[13]

It should be pointed out that many of the officers in General Stannard's 2nd Vermont Brigade had been trained while serving in the 1st Vermont Brigade, and those men played a decisive role in the battle of Gettysburg.

Lee began retreating back toward Virginia after he was defeated at Gettysburg. The VI Corps was ordered to pursue him. They followed him along the Fairfield Road. Wounded were everywhere; some were treated by doctors, but most were unattended. Lee left a strong force at Fairfield Pass to cover his retirement. Sedgwick decided not to attack them, but did leave Neill's brigade there to keep the rear guard busy. The rest of the VI Corps marched toward Frederick, Maryland.

Proceeding due west through the Catoctin mountain range, they passed through the Highland Pass. It was dark and raining hard. The men had done so much marching that some had no shoes. On July 9, still following Lee's army, Sedgwick marched his men north and up the Antietam Valley almost to Hagerstown.

At the Potomac River, Lee's army was stalled because the river was in full flood stage. He couldn't move his men across. Northern cavalry units were attacking him.

To take the pressure off, Lee rushed a reinforced brigade through Funkstown, with orders to push back the Union troops that were pursuing him, namely the VI Corps. The Vermont Brigade formed the skirmish line of the corps. Colonel William W. White's brigade was made up of the 7th, 8th, 9th, 10th, 11th and 59th Georgia, who attacked the Yankees with strength and vigor. The Union cavalry tried to hold the enemy in check, but, realizing they couldn't hold much longer, General John Buford rode back and requested help from General Howe.

The Vermonters rushed to aid the cavalry. When they arrived, the troopers were just about out of ammunition, and Buford was pulling them off the ridge they had held. A race was on to see who would reach the ridge first, the men from Vermont or the men from Georgia. The Vermonters made it in the nick of time and secured the position. The ridge was almost two miles long, so L. A. Grant placed the 4th Vermont on the right flank of the brigade, the 5th, on the left and two companies of the 2nd between the Antietam Creek and the 5th Vermont. He held the rest of the 2nd in reserve. Howe sent a battery forward. The men of the 3rd and 4th Vermont gave support.

The attacking Georgia Brigade was a veteran unit. They had seen constant service in almost every battle of the Army of Northern Virginia. Two Confederate batteries opened fire on the lines of the Vermont Brigade. The enemy assault was beginning. The 3rd and 4th Vermont rushed forward. Fighting fiercely, they held the line which was nearly two miles long. They beat back three determined charges with tenacity and gave up not one foot of ground. The Southerners fell back. The Vermonters jumped up taunting and yelling to the retreating troops, reminding them that they surely were not fighting a militia unit, but seasoned, veteran fighters and that they should come back and fight. Colonel Charles Stoughton of the 4th was seriously wounded while doing that. As he jumped up he received a head wound that eventually caused him to lose his right eye. Six months later he was forced to resign, but after the war was breveted to brigadier general for past gallant service.[14]

The battle at Funkstown was borne on the brigade's flag with pride. The men from the Green Mountain state felt that they had evened the score. The 1st Vermont cavalry had taken heavy losses at Gettysburg, and the winning of the Funkstown battle was in payment for those losses. The War Department listed that engagement at Funkstown as Gettysburg on the Vermont Brigade's record, incorporating it with that battle even though it took place ten days later.[15]

Colonel Charles B. Stoughton
4th Vermont Infantry

Some historians have felt that after the VI Corps stopped Lee's army at Funkstown, they should have been ordered to go on, and with support, attacked the rest of Lee's army and perhaps ended the war sooner. Instead General Meade halted his advance forces and started to bring up his reserves. While that was being done, Lee and his army crossed over the rushing Potomac, and escaped in the fog and rain on July 13. That was a big disappointment to the men of Vermont, and many others.

The VI Corps started back to Virginia on July 15. They covered many miles and crossed the Potomac on August 10. The bands played "Carry Me Back To Old Virginia" as they marched. They finally went into camp at Warrenton for a well deserved rest. In his report about Funkstown, General Sedgwick stated that the remarkable conduct of the Vermont Brigade deserved the highest praise.

Brevet Major General Martin T. McMahon was a colonel at the time of the action at Funkstown and also chief adjutant of the VI Corps. He wrote in his report about the heroic action at Funkstown, which he referred to as the battle of Beaver Creek. He finished his report with this final statement: "The history of war furnishes few instances such as this, yet the Vermonters did not seem to think that they had accomplished anything out of the usual line of duty."[16] That report was published twenty-six years after the battle.

CHAPTER IX

Keeping the Peace

The officers and men of the Army of the Potomac were just about worn out. General Sedgwick in a letter to his sister said that he was very tired and that he hadn't taken his clothes off since they had crossed the Rappahannock River back in June.[1] At camp in Warrenton, the men's health improved and they were well fed. They loved the abundant, ripe blackberries which grew in the area. Most of the Vermonters' time was spent drilling, standing for inspections and picket duty.

There, the men of Vermont, while on picket duty, were again made aware of the black man's plight. Large groups of black fugitives passed through their lines often. The Vermonters tried to help them whenever possible. Useful information was passed to the Union soldiers by those honest and humble people. The Vermonters also found them to be religious, with great faith in the Bible. The former slaves apparently never doubted for a minute that the North was going to win the war, and the soldiers had a good feeling when they helped them on their journey to a new life and freedom.

The draft riots, in the summer of 1863, were a tragedy and a disgrace. Most people would have liked to forget them. When the draft was voted in, the governor of New York was among those opposing it. There was much confusion about the rules, and there were different rules for different people. If you were rich enough, you could pay someone else three hundred dollars to go in to the service in your place. The Irish of New York, the largest and poorest

64

working class, were the ones most affected by the new draft law, and they showed their feelings about it by rioting. They were angry about the unfairness and also upset by the perception that blacks were taking most of the jobs, as they would work for lower wages. Blacks were hung from trees and lampposts. Asylums, draft stations, and armories were broken into and then ransacked and burned. Civilians, police and soldiers were killed and wounded. That happened not only in New York, but in the cities of Boston, Troy, Poughkeepsie, and Jersey City.

Major General John A. Dix, commander of the New York area, asked for troops to help put down the riots. Two brigades of Regulars were sent first, but they were not enough. The government, realizing the need for more troops, asked for the best volunteer troops the army had. General Sedgwick was asked to send his best brigade from the VI Corps. Without hesitation, he designated the Vermont Brigade to go.[2] They were selected because of their fine reputation for courage and reliability.

Riot control certainly was going to be a different type of fighting than the Vermont men were accustomed to. The men were rushed secretly by train to Alexandria.[3] Others from the 2nd Division were not aware of the Vermonters' departure.

Other fine units were also being sent north. Included were the 1st Minnesota, 7th Michigan, 14th Indiana, 4th and 8th Ohio, and the 37th Massachusetts. No regiments from the riot areas were sent to help. The government was careful what regiments were sent. Even the New York National Guard regiments stationed in Frederick, Maryland, were not sent to the distressed city.

At first the men of the Vermont Brigade had no idea where they were going. In Alexandria, Virginia, they boarded two transports, the *Ericson* and the *Illinois*. There was much confusion during the boarding. When they arrived in New York, most were glad to disembark because they had been jammed in like cattle. Sailors told the soldiers that the ships were loaded three times the capacity. Some were seasick. Many of the men still carried the mud and dirt of the Virginia countryside on their worn uniforms. Before going to do the job they were there for, new uniforms were issued and time was given to clean up.

Colonel L. A. Grant reported to Brigadier General Edward R. S. Canby. He told him that en route the *Illinois* had been involved in a collision in which one man was killed and several injured.

New York City was not the only trouble spot, and regiments were sent to different cities. The 2nd Vermont was in New York two weeks and then sent to Poughkeepsie. Arriving in the dead of night, they marched up the main street. That made a great impression on the citizens of that city. The realization that the troops were battle-tried helped to keep the peace and, while the regiment was stationed there, no trouble occurred. Many of the men's relatives and friends from Vermont were able to visit them.

The 3rd Vermont was sent to Newark, New Jersey, where they found plenty of trouble. They had to mount guard over the 33rd New Jersey regiment, which had been filled up with mostly bounty men who were trying to desert every chance they could. A small guard of Regulars had been pulled out by General Dix. The unit was too small and couldn't do the job of quelling the desertions. The very first night the Vermonters were on guard, bounty jumpers attacked them. The bounty men had made a grave mistake. The men from Vermont had been fighting and dying for the past two years to keep the Union and preserve the country. The men of the 3rd had no qualms about fighting those bounty men. Those substitute soldiers were only there to make a buck. They used the chaotic draft system just to make money.

In the short but savage fight, the Vermont men shot seven of the attackers. Three of those died and four were wounded. When it was over, the desertions came to an abrupt stop as those thugs realized that the men of the 3rd Vermont meant business. The money-hungry bounty men hated the soldiers, but feared them even more. When the Vermonters finally left Newark, they left with few regrets.[4]

The 4th Vermont spent most of their time in and around New York City. The 5th and 6th were sent to Kingston, New York, where a draft was to take place. Surprisingly, there was no trouble, and the three weeks the Vermont men spent there became a pleasant visit.

Their peace-keeping duties finished, all the Vermont regiments went back to Alexandria, Virginia. Behind, they had left a job well done, and most people that they had come in contact with had nothing but praise and respect for the men from the north country. Their good reputation was enhanced.

On September 16, in a torrential downpour, the Vermont Brigade was escort for a large supply column, consisting of a one hundred and fifty mule team and a thousand head of beef cattle, on their way to the Army of the Potomac. The march was slow. While marching, men took notice of a problem. They saw ten thousand men of the XI Corps all guarding one rail line, the Orange and Alexandria Railroad.[5] The line was constantly being raided by guerrillas or Southern partisans. Men who were farmers by day ventured out by night to plunder and steal. They sometimes would go out for a week or more and create mayhem, killing and capturing the Union soldiers. Although they were small in number, less than a thousand in the area, they created a major problem. That problem really never was eliminated, and whole areas of the country remained under their control right up to the end of the war.

It appeared an easy duty to guard the line, and some men threw a few digs at the XI Corps men. They asked them how they got the easy duty, suggesting that it might be because they were such good runners in times of battle. The soldiers of the XI took the joking in good favor. It would not have been wise to start any fighting between those two units although fighting had occurred between units from different regions before.

On September 23, the Vermont Brigade returned to the VI Corps in camps at Culpeper Courthouse. As the Vermonters entered, they were given rousing shouts and cheers from different units. One was the 10th Vermont who had just joined the VI Corps and had been put in the 3rd Division.[6] The men swapped stories of back home and enjoyed the friendly visit with each other.

When the Vermont Brigade rejoined the 2nd Division, all the top brass and General Neill's brigade were drawn up in review to welcome them back. It is interesting to note that Neill's brigade, a companion brigade to the Vermonters, showed so much respect to them. They too, were a gallant, fighting unit, made up of the 7th Maine, 43rd and 49th New York, and the 61st Pennsylvania.[7] They would be shoulder to shoulder in future battles with the Vermonters in some of the bloodiest fighting of the war.

The holes in the Vermont Brigade were filled with new recruits, who were distributed to the 2nd, 3rd and 4th regiments. They were a welcome addition. The state of Vermont wisely decided to keep the existing regiments intact and build them up as needed, instead of making new units. In doing that, each unit had veteran soldiers along with the new recruits.[8]

Many states had not followed that policy, but instead made up new regiments so that officers could be given commissions and have men to lead. That was purely a political maneuver. Mr. Ropes of Massachusetts, a military critic and analyst of the time, said it all when he said that the greater part of the Northern states blindly and recklessly threw away manpower who had long service and experience when new regiments were formed, instead of filling in the older ones.[9]

CHAPTER X

Stalemate at the Rappahannock

After a quiet two weeks the VI Corps relieved the II Corps from the lines that ran for two miles along a small stream called Robinson Run. Even there, Southern pickets on the other side and the Vermonters talked with one another, joking and exchanging newspapers. It was a welcome change from the usual exchange of battle, and the men knew it would be short-lived.

General Lee had learned that two Federal infantry corps had been transferred to a Western theater of war and took that opportunity to attack the Army of the Potomac. In a series of marches and counter marches both armies tried to maneuver into flanking positions.

The Vermont Brigade, leading the VI Corps, crossed the Rappahannock River and marched, with eight days' rations, to Brandy Station. Finding no enemy, they marched on to Bristoe, twenty-five miles from where they had camped the night before. Still, there was no sign of the enemy. At daybreak, the next morning, the brigade stood to arms, as they were expecting an attack by the Confederates. None came though, as Lee had decided not to fight at that time. He felt he needed more reinforcements and retired across the river.

On the 18th of October, the VI Corps marched back to their old camps. Along the way they met Brigadier General George A. Custer's cavalry brigade, who had recently been in a battle with Major General James E. B. Stuart's horsemen at Buckland Mills.

Custer's men had taken quite a beating and were in full retirement. They were at full gallop, being chased by Confederate cavalry, and rode right into the 2nd Division's lines. They were happy to see friendly troops. The 1st Vermont Cavalry was one of those regiments. Upon hearing that the Rebels were in hot pursuit, the 7th Maine and 6th Vermont were rushed forward to engage them. The two regiments had no sooner been placed across the road when a Federal light battery galloped through them, closely pursued by Confederate horsemen. They were almost captured. A heavy volley from the two regiments stopped the wild pursuit in its tracks.[1] After firing only a few shots in reply, the Southern troops retired back down the road.

The next day the Vermont Brigade marched on and finally reached Buckland Mills, the scene of the fight between Custer's and Stuart's men. Dead Union troopers were lying along the roadside everywhere. Their clothing had been stripped from them and all their equipment taken. Only their undergarments were left. Sights like that were hard to take, especially for the newer recruits. It made everyone realize just what they were into, a total and unrelenting war.

The brigade finally went back to camp at Warrenton and the first thing they did was to be reviewed by the "top brass". That happened quite often with the Vermont units. They were a great fighting unit, and the officers and others in charge liked to show them off. The men could have done without it though, because the weather had turned cold, and standing at attention in such weather was not too comfortable.

Generals and officials in Washington were putting pressure on Meade to go on the offensive against Lee. Major General Henry Halleck led the list of those urging Meade to do something, especially since the last campaign had been a fruitless one. The troops were tired from so much marching, and men had been captured or wounded by the many guerrilla bands that had infested the area.

So, on November 7, the brigade broke camp and started marching back toward the Rappahannock River. The Vermonters hoped the next campaign would be better organized and surely more rewarding. Reaching the Rappahannock Station, the regiments fell out and ate their rations; the opposing pickets just a few yards away, neither side paying any attention to the other. In modern combat, soldiers rarely see their enemies up close. In the Civil War some of the most savage and bitter battles in American history were fought at close range. In sharp contrast at times those same troops fraternized with each other, speaking the same language.

At one o'clock in the afternoon, the VI Corps was lined up for the coming engagement. The 1st and 2nd Divisions were in two

lines with the Vermonters in the second line, curving toward the
river. The skirmishers of the 5th Vermont were out in advance. As
the VI Corps moved forward, the Confederate skirmishers fell back
into their main line. The men of the 6th advanced to higher ground.
Artillery fire from both sides opened up. Most of the Vermont Brigade was well protected from the heavy shell fire because the men
were lying over the crest of the hill. The firing continued for over
three hours. One soldier of the 4th Vermont lost a leg in the exchange of cannon fire. He was the only casualty.

Brigadier General David A. Russell's 1st Division which formed
the left flank of the line, stormed the Confederate fortified positions,
with orders not to fire their guns and to use the bayonet, until they
were in the entrenchments. With six regiments, they captured over
thirteen hundred officers and men along with eight battle flags.[2]
That was to be one of the most successful attacks of the entire war.

The Confederate commander, General Jubal A. Early, destroyed
his end of a bridge and retired to prepared positions below the
Rapidan River. General Sedgwick ordered a pontoon bridge be put
across. The men of the Vermont Brigade had crossed that river so
many times that they had lost track of the exact number.

After crossing, the Vermont Brigade went into camp at Brandy
Station. There they witnessed the branding of two deserters. Desertions from the army were getting out of control. The records showed,
at that time in the war, that eighty-five thousand men had fled their
units.[3] Every day the count rose. Very tough policies were put into
effect. Men were hung by their thumbs, branded, strapped to poles
with hands and feet tied, strapped to tilted cannon wheels and sometimes whipped. Records show that two hundred and sixty-seven
men were executed in the Northern armies by firing squads.[4] It was
policy to have the regiments and brigades march into a large U-
formation and watch the firing squad do their duty. That was done,
of course, to impress upon the men that desertion was not to be
tolerated.

Two men from the Vermont Brigade were executed during the
course of the war; a small number, considering that brigade did so
much heavy fighting in the forefront of battle. One of those soldiers
was John Tague of the 5th Vermont, who was a New Yorker. A constant troublemaker, he had deserted three times before. He was
reckless and indifferent right up to the end, even helping to unload
his coffin and carrying it to the grave site. George Bowles of the 2nd
Vermont came from Arlington, Vermont. He had never been a troublemaker, but had deserted for some unknown reason and would pay
the price, execution. Oddly enough, George Bowles had a brother in
the same company and regiment, named William. William would

later be wounded in savage fighting at Cold Harbor. Three months after he also would desert, never again to return to the army rolls.[5] Records show, by the end of the war, over two hundred thousand men were listed as deserters.

The Army of Northern Virginia was still stationed at the Rapidan River. Lee's men had built strong fortifications along its banks. That river ran into the Rappahannock River, somewhat to the south.

Meade was still being prodded by people in Washington to attack Lee, as they felt he was vulnerable, due to heavy losses and the dispatch of some of his men to the Western theater. Meade decided to march three columns across the Rapidan below the mouth of a muddy, little stream called the Mine Run. He hoped to flank Lieutenant General Richard S. Ewell and his II Corps, attacking him at the rear of his positions.

The November weather was as usual bitter cold, rainy, with sleet at times and just plain miserable. The III Corps was supposed to be the first to march. The VI was to follow a few hours later. Marching on their appointed time, the VI Corps reached the camp of the IIIrd on time. They found the men still sleeping and it was past time to move on. That caused the men of the VI Corps to have to stand around for hours in the mud and cold.

On the march Major General William H. French, commander of the III Corps, came to a fork in the road. Apparently confused and unable to make a decision as to what road to take, his corps waited for several hours before he finally ordered them to march down one of them, to a place called Robinson's Tavern. General Ewell attacked with one of his divisions, and that action stalled the III Corps' advance. Meade was informed about the attack, and finally had to order French to go on the offensive. It was obvious that French was a very timid leader. He attacked at last, and was strongly repulsed. The III Corps lost over a thousand men.[6]

Ewell's corps was ordered back to the heavily fortified positions along the Rapidan and the Mine Run. In the cold and rain, Meade moved his army into position to attack those strong entrenchments.

As the Vermont Brigade moved into their positions for attack, a messenger rode into headquarters countermanding the attack order. Major General Gouverneur K. Warren, commander of the II Corps, was supposed to attack also; but being an engineer, he had surveyed the fortifications to be attacked and reported to Meade that they were too strongly held, and with such ghastly weather it would be an almost impossible task. Meade called the attack off.

Not only was the weather deplorable, but there were no warm rations. Some men froze to death while on picket duty. Morale was poor. After marching around for weeks, being shot at, horrible weather, and preparing themselves for battle and perhaps death, it was for naught. Again they retired across the Rapidan River to their camp. The 3rd Vermont and 77th New York, with a battery, remained at riverside to guard the crossing.

On December 2, 1863, the brigade was met by supply wagons with fresh meat and other rations that were badly needed. For the last twenty-five miles, the men had only coffee to drink, and no food.

In that senseless and very frustrating campaign, the Vermont Brigade lost more men than in many earlier battles. The rosters of their regiments showed thirty-six men listed as disabled or discharged, and another sixteen men died of exhaustion and disease.[7] It was with welcome relief when the men from the Green Mountains went into winter camp at Brandy Station.

Time was running out for most of the veteran three-year regiments. The government, including the state governments, offered all kinds of deals to encourage the men to sign up again. They were offered bounties if two thirds of a regiment re-enlisted. That would guarantee the continuing existence of the regiment. The greatest inducement, though, was a thirty-day furlough. Most of the men had not seen their loved ones for a long time.

It was said that the 5th Vermont was the first to sign over; in fact, the first in all of New England. Other regiments have claimed that feat, but there was little to substantiate their claim. However, the date and time the 5th Vermont re-enlisted as a group is recorded.[8]

The 5th returned to camp after furlough on February 29, 1864. Five hundred and ten men were listed on their roster. Four other Vermont regiments followed their lead and re-enlisted as well. When all was said and done, the brigade had over two thousand nine hundred men. The Vermont Brigade remained intact.[9] Very few brigades could match that record. Five officers who would now lead the brigade were: Colonel Newton Stone, of the 2nd Vermont; Colonel T. O. Seaver, 3rd Vermont; Colonel George P. Foster, 4th Vermont; Colonel Lewis, 5th Vermont; and Colonel Barney, 6th Vermont. Colonel L. A. Grant was promoted to brigadier general on April 27, 1864. Those officers were battle tested and had previously served their regiments at all times with great distinction. The brigade would need that experienced leadership in the coming battles during the last year of the war.

Another change that took place in the Union Army was the addition of Black regiments. Led by white officers, the men of those units were to become an asset to the Northern army. Twenty of the soldiers, accepted to become officers of those regiments, were promoted from the ranks of the Vermont Brigade. Before the war was over, their troops would do some heavy fighting and help win the war for the Union cause.

The men who were commissioned to lead the United States Colored Troop Regiments were as follows: Private Patrick F. Duggan, Corporal Marshall Montgomery, and Corporal Frelon J. Babcock, all from the 3rd Vermont. Private Charles S. Brooks, Private Andrew J. Dimick and Private Frank A. Howell came from the 4th Vermont. Private Stephen P. Joslyn, Sergeant Dan Mason, Sergeant Alexander W. Davis, Private Winslow S. Myers, Private James Tinkham, Sergeant Henry C. Cleveland, Private Horace L. Heath, Private Edwin C. Lewis, and Private Josiah Paul all came from the 6th Vermont. Corporal Frank E. Dow, Sergeant John Q. Adams, Sergeant Jabez H. Barnard, Corporal Charles J. Brown, and Corporal Nelson A. Summer came from the 11th Vermont.

Those men were promoted to the rank of lieutenant. The only two regiments that did not have anyone take a commission to lead in the United States Colored Troops regiments were the 2nd and 5th Vermont.[10]

All of those commissioned were volunteers. They would be partly responsible for the excellent records the black regiments would earn in the coming battles. The men from the Vermont Brigade led as they fought, with strength and endurance.

CHAPTER XI

Holocaust in the Wilderness

On March 10, 1864, Lieutenant General Ulysses S. Grant took command of the Army of the Potomac and all other Federal forces in the field. Although General Meade was officially in charge of the Army of the Potomac, Grant would make all important decisions.

The Vermonters, upon hearing that Grant was to lead the army, realized that a hard campaign must be ahead. They never dreamed just how hard it was going to be. History would tell us that the two-day battle in the wilderness was the most savage and brutal one in all of the American Civil War.[1] For the Vermont Brigade battle after battle, a total of twelve, followed in little better than ten months' time. With Grant in the field, the fighting style changed. Unlike the battles before, after which troops would retire to re-group, those harsh and grueling battles would be one continuous engagement after another.

Other changes that took place prior to the fighting were the breaking up of units and transferring men to different corps. The I and III Corps were broken up.[2] Those moves by leaders in Washington were senseless. Hard feelings of resentment were felt by the men of those corps. To protest, most of them refused to wear their new corps patches. Some even stitched them onto the seat of their pants as a gesture of defiance. Finally, an order was issued that the men would be allowed to wear their old corps patch if so desired. The men of the 3rd Division, III Corps, who were transferred to the VI Corps all agreed to wear the Greek Cross, such was the reputa-

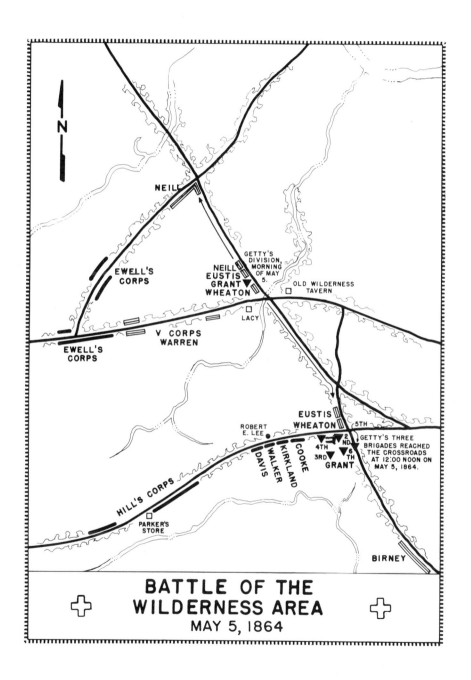

N

NEILL

EWELL'S CORPS

GETTY'S DIVISION, MORNING OF MAY 5.

NEILL
EUSTIS
GRANT
WHEATON

OLD WILDERNESS TAVERN

LACY

V CORPS WARREN

EWELL'S CORPS

EUSTIS
WHEATON

5TH

ROBERT E. LEE

COOKE
KIRKLAND
WALKER
DAVIS

4TH

3RD

2 ND

6 TH

GRANT

GETTY'S THREE BRIGADES REACHED THE CROSSROADS AT 12:00 NOON ON MAY 5, 1864.

HILL'S CORPS

PARKER'S STORE

BIRNEY

BATTLE OF THE
WILDERNESS AREA
MAY 5, 1864

tion of that corps.³ Another change was in the leadership of the troops in the Army of the Potomac. That was especially true in the Vermont Brigade.

General Howe moved to an artillery command in the Washington area. The 2nd Division was given a new commander by the name of Brigadier General George W. Getty. He was highly respected as one of the best field commanders in the Federal army and eventually would prove it.

The gray dawn spread across the sky on the morning of May 4, 1864, and the Vermont Brigade started on the march to Germanna Ford. The men carried fifty rounds of cartridges and enough rations for six days. Just before reaching the ford, the men passed by General U. S. Grant and his staff. The "Green Mountain Men" gave him a rousing cheer. That was certainly a compliment from those men as they gave very few cheers to any generals throughout the course of the war.

Grant's "Overland Campaign" was about to start, although many people advised against it. He knew, though, that he had the supplies and the manpower to go ahead; and that was just what he did. The cost in manpower was to be staggering, and as the campaign continued, whole divisions and brigades were put out of action, or driven from the field of battle. Losses mounted so high that Grant was given the nickname "Butcher Grant" by the soldiers.⁴ The newspapers also referred to him by the same nickname.

The Vermont Brigade reached the Rapidan River and crossed it with a little over two thousand, eight hundred men, arriving at Germanna Ford. The brigade marched down the Germanna Plank Road and camped at the crossroads of Germanna and Orange Turnpike. It was the morning of May 5, and to the west of their camp, General A. P. Hill and his III Corps were marching up the Orange Plank Road toward them. News of that advance was carried back to General Grant who was back down the Germanna Plank Road.

He was sitting on a stump, smoking one of his cigars when the message reached him. Grant realized immediately that the crossroads at the Orange Plank Road and Brock Road had to be held at all cost. He had to have a unit that he could depend on and he needed one quickly. He detached Getty's 2nd Division of the VI Corps to do the job. Getty's division had four brigades. Neill's brigade was immediately dispatched back to the VI Corps, probably to reinforce them. He quickly marched the other three brigades, along with his mounted staff, to the heavily wooded crossroads. Brigadier General Frank Wheaton, General L. A. Grant, and Brigadier General Henry L. Eustis commanded the three brigades. Getty and his staff, riding on ahead, arrived at the crossroads just in time.

Union cavalry, primarily the 5th New York under command of Colonel John Hammond, had been fighting A. P. Hill's men along the road. Hammond's troopers were being driven back along the Orange Plank Road toward the crossroads. As they retired, they shouted to General Getty that the Rebels were not far away. Getty ordered his staff to make a show of force until his troops could come up. They began shooting down the road, waving their flags.[5] Thinking they might have come up against a large Union force, the Confederate skirmishers came to a stop.

Lee didn't want to bring on a big battle at that time, because Longstreet's Corps had not yet reached the area. That was fortunate for the North. If Major General Henry Heth's division had reached the crossroads first, he would have split Grant's army in two, which would have been disastrous.

Finally, Wheaton's 1st Brigade reached the crossroads and fired a volley against Heth's men. That stalled the advance, but Wheaton's men took losses in the exchange. That brigade was a battle-tested unit, made up of the 93rd, 98th, 102nd, and 139th Pennsylvania and the 62nd New York.[6]

The Vermont Brigade came up behind the 1st Brigade. They advanced and went into positions on the left side of the Orange Plank Road, while Wheaton's men angled to the right. Eustis's 4th Brigade formed on the right flank of the 1st. The crossroads were secured. Then L. A. Grant advanced the 3rd and 4th Vermont, along with two companies of the 5th, as skirmishers, down the left side of the road under light gunfire. The 2nd and 6th Vermont were in the second line, making the Vermont Brigade the most advanced of Getty's division. The 5th was held in reserve. A two-gun section of Company F, 1st Pennsylvania, a light artillery unit, gave support in the first attack. Firing down the road, with the thick woods obscuring some of their view, they even wounded some of the Vermonters.[7] The guns fired so fast that one of them burst, thus decreasing their fire power.

General Hancock and his II Corps were ordered by Meade to support Getty; but due to narrow lanes and trails through the heavy tangled growth of forest, and artillery blocking them, the order was nearly impossible to carry out. Hancock rode forward to find out what the situation was. He talked with Getty and found out that two Confederate divisions were attacking on Getty's front and the fighting was getting heavier every minute.

Heth was putting more of his men into the battle. General Lee himself was directing the attack and whenever he attacked, he hit hard. Although he did not know the conditions of the terrain, Meade ordered Getty to attack immediately. Hancock had told Getty that he would support him as soon as his units got up to the battle area. Getty gave the order to advance.

The Vermont units were the first to engage the enemy in a savage fight. Advancing about a hundred yards, they received a blast of gunfire from the heavily wooded ridge to their front. They hit the ground, finding cover wherever they could. Many of them would never get up again. The Vermonters returned fire but were unable to see their targets in the "jungle". In fact, the woods were so thick that the fighting was being done by small units of men, as brigades that were put into the fight were easily split up. The Vermonters were ordered to advance again. As they stood up to fight, more rounds of bullets hit them. Taking cover, they returned fire into heavy, blinding smoke, which covered the area like a blanket, making the battle very confusing.

Brigadier General John R. Cooke's North Carolina Brigade received the Vermonters' gunfire. Also fighting with Cooke were the brigades of Brigadier General Henry H. Walker and Brigadier General William W. Kirkland which were moved up from reserve. The Vermont men were outnumbered two to one. The battle increased in fury. The two lines of the Vermont Brigade became one, and all five regiments were engaged in severe action to hold the line against the Confederates. The losses to the Vermont Brigade were staggering. Many of the officers were hit as they rode on horseback, directing their men. They made easy targets for the Southern sharpshooters.

Colonel Stone, the young officer leading the 2nd Vermont, was hit by sniper-fire and went to the rear to receive treatment. After the treatment of a leg wound, he returned to his regiment amid cheers from his men. As he rode, a shot rang out, and Stone fell to the ground mortally wounded in the head. He was dead when he hit the ground. His body was left where he fell during the battle. When the regiment moved back to better positions, the body was then within the enemy lines. Not until later when they advanced again was his body recovered and finally sent back for burial.[8]

Lieutenant Colonel John S. Tyler took command of the 2nd Vermont. Although very young, he fought and led well. While keeping his men up on the firing line, he too was shot, a bullet penetrating his waist. He refused to allow his men to take him to the rear because he realized that every man was needed on the firing line. That young hero died of his wounds before he reached his home in Brattleboro, Vermont.[9]

Colonel Pingree from the 3rd Vermont took over command of the 2nd. The fierce fighting continued, never letting up, but growing in intensity.

Colonel Foster of the 4th Vermont was badly wounded, also in the waist, as he rode among his troops. The 4th was then turned

USAMHI

USAMHI

Brevet Brigadier General
George P. Foster
4th Vermont Infantry

Colonel Elisha L. Barney
6th Vermont Infantry

over to Major John E. Pratt from Bennington, Vermont. Seven officers of that regiment were killed in that deadly fighting in the Wilderness. Ten more were wounded. However, the men from Vermont held their positions.[10]

While the savage fighting continued, Sergeant Carlos Rich, Company K, 4th Vermont, carried one of the wounded officers to safety. Thirty-one years later, he was awarded the Medal of Honor.[11]

Colonel Lewis from Burlington, Vermont, commanded the 5th Vermont. He was badly wounded in the upper arm. He survived the amputation, and a three-day trip to Fredericksburg, where his loving wife came to nurse him back to health. By a special ruling of the secretary of war, Lewis was assigned as colonel of the Veteran Reserve Corps. Later, he was awarded a brevet brigadier general's star for his actions in the battle of the Wilderness.[12]

As the 6th Vermont moved up to support the 3rd Vermont, Colonel Barney was shot through the head, later dying of his wound. He left a distinguished record as his legacy. He was from Swanton, Vermont, where over two thousand people came to his funeral. His family had sent six men to fight for the Union. On that brave soldier's coffin was placed a sword that he had taken from Colonel Stafford, 9th Louisiana, who had surrendered to Barney at Salem Heights.[13] Major Oscar A. Hale of Troy, Vermont, took over command of the 6th.

The heavy and brutal fighting continued. The men of Vermont fought hard and never backed off. During the fighting Captain R. A. Bird of the 6th Vermont, while leading his men, was wounded in the head. His men urged him to go to the rear but he refused. He continued to hold his place in the line. Then a second bullet hit him in the waist, knocking him off his feet. Even that didn't stop him. He advanced with his men until he again was hit by a bullet, which was the fatal blow.[14] Indeed, because of leadership like that the Vermont Brigade survived the terrible battle in the Wilderness.

The constant gunfire continued. Leaves and branches fell as if they had been cut with a knife. Anyone who raised himself more than a foot above ground met instant death. It was impossible to see the enemy. Heavy smoke from the battle hung in the hot humid air. Firepower was coming in on the left flank of the "Green Mountain Men", from the hard-hitting attack of Cooke's and Walker's brigades. The enemy had broken the Union line.

Brigadier General Gershom Mott's division took positions on the left of the Vermonters, and as his men advanced into the woods they attracted gunfire, which started a full scale retreat. Those who viewed the retreat thought it strange to see those veteran troops moving to the rear. Apparently, they all had had too much war and wanted out.[15] The Excelsior Brigade was the first to break.

Colonel Robert McAllister's brigade was able to hold on long enough for Hancock to rush fresh troops to fill the gap. Colonel Samuel S. Carroll and his brigade threw back the attack by the Confederates. At that time Brigadier General John Ward's unit made an attempt to relieve the men from Vermont. It was none too soon as they were exhausted and almost out of ammunition. Ward's brigade was made up of nine regiments. Under constant fire, it was almost impossible to relieve the weary and battle-fatigued men in the confusion. Three regiments from Ward's troops did relieve them finally.

The Vermonters were able to fall back to the log barriers; although only after several counterattacks were made by Major Dudley and the 5th Vermont. Those attacks, although not successful, did allow the other regiments to retire. The three regiments taking the place of the Vermont men were all veteran units. They had already been in over a dozen hard-fought battles. When that battle was over, records showed the Vermont regiments had three times more men killed and wounded. Never retiring unless ordered to, and staying in the thick of battle, resulted in those heavy losses.

The other two brigades of Getty's division also took hard losses, but not the number the Vermont Brigade had. When the losses of that terrible day were counted, it showed the Vermont Brigade had lost more men killed and wounded than the entire II Corps put together.[16]

The brutal fighting finally stopped when darkness set in at eight o'clock in the evening. The shooting slowed and then stopped. The Confederates themselves had been fighting all day and were just about done in. It has been said the darkness saved Heth and his men as they had not been reinforced and were completely worn out.

None of the Vermonters who lived through that day would ever forget it. Wounded were everywhere. Their cries for help could be heard all through the night. Sporadic gunfire went on through the night hours. Tired and dirty, the men tried to get some rest. That was almost impossible. Everyone knew an attack was going to be made first thing in the morning.

General U. S. Grant ordered the attack to start at four o'clock in the morning, but found out that many of the units were mixed up, so he moved that attacking hour to five o'clock, May 6.

On the Confederate side, things were no better. Their battle line was also mixed up. The men were tired out, and had had no rations for a long time. General A. P. Hill, corps commander, was not a well man, and he told Heth and Wilcox to let their men rest, and also informed them that General Longstreet's men would be up in the morning to relieve them. After Hill told them that, General Heth said he could never understand why Hill hadn't tried to straighten out the lines and reorganize before the next day's battle.

In the meantime, General Longstreet, along with the leading division of his I Corps, was resting at a place called Richard's Shop. That was a well-earned rest which in the future would pay big dividends.

The attack that General Hancock planned for the morning of May 6 would be a sledgehammer blow to the South. He planned to throw everything he had at them. He had the troops to deliver it. With Brigadier General James S. Wadsworth's V Corps Division facing on A. P. Hill's exposed flank, Hancock planned to attack in three lines of division strength.

The first line was made up of brigades led by Generals McAllister, Ward, and Hays. The second line consisted of brigades led by Colonel William R. Brewster on the left flank, and L. A. Grant with the Vermont Brigade on the south side of the Plank Road. General Wheaton's brigade was just north of the road and General Eustis's brigade was on his right flank. The third line was made up of Brigadier General Joshua T. Owen's and Carroll's brigades, with Brigadier General Alexander S. Webb's held in reserve. The men in the second line were the only brigades from the VI Corps.[17]

When the Vermonters jumped the log barriers and started the attack, they had two regiments on the right side of the road and three on the left. They engaged the enemy quickly. After a half hour of heavy fighting the opposing line broke, due to the overwhelming force. It was a devastating battle, fought among the bodies of soldiers killed the day before. The Confederates were driven back a mile to the rear. Prisoners taken were from North Carolina regiments. Some of those men surrendered, and, as they came toward the Vermonters, said that they didn't want to fight anymore that day. Other good fighting regiments fell back to the rear, exhausted. There were just too many Yankees for the Rebels to handle!

That moment was actually the high water mark of the Federal attack. In the confusion things began to go wrong for the Federal forces. As Wadsworth's regiments drove Kirkland's North Carolina Brigade to retreat, they became mixed into the lines and troops of Hancock's Corps. The firing stopped when they realized they were among their own men. That delay allowed the Southern brigades to regroup and come back into line. General Lee was at the Trapp farm. He saw his men falling back to the rear and could see that they were in a hurry. He shouted to Brigadier General Samuel McGowan and asked why his men were running like a flock of wild geese. McGowan replied that they were just trying to find a place to regroup.

Longstreet's First Corps arrived with fresh troops. Major Generals Kershaw's and Field's divisions attacked, one on the south side of the road and the other to the north. The Texas Brigade, rated as one of the better brigades in the Army of Northern Virginia, was one of the attacking units.

Hancock learned that only a small number of Burnside's men had arrived on the battlefield. He detached Eustis's brigade to the northern section of the battlefield. The troops continued to advance. The Vermonters fought their way to Colonel Samuel Carroll's brigade. They relieved them as they were almost out of ammunition. Continuing on, they suddenly found themselves in the front positions because the other brigades appeared to be falling back. Kershaw's division had hit the first lines in intense fighting. The Vermont men were holding a wooded ridge and had put up a barrier of logs and rails, anything that gave them some protection.

Kershaw's men came running, guns firing and bayonets ready. Charging and shouting the Rebel yell, they struck the Vermonters' lines in repeated charges. They were thrown back by the Vermont fighting men, the only part of the Union lines that held. During those severe attacks, the units flanking the Vermont Brigade gave way and the "Green-Mountain Men" received heavy fire on their flanks.[18]

In the fierce fighting, General Getty was shot through his shoulder. He continued to yell out orders to his men, while his horse was rearing. He held his men to the fight until he fainted and fell from his horse. His men placed him in a wagon and he was taken to Fredericksburg. General Wheaton took over command of the 2nd Division.

McAllister's regiments were still holding on the left flank in an unbroken line. Troops from two different divisions were attacking the Vermonters, who continued to maintain their position.

Wadsworth's division to the right of the Vermonters was hit hard by Field's charging brigades, including Brigadier General Edward Perry's Florida Brigade, one of the smallest in the Southern army. The ranks broke apart. As Wadsworth tried to rally his men, he was shot and then taken prisoner. He later died in the enemy camp. A fine leader, he was a great loss to the Union cause.[19]

With Wadsworth's division in retreat and the right flank of the Vermont regiments being pushed back, L. A. Grant ordered his regiments to fall back to the barrier. Reportedly, the Vermont Brigade quickly and deliberately took up their former position at the barrier on the Brock Road and awaited the attack of the enemy. Fortunately, other troops were moving into the intersection of the two roads. Colonel Seldon Connor placed the 19th Maine into position there. Many of the Vermont Brigade were using the Orange Plank Road as they retired to the barriers. Just as the "Green Mountain Men" got clear of the Maine unit, Connor gave the order to open fire on the opposition. That well directed volley stopped the Southern momentum. Connor was wounded in that exchange, which put him out of the fighting for good.[20] Other Union troops were gathering at the barrier, but some of the men and units didn't stop there. They just kept on going right out of the battle area. Colonel Sumner Carruth's 1st Brigade, IX Corps, did form to the rear of the Vermont men.

Timing is always an important factor. During the time that the Federal forces were starting to fall back, Longstreet and his staff rode forward to direct the attack on the Northern troops. As they moved along the Orange Plank Road, a volley of fire from Mahone's Virginia regiments cut down Longstreet and his staff. In the confusion of battle the Virginians mistook the general and his men for the enemy. Longstreet was seriously wounded and one of his officers, General Micah Jenkins, was killed.[21]

Longstreet's command went to Brigadier General Charles W. Field. Then as senior officer, General Anderson took charge. When Lee found out about the mixup of troops and the utter confusion, he ordered the attack to stop. There was much difference of opinion about that order. Some said the attack shouldn't have been stopped and others, who perhaps were in a better position to know, agreed that with all the intermingling of the forces a strong coordinated attack couldn't be made at that time.

When General Lee finally did attack again, he hit hard. Nine brigades of infantry were used. Those barriers that the Federals had put up earlier paid off. Getty's two brigades along with most of Hancock's II Corps were holding a strong position. Then on the left flank of the Union line, the log barrier caught fire and the soldiers fell back from the smoke and fire. Colonel John W. Henagan's South Carolina brigade stormed the barrier at the point where the fire was, and, with the help of Anderson's Georgia brigade, planted their colors on the smoking, burning logs, but only for a short time.

As the Vermont Brigade continued to hold their line, fighting with determination, Captain Edward B. Dow's 6th Maine battery fired round after round of canister.[22] Carroll's brigade was sent in to drive the enemy out. It was a short and grueling hand-to-hand fight.

All along the Confederate battle lines their forces began to fall back. The Vermonters continued their firing on the troops. They never let up. Theirs was some of the heaviest and hardest fighting of the battle, but they never gave up their positions as other brigades and regiments had done. Hancock was wise in keeping the Vermont men there. During the two days of fighting he never moved them, although they weren't part of his corps. He realized their dependability and fighting spirit.[23]

On the morning of May 7, the Union high command was unaware of the exact position of the Confederate forward battle line. Hancock sent the 2nd Brigade of General Birney's 3rd Division out on the south side of the Orange Plank Road. In conjunction with that scouting movement, L. A. Grant also sent out a line of skirmishers onto the north side. They were under command of Major Richard B. Crandall of the 6th Vermont. In front of Birney's division Hancock had also sent the 1st U.S. Sharpshooters regiment as advance skirmishers. He had also placed twenty men out front, who had been caught hiding in the rear of the Union lines. The sharpshooters were ordered to shoot any of those men if they tried to run away.

No enemy was sighted. All they found were many corpses, in every position, wearing either the blue of the Union or the butternut color of the Confederacy. The Vermont soldiers found a large cache of rifles which apparently had been collected by the Rebels and then left behind. The guns were sent to the rear by wagon. By that afternoon, finding no enemy troops, the Vermont Brigade rejoined the VI Corps. They were glad to be back among the friendly familiar faces of their corps.

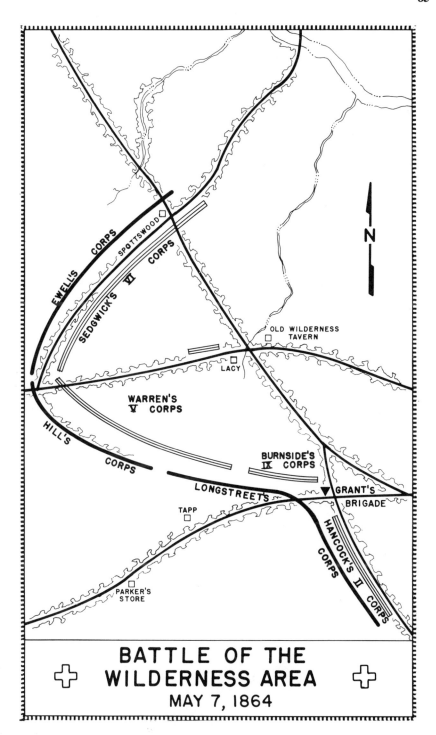

BATTLE OF THE
WILDERNESS AREA
MAY 7, 1864

The Vermont Brigade paid a staggering price fighting in the "slaughter pen" of the Wilderness. They lost 1,234 officers and men in two days of battle. Of that number, there were 342 killed, 947 wounded, ninety-six missing and two deserted.[24]

The battle of the Wilderness was at a stalemate. Neither General Lee nor General Grant was defeated. The one plus that Grant had to his benefit was that he had inflicted so many casualties on Lee's forces which was something Lee couldn't afford. Lee's army was starting to bleed to death.

CHAPTER XII

Battles at Spotsylvania

Under its earlier commanders the Army of the Potomac would usually retire and regroup after every major battle. They would count their losses. That didn't happen after the battle of the Wilderness, though. U. S. Grant was moving south to fight against the Army of Northern Virginia. His officers and men agreed with the change of procedure.

General Lee knew Grant well and realized that he was a fighter and would not retire. Lee sent Anderson's I Corps on a forced night march to Spotsylvania. Lee ordered a rough road cut through the forest to aid Anderson and his men to reach their destination quickly.[1] The forest was hot and smoky from the remaining fires and needless to say the troops didn't stop to make camp. The decision not to stop would pay high dividends in the coming battle.

The Federal army was also en route to Spotsylvania, but due to poor communications and misunderstandings between the cavalry and infantry units, the movement of the troops went from bad to worse.

Two Confederate cavalry brigades were making it almost impossible for the Union soldiers to move by felling trees and sniping at the advancing Yankee forces. And if that wasn't enough trouble for the advancing troops, two Federal cavalry brigades did not receive their orders and did make camp, thus blocking their infantry. That caused a violent argument between Generals Meade and Sheridan.[2]

Meade was finally able to get his men on the march, but the time lost would be costly. Lee's troops had arrived first at Spotsylvania and were able to fortify positions around the area.

As the Vermont Brigade left the battlefield of the Wilderness, they were ordered to be the rear guard for the VI Corps as they marched towards Spotsylvania. Unfortunately, several hundred of the wounded had to be left under the care of Surgeon Edwin Phillips of the 6th Vermont. Marching by way of Chancellorsville, the Vermont Brigade was ordered to guard the artillery and supply trains there.

In the meantime, the advanced Union cavalry tried to dislodge the Confederates from their well entrenched positions at Spotsylvania. They failed, and grudgingly called on the infantry to do the job. General Warren's troops were also unable to break through. He got into trouble and called for support. General Meade ordered the VI Corps to the support of Warren. They went on a forced march in the heat of day, and arrived at the scene of the battle just before dark.

The Vermont Brigade was ordered to the extreme left flank of the VI Corps. While marching the Vermont Brigade received just praise and recognition for their gallant deeds and heroic actions performed at the battle of the Brock Road. As the Vermonters marched past on their way to take up their positions, the regiments of the VI Corps broke out in a hurrah after hurrah. That was a great tribute, coming from those men of such a great fighting corps.[3]

Meade rode up to General L. A. Grant. He informed him that there was to be no attack that night, realizing the men had been marching all day in the heat. Before he left, he congratulated the Vermont Brigade on their valiant fighting in the Wilderness, and thanked them for getting there so quickly.[4]

Lee had chosen positions for his men wisely. The safety of those positions was helped by the lay of the land. The lines ran south to north and then went into a large bend to the east, and then turned south again. Turning slightly east again, the end of his lines rested at a small creek. The bend where the line made a U-shape came to be called the "Mule Shoe", by both the North and South. Later, after the battle, it would be called the "Bloody Angle". They would have good cause to call it that.

General Sedgwick, commander of VI Corps, was killed by a sharpshooter on May 9. While directing the action he advanced too far forward and became a good target. His death was a hard blow to the Vermonters. "Johnny", as the general had been called by his men, was considered one of the best and well liked generals in the entire army. He respected the Vermont Brigade highly and showed it more than once, by putting them where the need was the greatest. The Vermonters never failed him.

After the men of the Vermont Brigade learned of Sedgwick's death, they sent out a detail to find the marksman who had killed him. Sergeant Sanford Gray, originally from Wheelock, Vermont, found a concealed position with a dummy dressed as a soldier, propped in a firing position. The sergeant waited at that position until he saw a Confederate soldier moving toward the hiding place. Gray shot him dead. The body was examined and his rifle was found clutched in his hand. Although there was no definite evidence, the Vermonters liked to think that that soldier was the one who had killed their general.[5]

On May 10, Colonel Emory Upton, in command of the 2nd Brigade, 1st Division, of the VI Corps, asked his superiors if he could implement a new plan of attack. He asked if he could pick his own twelve regiments. His plan was to attack, with support, at one point. It was hoped, that with such concentration, they could break the Confederate line. Major General Horatio G. Wright, who had succeeded command of VI Corps, told Upton to put his plan into action. Picking twelve veteran regiments, Upton organized them into four lines. The first line consisted of the 121st New York, 5th Maine, and 96th Pennsylvania. The second line had the 6th Maine, 5th Wisconsin, and 49th Pennsylvania. The three regiments of the third line were the 43rd and 77th New York and 119th Pennsylvania. The fourth line was made up of the 2nd, 5th, and 6th Vermont. The 2nd was under the command of Lieutenant Colonel Samuel Pingree, the 5th under Major Dudley and the 6th was under Lieutenant Colonel Hale. Commanding all three regiments was Colonel T. O. Seaver.[6] Four companies of the 3rd Vermont also took part in Upton's charge as advance skirmishers. The 65th New York, under the command of Colonel Joseph E. Hamblin, also joined in this charge.

The attacking division moved as quietly as possible to within one hundred yards of the enemy positions. The men had already taken off all excess gear. The trees in the area were being cut by rifle fire as the men waited for the order to attack. To the right of Upton's men heavy artillery fire could be heard. They were firing on the V Corps as they attacked and were repulsed. Many of the soldiers were killed at once or burned alive by the surrounding burning bushes. The brush was tinder dry and the gunfire ignited it easily.

A little before six o'clock in the evening, as the gun fire began to let up, VI Corps' artillery opened fire. Round after round was hurled into the strong fortified, rebel entrenchment. For ten min-

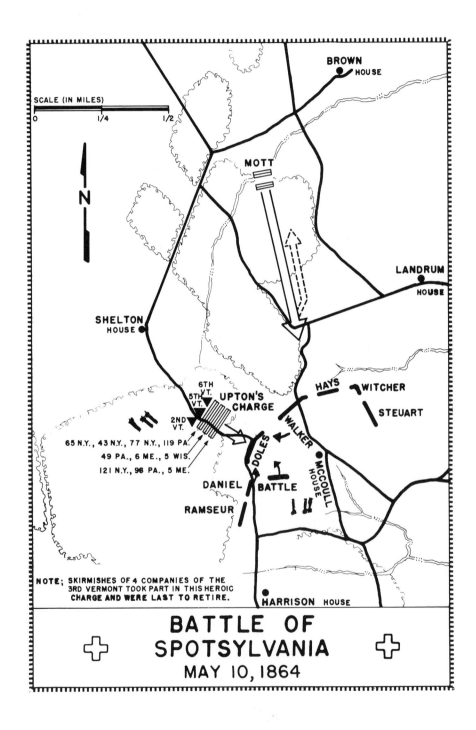

BATTLE OF
SPOTSYLVANIA
MAY 10, 1864

utes the shells poured into the front line positions. As the artillery ceased, the gunners lifted their sights and continued to pound the second line of Lee's forces. Then it was up to the charging infantry regiments to do the hard man-to-man fighting.

Jumping to their feet, Upton's attacking soldiers with loud yells and a hurrah charged the Rebel lines. They were met with heavy canister and rifle fire. At the barriers, a murderous hand-to-hand fight ensued. Brigadier General George Doles' Georgia Brigade fought back ferociously. Finally the Federal forces overpowered them, and the prisoners taken were sent to the rear.

Mr. Charles A. Dana, assistant secretary of war, was on the staff of General U. S. Grant. When he sent his report of Upton's charge to the secretary of war, he stated that General Doles' Georgia Brigade had been captured. The brigade consisted of the 4th, 12th, and 44th regiments. Nine hundred and fifty officers and men were taken prisoner, including Colonel William H. Peebles.[7]

Charging on to the second position and after heavy fighting, the Union men captured a battery of Confederate artillery which had done much damage. After taking over nine hundred prisoners in all, Upton's men put dirt and sods into the muzzles of the captured guns.

General Gershom Mott's division had been ordered to support Upton's brilliant charge. But, as soon as the Confederates started firing upon his men, they retired to the rear. It was strange that veteran troops would act in that manner; but many of those men were due to go home soon, their three years up, and that might have had a bearing on their actions.

Before the initial charge, Colonel Upton had given explicit orders to the commanders of the four attacking columns. He had told Colonel Seaver to hold his regiments back and only put them in where needed on the left flank. When Upton saw his troops being forced back by Southern brigades, he ordered his men to form side by side against the breastworks to the outside. He then rode across the field to bring up the Vermont regiments under Seaver.

In his official report of that engagement, Upton stated, "I rode back to bring up the Vermonters of the fourth line, but they had already mingled in the contest and were fighting with a heroism which has ever characterized that elite Brigade!"[8] Colonel Seaver was awarded the Medal of Honor for his actions in Upton's charge, though not until twenty-eight years later.[9] Colonel Upton was promoted to brigadier general for leading that fearless charge.

Lee brought up seven more brigades and rallied his forces against the breakthrough of Upton's surging regiments. He drove the Federal units from the "Mule Shoe". Ordered to retire, all except some of the men of the Vermont Brigade did so. Those men were still holding their positions in the "Mule Shoe". Learning that they had not retreated, Upton rode back and told them to leave. They then told Upton that, if he sent more ammunition and rations, they could hold their positions for months. General Wright heard about the Vermonters' refusal to retire and rode to General Ulysses S. Grant to ask what should be done. Grant, without wasting a second, told him to send in more men and to hold the position.[10] When Wright returned to the Vermont Brigade, they had, under special orders from Brigadier General David A. Russell, finally pulled back to the original starting lines in the woods.

Grant realized that that form of attack could be very successful. He stated "today a division, tomorrow a corps."[11] Upton's attack had broken the line and with a larger body of men, he planned to attack again in the same manner. He sent a message to Washington and told them that he proposed to fight it out on that line if it took all summer. And well that might be, as he realized just how strong Lee's positions were.

Grant made plans for a second hammer blow on the "Mule Shoe". Early in the morning of the 12th of May, Hancock's II Corps was ordered to make a grand assault. Lee was not prepared for them. Hancock's troops were knee-deep in the battle, but the opposition was tremendous. The weather was miserable, rain and fog all day. Hancock sent two divisions and later a third, to attack on the north side of the "Mule Shoe". Many of the Confederates' rifles misfired because of dampness. Their powder was of a poorer quality, and the men had been out in the wet longer. That attack was somewhat more successful and four thousand men and twenty cannon were captured. Hancock required help, and Grant sent General Wright and the VI Corps in support. They were ordered to Hancock's right flank because Lee had rushed three divisions there to aid in throwing back the attack.

The Vermont Brigade charged the enemy and took heavy casualties from artillery fire. They continued to press on to the barriers. It was only eight o'clock in the morning. Brigadier General David A. Russell's brigade was hard pressed. L. A. Grant was ordered to take the 4th and 5th Vermont regiments to help him. They took and held a part of the breastworks on the right flank of the angle in support of Wheaton's brigade.

Colonel Seaver came up with the rest of the Vermont Brigade. Leaving the 4th to hold the position and putting the 6th Vermont in reserve, L. A. Grant took the three remaining regiments to the western side of the angle. There they fought against Brigadier General Samuel McGowan's attacking South Carolina brigade.

Inside the breastworks was a scene of horror. Rain that fell formed puddles which eventually turned red from the blood of the killed and wounded. It was a nightmare for both sides. The savage fighting at that bloody angle went on hour after hour. The firepower was so heavy at that section of battle that trees over a foot in diameter were cut down by the guns and the limbs cut up like matchsticks. Union artillery, rolled into place by hand, fired into the opposing lines. During that agonizing battle the men of the Vermont Brigade realized the fighting at the bloody angle was four times more deadly than the fighting of May 10. The numbers of losses on both sides proved that. The Vermonters fought all day for eight hours straight. Dead and wounded lay everywhere, some piled two and three on top of each other. Stabbing with bayonet, jumping on top of the breastworks and firing down on the enemy, the Vermonters continued the fight. Any Confederate showing his head above the

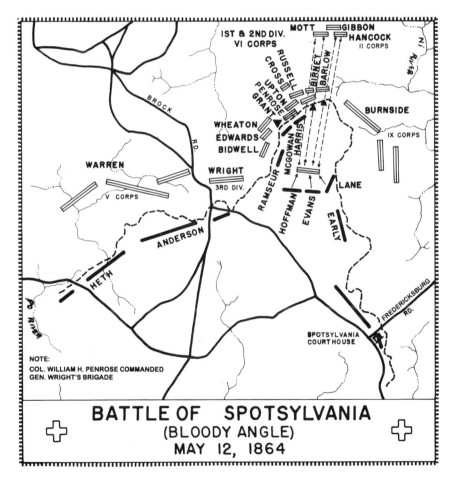

BATTLE OF SPOTSYLVANIA
(BLOODY ANGLE)
MAY 12, 1864

breastworks met instant death due to the accurate firing, but the Mississippi and South Carolina regiments held.

A lucky and brave Private William Noyes of the 2nd Vermont, while on top of the breastworks, fired over thirty shots into Rebel lines, even though he was exposed to the enemy. His hat was shot off. He was a sitting duck, like many others, but performed his duty without hesitation. He received the Medal of Honor twenty-eight years later.[12]

The Vermont Brigade suffered severe losses at the "Bloody Angle", many of them commanding officers. At that time Colonel Pingree was in command of the division skirmish line. For that reason Captain Dayton Clark took command of the 2nd Vermont. He led his men, in much of the hand-to-hand combat. He also received the Medal of Honor twenty-eight years later for distinguished conduct.[13]

There were many brave deeds throughout the war, some never officially recorded. One of those deeds was performed by Sergeant Warren Gifford of Danby, Vermont. While at his position with Company B, 2nd Vermont, a staff of colors of the 2nd North Carolina was planted directly in front of him. He attacked the color bearer, and bayoneted him. He took the colors off the field amid cheers from his comrades.[14]

At times a white flag was waved and the signal was in earnest. Other times it was a hoax, a tactic to get into the Union lines. That ploy was used on the 2nd Vermont. During the battle, a white flag was waved and the firing stopped. Confederate soldiers, carrying white flags, came forward as if to surrender. Lieutenant Henry Hayward of Company E looked beyond those soldiers and saw a large column of attacking troops just behind them. He alerted his comrades and called for help. The men of his company fired into the oncoming troops. The sneak attack was averted and the Union lines were not broken.

The Vermont Brigade was relieved of duty just as it was getting dark, although the fighting didn't cease until three o'clock in the morning. They were exhausted and almost out of ammunition. Groping their way in the darkness to the rear of their positions, the Vermont men found a place to rest. They had fought gallantly and also had done almost the impossible, inflicting heavier casualties on the enemy than they had taken and had held their positions until relieved. Along the front of the breastworks for a half mile, one could see men of the II and VI Corps lying dead in every grotesque position. The bloody angle had earned its name.

The Confederates were also worn out. Lee had established a second line and withdrew some of his troops to it. They had accomplished the difficult task of stopping the Federal troops from breaking completely through, holding their lines under inconceivable conditions.

On May 14, with the VI Corps, the Vermont Brigade marched two miles south and a mile and a half east of Spotsylvania Courthouse. It was a hot, dusty and tedious march. They ended up on the Ny River at Anderson House. There the 11th Vermont was added to the Vermont Brigade, none too soon.

The 11th Vermont had been organized as the 1st Vermont Heavy Artillery back in 1862. Like other heavy artillery units, it had been sent to guard Washington, D.C., but due to tremendous losses in the field, Grant used those regiments to swell the ranks of the battle-torn brigades. The 11th had the distinction of being one of the first artillery units to join the Army of the Potomac. They were added to the Vermont Brigade because General Sedgwick had requested them. Joining the Vermont Brigade with fifteen hundred strong, they brought it up to strength. That request would eventually save the "Old Brigade" from being broken up.[15] One hundred and fifty recruits were also added.

Most of the hard fighting around Spotsylvania was just about over by the time those recruits were added. Twenty battles and many small skirmishes had been fought. The veteran soldiers looked on the new men as outsiders. The men of the 11th knew they would have to prove themselves.

Grant believed that Lee had weakened his lines by moving his troops. The heavy losses didn't help him either. With that in mind, in the night and in poor conditions, Grant marched the II and VI Corps back to the lines and to their old positions around the Spotsylvania battlefield on May 17. In darkness and in the mud of the swamps, the "Green-Mountain Men" started attacking from the third line. In the chaos and darkness they found themselves somehow in the first line of attack. Steadying themselves, they dressed their lines for attack, but Meade called the attack off when he realized that Lee's positions were still strongly held. In the short time they fought, the Vermont Brigade took casualties; thirty-seven, most of them from the 11th Vermont. Their first

USAMHI

Brigadier General James M. Warner, 1st Vermont Heavy Artillery, later the 11th Vermont.

time in action had been a grueling and dirty fight for the men of the 11th.

Colonel James M. Warner led the 11th Vermont. He was shot by a sharpshooter and, although wounded, returned to his regiment. He set a good example for his men with that kind of leadership. The 11th would surely maintain the high reputation of the "Old Brigade".

At that time the Southern armies also received much needed reinforcements. The small Florida brigade added three new regiments. General Hoke's division from General Beauregard's command was sent from the Petersburg and Richmond defenses. The five brigades were a welcome addition to Lee's army.

On the night of May 21, 1864, the VI Corps started marching south to the North Anna River. General Wright had given the Vermont Brigade the important position of rear guard.

Knowing that Grant's army was on the march, Lee attacked every chance he could. The soldiers were attacked during the very first night. The Vermont Brigade was right in the fighting along with the 11th Vermont. Gun fire went on all night. The slightest movement drew rifle fire. By the morning of the 22nd, the 11th was able to start to withdraw. Under difficult conditions, dodging from tree to tree and crawling through bushes, they headed for a line of rifle pits a half mile to the rear. The Confederates were right on their heels. They made it to the pits, but holding that line wasn't going to be easy.

General Wilcox sent out two brigades of infantry. The Vermonters held their line with help from some Massachusetts men. Together they were able to repulse the attacking Georgia and North Carolina troops. On the third attack a North Carolina regiment planted its colors just to the right of the 11th. It appeared that their lines were broken. Then Captain Walker of the 11th moved his men facing right. They held the line until Colonel Seaver and the 3rd Vermont arrived and, with the help of artillery, drove the enemy back, thus restoring the lines of the Union. The Vermonters took several prisoners. Southern losses were high in that savage fight.

May 22, the VI Corps crossed the North Anna River. Grant found the Confederates too well entrenched there, so he marched on to Hanovertown, just fifteen miles north of Richmond. Again the march was done at night, and again it was raining. They were constantly fired on by snipers. Finally they went into camp.

The last two campaigns took a great toll on the Army of the Potomac. Most of the wounded were sent to the town of Fredericksburg, which became one big hospital. So many of the wounded were from Vermont, the people of Vermont wanted to help. They knew the care would be only fair, so they sent doctors to help.

Eventually, the wounded from Vermont were removed to special hospitals that were set up in Burlington, Montpelier, and Brattleboro, Vermont. Over fifteen hundred men were moved.[16] Their care was excellent and because of that, many lived who might otherwise have died.

Years later when official records were published, it was revealed that General Ulysses S. Grant had requested those heavy artillery regiments and reserve regiments a month before he started his Overland Campaign. The records showed that on May 1, orders had been issued to send forty-eight thousand men to the Army of the Potomac. Grant must have realized before he ever started the campaign that he was surely going to take heavy casualties, and he was smart enough to prepare for that eventuality.

CHAPTER XIII

Assaults at Cold Harbor

On May 22, 1864, the Vermont Brigade started their retirement from the battlefields around Spotsylvania Courthouse. By the 25th of May they reached the railroad near Gordonsville. There was heavy and steady skirmishing with the Confederates most of the time.

The VI Corps was detached and sent to Cold Harbor. They were sent to relieve the outnumbered men of Sheridan's command. The Vermonters had to endure another brutal march. They had been skirmishing in the swamps for a few days before they embarked. Heat and thirst were constant companions. The dirt roads produced clouds of dust, making it almost impossible to breathe. The men were covered with it, so much so, that anyone looking at them couldn't tell if they were Federal or Confederate troops. As they marched along, some fell from sniper fire and others from heat exhaustion.

One of the soldiers who fell by the wayside was Julius Moreau. He was then captured and later joined the Confederate army so that he wouldn't die of starvation. Later in the war he was recaptured by Union forces, after which he took an oath of allegiance to the North and near the end of the war was mustered out of service.[1]

Cold Harbor was of particular strategic importance because three or four roads crossed there. A short distance down one of the roads flowed the Chickahominy River, and the city of Richmond was only five miles away.

General Philip Sheridan and his cavalry troopers had been sent to Cold Harbor earlier to secure that vital crossroads. He sent a message back to General Wright that he wouldn't be able to hold the position much longer. The fighting was continuous and it was difficult for cavalry to hold against infantry for very long. His men and horses needed relief.

A few days earlier General Grant had ordered Major General Benjamin Butler to dispatch two corps of infantry to reinforce the Army of the Potomac. Major General William E. Smith's XVIII Corps, along with units of the Army of the James, were sent.[2]

"Baldy" Smith, as he was called, was himself a Vermont native. He had helped form the Vermont Brigade at the beginning of the war and had led the 2nd Division of which the Vermont Brigade had been part.

The men of the VI Corps did relieve Sheridan's men just in time, as they were nearly out of ammunition. Wright was given orders to attack the enemy immediately, but Smith and his units had just arrived at Cold Harbor and were not in their positions. That was due to another mixup of orders.

Grant planned to make a major attack on the strong fortifications built by Lee's troops. Unfortunately for the Union those strongholds would never be taken or really penetrated, except for one small break made by Brigadier General James B. Ricketts' division of the VI Corps. Also, the plan of attack was delayed due to heavy rains, and it was not instituted until late in the day of June 1.

The Vermont Brigade was in the first line of attack. The other two brigades of the 2nd Division were to the rear. The Federal artillery opened fire. About the same time the Confederates started an attack to the north and left of the Union line. General Neill, commander of the 2nd Division, ordered L. A. Grant to meet that attack.[3] The 4th and 6th Vermont along with Major Charles Hunsdon's battalion of the 11th Vermont were turned to meet the heavy rifle fire. The 5th Vermont was rushed to the assistance of a

USAMHI

**Colonel Charles Hunsdon,
1st Vermont Heavy Artillery**

Federal battery which was under severe gunfire. The 2nd Vermont, commanded by Lieutenant Colonel Pingree, along with a battalion from the 11th, under command of Lieutenant Colonel Reuben C. Benton, joined General Russell's division in the main assault. Those fortifications were almost impregnable, and the charge lasted only about twenty minutes. Ricketts' division was the only unit to break the Confederate lines.[4] Due to the heavy enfilading gunfire on both of his flanks, his men had to finally give up their position. All along the Northern lines their attacks were stopped cold.

The Federal soldiers had to dig in, trying to take cover as best they could. That was hard to do because the area in front of the enemy fortifications was mostly open fields. Along in front of the five miles of Confederate lines, the Union dead and wounded lay by the hundreds. The 2nd and 11th Vermont suffered thirteen killed and one hundred sixteen wounded in that first attack at Cold Harbor.[5]

Grant, for some reason, thought his troops had broken the opposing lines, and ordered a second charge for the morning of June 2. Hancock's II Corps, just coming up to the battle line, was placed on the left flank of the Vermont Brigade. They had been marching all night and were in no condition to do battle. William F. Smith's regiments had taken severe losses the day before and were almost out of ammunition. All those problems were not taken into consideration by Grant, although they delayed plans to attack the second time.[6]

The plan to go on the offensive was postponed until the next day, which proved to be a costly delay as it allowed Lee to bring more troops into the area. In the gray dawn of the 3rd of June, three brigades of the 2nd Division, VI Corps, attacked the fortifications again. The men were in three lines. The Vermont Brigade was in the second line. Wheaton's brigade was in the first line, they stormed the enemy and drove in their advance skirmishers. Captain Alexander Beattie of Company F, 3rd Vermont, amid heavy gunfire and the smoke of battle, carried one of his wounded men to safety. He later received the Medal of Honor for his deed.[7]

Wheaton requested relief for his brigade. General L. A. Grant ordered the 3rd and 5th Vermont into the forward rifle pits and used the rest of the brigade for support. The "Green Mountain Men" held the front lines.

U. S. Grant told his officers to attack again and again, if they thought they could succeed. Some units advanced further than others, and in doing so exposed their flanks. Concentrated Rebel fire into those exposed areas stopped the troops from continuing to advance and caused tremendous Union losses. The assaults were fruitless.

The men of Vermont dug their trenches deep, and piled logs, rails, sods, and rocks up high; anything for cover. They were very close to the enemy lines and under constant fire. In fact, no movement could be made at all during the daytime. Only during the dark of night could the reliefs and rations be brought up. It was a living hell. With so little food and water it was unbearable. The heat was intense and the dead lay everywhere. Those courageous men held their positions for ten grueling and horrifying days.[8]

During the time that the wounded and dead lay on the battlefield in the open, and after the attacks of the 1st and 3rd of June, the officers of the Union regiments requested a truce so the dead could be buried and wounded removed. General U. S. Grant sent a request to General Lee for that truce, but it apparently was not worded correctly. Lee asked for clarification of the request. Those delays took time and by the time the truce was put in place, almost all of the wounded had died.[9]

On June 9, near the end of the battles at Cold Harbor, Mr. Charles Dana, serving on Grant's staff, sent his usual report to the secretary of war. In that report he stated that when the truce finally came, the Union soldiers went into the field of battle to bring the wounded in. They were only able to bring two men back alive. That left four hundred and thirty-two men dead. That blundering left the men with a futile feeling about the tragic and horrifying battles at Cold Harbor.[10]

On June 12, 1864, the Vermonters left their positions and started a march toward Petersburg. The battle at Cold Harbor had been a disastrous failure. It was obvious that the fighting spirit of the men of the Army of the Potomac was pretty low after that costly battle of Grant's overland campaign.

After the war many officers stated that those attacks were senseless and should never have been ordered. The men in the ranks paid the price, but they would earn high honor a year later when final victory would be theirs.

During those ten days, fighting continued by other units which took heavy losses. Reports came back and newspapers reported that troops were refusing to advance. Of course, that wasn't true. U. S. Grant himself verified that none of his men in his command refused to advance when ordered to do so. He did say the attacks at Cold Harbor were ones he wished he hadn't ordered.[11]

The whole Army of the Potomac appeared to be moving toward Petersburg. The VI Corps was no different. They followed the route of the IX Corps and soon passed them in the line of march. Grant had sent Phil Sheridan and the cavalry, along with General Warren's V Corps to screen the movement of his other units. Warren's men used diversionary tactics, skirmishing with the enemy to keep them busy.

June 12 was a warm day. Although the roads were dusty, the men did notice they had reached a part of Virginia that was quite pretty. The war had not reached that area yet. The brigade crossed the Chickahominy River at Jones Bridge, twenty-three miles south of Cold Harbor. They went into camp one mile south of the bridge.

The next morning, as the soldiers marched, they saw even prettier countryside, fields of corn, beautiful trees and fine looking homes. That was a big contrast to other areas the Vermonters had seen as they fought to help to preserve the Union. They reached the James River on June 15. A pontoon bridge, over two thousand feet long, had been built and they proceeded to guard it. As the men marched across, the bridge swayed and tossed with the wind and currents. Most of the Northern army crossed there, including the 2nd Division of the VI Corps but the 1st and 3rd Divisions went by steamboat. The Union army on the march, including troops and supply wagons, measured fifty miles long.

Marching to positions near Petersburg, the Vermont Brigade relieved General Brooks and his units who had secured those positions the day before. The men from Vermont thought that Petersburg had already been taken and much to their surprise, they found that only the first lines of the defenses had been penetrated and the city was still held by the enemy.

Some of the fighting up to now had been done by black soldiers. They were fine fighting men, but at that time in our history, the black soldier earned only seven dollars while the white soldier earned thirteen dollars. It took many months into the war before the injustice was corrected. A black soldier was never commissioned as an officer, although Governor Andrews of Massachusetts had commissioned a sergeant major to a lieutenant, but the Federal government refused to acknowledge it. It took nearly another one hundred years before black and white units were integrated.

While in the trenches in front of Petersburg, some of the men of the Vermont Brigade were due to be mustered out of service because their enlistments were up. Two hundred and twenty-two men of the 2nd Vermont were to go home. They were part of the senior regiment of the brigade. General Neill commended them for their dedication to duty and their great fighting record. The state of Vermont sent new recruits, replacing those veterans. That was a good policy, as having all the men from the same area created pride in the units. That is one of the main reasons the Vermont Brigade remained strong and had great spirit.

On the 18th of June, an assault again was mounted on Petersburg's defenses. It wasn't until over seven thousand men were killed and wounded that Grant realized that Petersburg would never be taken by direct attack. The fighting was intense and the Northern troops were unable to penetrate the city's defenses. The men fought with the heat and dust, making it hard to see or breathe. The failure of that contest was blamed on General "Baldy" Smith, although the real blame should have been the poor lines of communication that existed between U. S. Grant and his corps commanders.[12] Also many of those commanders failed to attack as soon as they were ordered to do so. The Vermonters were lucky, they were not engaged in that battle.

The VI Corps was again ordered to march. They were ordered to the southwest end of the Union lines and were told to cut one of the rail lines that was supplying Lee's army in the defense of Petersburg. The XVIII Corps relieved them and they proceeded toward the Weldon Railroad.

CHAPTER XIV

Disaster at Weldon Railroad

On June 21, the VI Corps marched toward their destination. They moved through the night and finally arrived at the Williams House which was located at the very end of the Union lines. The II Corps was ordered to follow them and support the VI Corps on their left flank. Marching at night protected the men from sunstroke and heat exhaustion, a natural enemy of the foot soldier. Temperatures were climbing near the hundred mark.

As the II Corps moved to link up with the VI Corps, to their left, they were hit a disastrous blow. General A. P. Hill's forces found a hole in the Federal lines between the two corps. He mounted a surprise attack against Major General David B. Birney. Suddenly the men of II Corps were overwhelmed. Over two thousand prisoners were taken by Hill, with little loss to his own units.[1] Many veteran units were put out of action.

General Wright ordered the Vermont Brigade to the left flank of VI Corps. General L. A. Grant moved the 3rd Vermont, along with Walker's battalion of the 11th Vermont, way out on the left to guard against any attack from that quarter. On the right, units were moved to better tactical positions. Skirmishing with the enemy, they were able to drive the Confederates back into their main battle line. By the time that was accomplished, it was very late at night on June 22. Having halted the advance of the enemy, the men dug in to get some rest. The 4th Vermont was put out to act as advance skirmishers.

In the morning, a scouting party was sent out under the command of Captain Beattie of the 3rd Vermont. They found the rail line that they were to destroy and sent back a message that more men would be needed. A large force of pioneers was sent to help pull up the rails and tracks. Fleming's battalion of two hundred men from the 11th, was also sent for added protection. At the same time circumstances led to confusion about the placement of the troops. The terrain was rugged and hilly, with patches of heavy woods.

Wheaton had ordered General L. A. Grant to send more men to the skirmish line. He wanted to strengthen the forward lines, so he sent the rest of the men of Fleming's battalion. They were directed to the wrong position by a staff officer.[2] They found themselves a mile in front of the Vermont Brigade's position; high ground that the Vermonters were holding.

Realizing that the area they held was a key position, when L. A. Grant was ordered to leave, he thought better of that and went to explain why he didn't want to move his men. At headquarters, he first spoke with General Wheaton, division commander. Receiving no satisfaction, he went to the corps commander, General Wright. Together they rode to the crest of the hill held by the Vermonters. Heavy fighting was occurring. Wright told L. A. Grant that if it became impossible to hold, he should retire to his right flank to link up with Ricketts' units. The direction given by Wright was a mistake. The area on the right flank had been held by the 87th Pennsylvania, but they had retired from that position because of heavy firepower. Trying to find out exactly where the Confederate troops were, L. A. Grant sent out a hundred men of the 4th Vermont as skirmishers into that abandoned area.

Meanwhile, more than half a mile of track had been torn up. The men could see A. P. Hill's advancing units moving toward them. The pioneers and sharpshooters withdrew under orders from Beattie. He also informed Captain Safford, 11th Vermont, to retire his men. Colonel Samuel Pingree pulled back some of his skirmishers. The Southern force which was attacking were men of Brigadier General William Mahone's division. That division had twenty-seven infantry regiments.[3] Wright still had not ordered artillery into that battle area.

The 4th Vermont's lines ran through heavy woods and very little could be seen beyond the trees. The 12th, 16th, 19th, and 48th Mississippi regiments charged through the woods suddenly, hitting the front lines of the 4th and 11th Vermont. Brigadier General Joseph Finnegan's Florida Brigade advanced through the open right flank.[4] Wheeling right, they came in on the rear of the Vermonters. In the short fight that ensued, fifty men escaped with the colors of the 4th Vermont so the colors did not fall to the enemy.

The 11th Vermont was engaged in heavy fighting. Part of Major Fleming's battalion was cut off and outnumbered; two hundred and seventy officers and men were forced to surrender.[5]

The soldier who carried the colors to safety was Sergeant James Drury of Company C. He was an Irish lad who had enlisted at Chester, Vermont, in August 1861. At the close of the war, he was promoted to 2nd Lieutenant and received the Medal of Honor twenty-nine years later for his heroic deed.[6]

June 23, 1864, was a dark day in the history of the Vermont Brigade. Due to confusion and mix-up of battle, thirteen men of the Vermont Brigade were killed and four hundred and one men were captured. More than half of those men died in the hell holes of Confederate prison compounds at Andersonville, Georgia, and Columbia, South Carolina. The men who were released at the end of the war were broken in health, and many died shortly thereafter. Seventy percent of the Vermonters captured at Weldon Railroad died because of their imprisonment.[7] They were young, healthy men when they went into prison; the people of Vermont could not understand why and how they had died.

The loss of so many men, and the blunders made in the field on that dark and disastrous day must be blamed on General Wright. He had not allowed the pickets to retire. He also did not know that the Vermont Brigade's flank on the right was not covered. Very few reports were ever written about that disastrous engagement. After the war, the few reports or letters which were written seemed to blame General Wright.

June 23, Colonel Theodore Lyman, aide to Major General George Gordon Meade, was sent to VI Corps' headquarters. Although he was probably sent to carry messages, Lyman stayed with Wright throughout the entire engagement at the Weldon Railroad. After the war, Lyman wrote his observations and reported that Wright's divisions were not connected, stating that the wings were in the air. He also stated that Wright didn't know what positions his divisions held. In one letter he wrote that Wright was not fit to command a corps.[8]

It was reported that Meade, throughout the fighting at Weldon Railroad, sent many orders to Wright to attack. At four o'clock in the afternoon Wright had not yet ordered the attack. He was hesitant and undecided. Only as darkness crept in did Wright give the order to dig in. Meade's last communication to Wright summed up the blunders at the Weldon Railroad on June 23. It stated, "Your delay has been fatal."[9] Many believed that if Getty had been in command, that disaster would probably never have happened. Good leadership wins battles.

Up to that time in the war, prisoners had been exchanged evenly; allowing them to go back to their own armies. Ulysses S. Grant felt strongly that that policy helped the South, so he cancelled the policy. Unfortunately, some officers and men with political pull were still able to be exchanged. The ordinary soldier in the ranks was not allowed that special treatment and consequently, thousands died in the prison camps. Many of the Vermont soldiers who were captured at the Weldon Railroad might have survived if Grant and Secretary of War Stanton had not changed and enforced the method of exchange.[10] Most of those deaths occurred within a few short months of their capture.

CHAPTER XV

On to Washington —
The Marching Campaigns

June 28, the Vermont Brigade went into camp near a house owned by a Mr. Williams. The next day they marched to Reams's Station. The skirmishers of the 3rd Vermont were out in front. When they reached the station, they were met by a Confederate force which had just repulsed a small Union cavalry unit. They were part of General Mahone's division; men from Finnegan's Florida Brigade. The Vermont Brigade, realizing their situation, quickly formed their line of battle. After a very short exchange and very little shooting, Finnegan's men retired and Reams's Station was then in the hands of the Vermont men.

The Vermont Brigade was not engaged in any more fighting at the station, and the next day they were able to destroy a large section of track. Afterwards they were ordered back to the area near the Williams house, just four miles south of Petersburg.

At that time in the war, many other great units of the Army of the Potomac were falling apart. Heavy losses among the veteran soldiers, new and untried regiments, and poor leadership contributed to their decline.

The Vermont Brigade entered the next campaign with two thousand six hundred officers and men. Men left from Major Fleming's battalion were put into two remaining battalions of the 11th Vermont.[1] Under the command of General Lewis A. Grant and with General George W. Getty again in charge of the 2nd Division, VI

108

Corps, the "Green Mountain Men" knew they would have excellent leadership in the coming campaigns.

The war in the Shenandoah Valley was not going well for the Union. The Army of the Shenandoah had been defeated at New Market and forced to retreat to Harpers Ferry. Major General Franz Sigel was relieved of command there, and Major General David Hunter took over.[2] Hunter took the offensive and won a small victory at Piedmont. General Lee sent his Second Army Corps, led by General Jubal A. Early to help relieve his situation at Petersburg. That corps was made up of some of the toughest and roughest men in the Confederate army. Many historians later would say that they were the best infantrymen in the world.[3] Hunter retreated down the Kanawha Valley instead of retiring toward the defenses of Washington. By making that mistake, he took himself right out of the war, leaving the Shenandoah Valley and the areas of northern Virginia and Maryland wide open to Early and his men.

On July 9, U. S. Grant sent the 3rd Division of the VI Corps to Baltimore to reinforce the few trained militia troops there. That same evening, the 1st and 2nd Divisions, VI Corps, broke camp and marched to City Point, Virginia. They were force-marched on a dusty road, in the dark of night. That was a saving grace as there was no sun to bake the men, and that saved them from sunstroke. At City Point there were transport steamers that would take the men down the James River, out to the Chesapeake Bay and then up the Potomac River to the docks at Washington.

On their arrival at City Point, tired and ragged, the men were fed before boarding. The Sanitary Commission gave out food. The meal consisted of hardtack, pickles, and coffee. Even though those rations might not seem too appealing, the men ate and enjoyed every mouthful.[4] The men boarded the steamers soon after, packed in with practically no room to breathe. The conditions on board were disgraceful. The transports were in disrepair and filthy. They sailed out and reached the Chesapeake Bay by evening. Resting, along with the gentle sea breeze, did much to refresh those tired, hardy veterans. General Getty had left earlier on a smaller and faster steamer, in order to reach Washington before his men.

Meanwhile, at the railroad junction at the Monocacy River, Maryland, the small force of militiamen and General Ricketts' division were involved in a battle with General Early's Second Corps. Although the Union forces were defeated, thus leaving the defenses of Washington open to Early's attack, they delayed him and wore down his troops.

Washington was in a state of turmoil. Some people already had left the city. Most of the citizens and the non-combat personnel who remained didn't know what to do. There was little or no organization, and no veteran troops in the city. Most of the generals were staff members and had very little, if any, experience in fighting. The one thing they all did have in common was their willingness to defend their city.

Dr. S. J. Allen on Getty's staff was one of the first officers to disembark from the steamer at Washington. He was met by President Abraham Lincoln. Looking very tired and drawn, Lincoln had been waiting impatiently for the troops to arrive. He asked the doctor what troops the steamers had transported. Allen told him, General Getty and his staff. Lincoln replied that he was not there to see generals, but was there to see the Vermont Brigade and the troops of the VI Corps.[5] Lincoln had a great admiration for those units. The president kept track of all his troops and knew who was doing the fighting. He kept up with the casualty reports and knew of the many losses of the Vermont Brigade, especially those lost in the battle of the Wilderness.

When the troops finally did start to disembark, President Lincoln stopped a soldier and asked him for a piece of hardtack. He took a bite now and then, and talked to the men as they fell into ranks.

Crowds began to gather as the soldiers marched up Seventh Street. Voices became louder as the people found out that the men were the battle-hardened men of the VI Corps. They began to shout, "It's the Sixth Corps. We are saved".[6] As they marched by, people gave the men cool water to drink. Some of the rugged soldiers were lost to the many pubs, as they were looking for something stronger to drink than water. The people of Washington were very grateful to the men of the VI Corps for their timely arrival.

Marching out on the Seventh Street Road toward the defenses of Washington, the Vermont Brigade reached Fort Stevens, and the 2nd and 3rd Vermont were posted in the rifle pits on the left flank of the fort. Major General Robert E. Rodes' Confederate division had advanced and the firing was heavy. Eighty selected marksmen under command of Captain Beattie, 3rd Vermont, were sent to deal with Southern sharpshooters occupying a house directly in front of the Vermont Brigade's positions. The enemy was driven out. One of the Vermont marksmen was killed and six more wounded in that action.[7] Fifty more men were then added to that unit from the 4th Vermont and later in the day they took part in stopping Rodes' advancing units.

The main attack was made by the 3rd Brigade, 2nd Division, under command of Brigadier General Daniel D. Bidwell, on the afternoon of July 11. The men moved out of the forts and formed two lines of attack. Early's units increased their rifle fire on those exposed lines. Union artillery opened fire just before the 3rd Brigade attacked. They charged, and, through the thick smoke of the artillery fire, fought a short but hard fight and finally drove the Confederates from their prepared positions.

President Lincoln saw that whole battle, along with his wife and most of his Cabinet. General Wright had given the president an invitation to witness the fighting, but thought he would decline it. He was wrong and the president and his wife and staff had come into the forts. The president was standing in a parapet during the fighting and just a few feet away an officer was shot and wounded. That was too much for General Wright, and he ordered the president to get down and go to a safe place or he would have him carried there.[8]

On the night of July 12, General Early, realizing that his men were vastly outnumbered and exhausted, decided to retire from the defenses of Washington.[9]

Meanwhile, the Vermont Brigade and two divisions of the VI Corps and one from the XIX Corps marched in pursuit of General Early's retiring troops, with the hopes of destroying them. At first the Vermont Brigade formed the rear guard. The march was boring and tiring. The supply wagons on the narrow roads kept the march at a slow pace. By marching all night they covered twenty miles. The men fell out for a quick breakfast and short rest in the early morning. It was army policy that if your unit was rear guard one day, the next day it would lead the column.[10] The Vermont Brigade, then in the lead, reached Poolesville in the afternoon of July 14. They marched forty miles in the summer heat and on dusty, narrow roads in just over twenty-four hours.

There was much changing of command and much confusion during the campaign. No one leader controlled all units. That was due to the many conflicting orders that came out of Washington. Gen-

USAMHI

Lieutenant Colonel Horace W. Floyd, 3rd Vermont Infantry

eral Getty took over command of the VI Corps. General Wright was put in command of the forces pursuing Early.

The Vermont Brigade, still leading the forces, crossed the Potomac at Whites Ford and Conrad's Ferry. The enemy could be seen on the other side, but as soon as they saw the Union troops they ran off into the woods. Although the river was only three feet deep in most places, the current was very strong. The men made ready to cross and as they did, many took a dunking in the cool water, toppled by the rushing river. The men didn't seem to mind. The summer heat and choking dust of that long and arduous march were soon forgotten in the cool water of the Potomac. On the other side of the river, they met General Ricketts' 3rd Division coming from the Baltimore area after the battle of the Monocacy. They rejoined the VI Corps, making it complete again.

During the pursuit of Early's army, the 3rd Vermont lost one hundred and sixty-five officers and men because their enlistments were up. Those were veterans, hardened to the fighting, who would be missed. Two of their best officers, Colonel Seaver and Lieutenant Colonel Pingree were among them. They had performed heroic deeds. Seaver would eventually win the Medal of Honor for previously leading a gallant charge at the battle of Spotsylvania Courthouse. Pingree also would win a Medal of Honor for a brave performance in his duty leading the charge at Warwick River, the first attack of the war. Those leaders would be hard to replace. Lieutenant Colonel Horace Floyd then took command of the 3rd Vermont.[11]

The Vermont men had their first view of the beautiful Shenandoah Valley when they marched through Snickers Gap in the Blue Ridge Mountains. That valley had been a battleground all through the war and its farms had supplied the Confederate forces with food, horses and many other things during the first three years of the war. In the next five months the Vermonters would come to know the valley very well, and would participate in some of the Union's greatest victories there.

As the VI Corps proceeded in their quest to destroy Early and his men, other forces under General Hunter and Major General George Crook, further up in the Valley, almost trapped his forces. After a sharp action, Early was able to escape to Strasburg, just below Winchester. Hearing about that action, General Wright thought that the VI Corps would not need to continue their pursuit. U. S. Grant wanted them back at Petersburg and Wright started them marching toward Washington. On July 21, the Vermont Brigade recrossed the Shenandoah River, and again marched over the hot and dusty roads of the Blue Ridge Mountains. It was in the dead of night when they marched back through Snickers Gap. They passed the tired XIX Corps; never slowing their pace. With only a few short rests, the brigade marched through Leesburg and on to Dranesville. Exhausted but determined, they continued to Tenallytown, just north of Washington.

On July 23, they went into camp for a well deserved rest. Much was asked of those Vermont men and they responded well. They had just finished marching through territory which was mostly controlled by the South. Large and small guerrilla bands or partisan raiders roamed the area. Although Lee deplored them, they did much harm to the enemy, capturing them and most times killing them. Needless to say, the knowledge that those bands were around, helped the brigade to march as they did. They knew that if they fell out of the line of march and were captured, they could be robbed, sent to the hell-holes of Southern prisons or die.[12]

It will never be known how many Union soldiers were lost on those sometime futile and grueling marches. The main problem while marching was the lack of water. That was one of the main reasons the men might leave the line of march. Another major problem concerning the moving of troops and orders on the field was caused by Major General Henry W. Halleck, or "Old Brains", as he was sometimes called. He was stationed in Washington after being in the field, because President Lincoln thought he would be of value there. He had much power, but was a stupid and blundering man. He knew nothing about fighting and winning a war, and his orders were the cause of many soldiers' deaths.[13]

For the next three days, the Vermont Brigade, while resting, was refitted with new clothing and shoes. Some of the troops had come into camp with no shoes at all. They had been worn right out from the hard marching they had done.

The 11th Vermont then was sent into the forts around Washington. They had just arrived there, when they were sent back to the Vermont Brigade again, all within a day and a half. The temporary assignment, was originally intended to last until the end of the war.[14]

General Early inspired the order for their return because, when he found out the VI Corps had returned to Washington, he decided to attack General Crook's command at Kernstown. Defeating the Federals, Early took control of the Shenandoah Valley again. The VI Corps was hurriedly dispatched back to the Valley.

On July 26, 1864, the Vermont Brigade started their march back toward the Shenandoah Valley. By the 28th, they crossed over the Monocacy River and marched to Jefferson, Maryland, just the other side of South Mountain. It is hard to imagine how tortuous and grueling that strenuous marching was. The miles and miles of travel those men endured was taken for granted by the Union generals. Moving along the Potomac River, they reached Harpers Ferry. They had come seventy-five miles in a little over three days. Wright's troops and Hunter's troops combined at that time and Hunter took command.[15]

Then another idiotic order came from General Halleck. He ordered Hunter to move his men back into Maryland to stop an invasion by Early. Hunter wired Halleck that the VI Corps was in no condition to make another quick march. Halleck refused to listen and ordered Hunter to march his forces. So the VI Corps started toward Frederick, Maryland.

It was hot and humid the day the Vermont Brigade reached Harpers Ferry. The corps marched down into an area which was formed like a basin. Here, the men had to wait for hours in order to cross the long pontoon bridge that spanned the Potomac River. The 2nd Division was lucky as they crossed in the cool of night. The Vermonters were only able to march a few miles, due to the congestion of troops, supply wagons and artillery. The road was narrow there and things got bottled up.

The next day was Sunday. The men of the Vermont Brigade would always remember that particular march, as it was one of the hardest they ever had to endure. The heat was overpowering, and the dust from the long dirt roads rose up and choked the men. The men of the 11th Vermont probably suffered the most because, when they had been detached from the brigade earlier, they had not been issued new shoes. They were marching with bare and bloody feet. Soldiers were falling out by the hundreds. Because of that, the mounted officers and the corporal's guard took the colors of the regiments on to Frederick City.[16]

The brigade was strung out along the road for twenty miles. Men lay exhausted by the roadside. Others staggered along, but still carried their rifles. How many died because of the severe, unrelenting heat or sheer exhaustion can never be known. Losses were at least in the hundreds. Many of those men who did survive that march were permanently broken in spirit and left the ranks, never to return. The VI Corps lost more men on that march than were lost in many of their battles.

Nothing was accomplished by that needless maneuver. The orders for the march had come about because Brigadier General John McCausland, nicknamed "Tiger", had been sent by Early on a raid into Maryland and Pennsylvania in retaliation for General Hunter's acts of destruction in the Shenandoah Valley.

The Vermonters stayed two days at Frederick City. On August 3 they marched to the small town of Buckeystown, where the beautiful Monocacy River flowed past their campsites. The men bathed in the river, lay in the sun and got some of their strength back. They did only light duty. They would be ready to fight in the next campaign when General Getty returned to command.[17]

CHAPTER XVI

Battles in the Shenandoah Valley

During the summer of 1864 leaders in Washington realized there was a need for change in command of the armies. It was decided that one man should be given control of all the northwest territory of Virginia. They knew that the man picked would have to be a tough fighter and a person who believed in really getting the job done. General Ulysses S. Grant selected Major General Philip H. Sheridan. That leader could be described as the "General Patton" of the Civil War.

General Sheridan was given three infantry corps to command: the VI, VIII and XIX, the last two having only two divisions. He was also given two cavalry divisions, commanded by Brigadier General Alfred T. A. Torbert and Brigadier General Wesley Merritt.[1]

Sheridan organized his army at Halltown, Maryland. He wanted to bring together as many troops as he could. His forces had shrunk, for many reasons. Some had completed their enlistments and were on their way home. Losses on the battlefield had taken their toll. Sickness and fatigue played a role. Desertions from the ranks and many stragglers too tired to keep up caused the ranks to dwindle.

The Vermont Brigade's numbers were at their lowest. The VI Corps had less than twelve thousand men. The numbers were due to the severe conditions on the hundreds of miles they had marched.

The Vermonters realized that they were to be a part of the new Army of the Shenandoah. As the army was being reorganized, the men felt that they were under a different kind of leader. The Vermont Brigade was transported by rail, through Monocacy Junction, through Harpers Ferry and finally to Halltown. Those trips by rail were adventures in themselves. The men were packed in the cars like cattle. Some had to ride on the top of the cars, some were injured, and there were fatalities.

The cavalry units were re-organized. Instead of sending them out alone scouting and raiding, Sheridan made them a part of his army. That would prove to be a wise move, as the cavalry would play an important part in winning the battles in the Shenandoah Valley.[2]

The Federal army, under Sheridan, broke camp on August 12, 1864. They marched by way of Clifton and Newtown to Cedar Creek. That march took three days. The cavalry, artillery, and supply trains kept to the dusty roads, while the infantry marched through the fields and woods next to the roads. That allowed the men to move right along, and not eat the dust from the roads. The heat was intense.

At Cedar Creek the Vermonters were involved in a light skirmish against Early's troops. Several men of the 2nd Vermont were wounded. They had been the advance skirmishers for the brigade. Early withdrew to Strasburg to position himself better and to strengthen his army.

Sheridan followed him. When the Union general reached Strasburg, he found Early's positions very strong. Sheridan decided to withdraw to Cedar Creek, to regroup. Looking over the surrounding country, he realized the area would be hard to defend. Rations were getting low. A supply train had been attacked by Colonel John S. Mosby's men and destroyed.

Scouts reported that General Kershaw's crack infantry division was on the way to join Early's forces. Sheridan decided to retire back down the valley toward Halltown. As the men marched through the town of Winchester, the residents taunted and jeered the Union troops. General Torbert and his cavalry, along with the 1st New Jersey Brigade, were left as rear guard for the VI Corps as they marched to form new positions.

The New Jersey Brigade, under Colonel William H. Penrose, came under heavy attack by large Confederate units. With only three regiments, they were able to hold their positions until it started to get dark. Those gallant men were finally driven out of their positions, losing over four hundred men; killed, wounded, or captured.[3] That brigade was a VI Corps outfit, 1st Brigade, 1st Division. Many battle honors were inscribed on their brigade flag. As they retreated back through Winchester, the townspeople attacked them as well. Indeed some of the soldiers were captured by the armed townspeople.

In the town of Clifton, the men of the VI Corps hurriedly ate the last of their rations and at midnight on August 17, along with the Vermont Brigade, they marched on to Charlestown. They made camp a mile and a half from the center of town. The rest of Sheridan's army camped around the town. In the coming engagement, Sheridan would take note of the Vermont Brigade. Charlestown, like Funkstown and Savage Station, is passed over very lightly by historians and writers. But if the truth were known, had those battles been lost, the South would have been stronger and that would have changed the course of the war.

The Vermont Brigade was in camp at a place called Flowing Spring. They were doing picket duty on the left flank of the Union line. L. A. Grant had ordered them to that duty as he was aware they were the most reliable and would not allow any surprise attack to take place. It was a quiet Sunday morning when the brigade was readying for inspection. Suddenly heavy gunfire broke out in front of them. The pickets fell back through the fields. The bullets of the advancing Confederates cut through the camp. Luck would have it that the Vermont men were up and ready. General Getty ordered L. A. Grant to attack, to drive the enemy back.

L. A. Grant lined the Vermont regiments up along the edge of a large field. He put the 3rd, 4th, and 6th regiments in the first line. The 2nd, 5th and 11th were in the second line.[4] The order to advance was given and the brigade moved across the field at a slow trot. A large cornfield was hiding the Confederate riflemen. The Vermonters charged right into the cornfield. The fighting was fierce, but they drove the enemy from their position and back over the hill, to the next hill. There the men from Vermont dug in as ordered.

Two battalions of the 11th Vermont did not receive the orders to dig in and they continued their advance on the left side of the line. The men did not receive their orders because Lieutenant Colonel George Chamberlain, commander of the 2nd Battalion, was shot and wounded through the stomach while riding his horse. Consequently, no one was in command of the charging 11th.[5] Chamberlain was taken immediately from the field, and died from his wounds the next day. The 11th advanced another half mile before General Getty realized what was happening and rode to bring the impetuous group of Vermont fighters back. After a wild ride, he finally stopped their advance and returned them to their lines. During that action, Getty had his horse shot out from under him. He wasn't hurt and returned to the brigade's lines. Getty's brave action saved many lives. If the 11th had been allowed to continue, they would have run into the tough veteran division led by General Rodes.

The brigade now held a line over a mile long. The Southerners attacked in heavy numbers. The "Green Mountain Men" fired from behind stone walls and rail fences. They took cover wherever they could, and continued to hold the line. The 6th Vermont was at the center of the line and took heavy punishment but still held. Major Walker's battalion of the 11th Vermont was holding the line of the left flank. They received heavy rifle fire from the enemy behind a stone wall to their front. One of the brave men who was killed was Color Sergeant Daniel Field.[6]

In the center of the Vermont Brigade's lines, just to the right of the turnpike, stood a fine brick house owned by John Packet. The house had been protected by the Federal forces. It was occupied, though, by Southern women. Their men had gone off to fight for the Confederacy, but they refused to leave the house and showed a great deal of courage in the action that followed. General Getty ordered sharpshooters to be put in the house. Heavy firing was coming from North Carolina regiments. Men of the 11th Vermont were placed in the windows. With that advantage they were able to fire into the Confederate ranks, silencing much of the enemies rifle fire. Then the Southern troops put a battery of artillery on top of a nearby hill and proceeded to shell the house. Nine shells landed inside the house, killing and wounding some of the sharpshooters. One of the shells landed and exploded in the cellar where the women were hiding. They fled to the Vermont lines in the rear.[7]

Major Walker finally ordered the men out of the house. For the rest of the day, the Vermont Brigade held their positions. Mules were used to haul ammunition to the Vermont Brigade. Later, it was also reported, that fifty-six thousand rounds of ammunition were used by the men from Vermont in that battle.[8] General Ricketts' division was ordered to the left flank of Getty's division to explore and feel out the opposing positions. Some of the Vermont Brigade's officers were behind the Packet house, having a quick lunch when Ricketts' men marched past jeering and taunting the Vermont men, saying that there must be no enemy around, as they were not fighting.

Marching on to the top of the hill, to a stone wall, suddenly a double line of Confederate infantry stood up and fired a volley into the surprised ranks of the Union soldiers. The Union troops turned and fled back down the hill, never firing a shot in return. They ran past the laughing Vermonters who were glad to see them go.

Sheridan decided to withdraw his troops from the exposed positions they held. He left the Vermont Brigade as rear guard. Those courageous men held their line until three o'clock in the morning. Finally they retired to the prepared lines at Halltown.

Sheridan entered the Union lines together with the Vermont men. That had been the first time he had seen the Vermont men fight. He was pleased with what he saw and knew that he had the troops to do the job. The Vermont Brigade lost forty men in that battle and one hundred more were wounded.[9] The battle at Charlestown was a proud battle honor for the men of the Vermont Brigade. Against veteran troops, they held the line and retired only when they were ordered to do so.

Early, on the offensive, advanced his units to the Federal lines at Halltown. Finding the Northerners too strong, he pulled his men back to their old positions outside of Charlestown.

On August 28 Sheridan followed Early's men with the VI Corps leading. They marched straight through Charlestown. As they went, the band played "John Brown's Body" just to remind the Southern people that his spirit was still marching on.[10]

Sheridan's army was gathering strength. Units were joining him every day. The XIX Corps rejoined him. General Crook's small VIII Corps was also added. The Union cavalry under General Merritt was becoming a strong fighting force and that fact would control the outcome of most of the battles fought in the Shenandoah.

Fighting continued with engagements against Early's troops at Smithtown and Leesburg. Then, Early retired his men to the town of Martinsburg. After fierce fighting he had to regroup.

September 14, Kershaw's crack infantry division, under General Anderson, left the Shenandoah Valley, recalled to reinforce Lee outside of Petersburg. Sheridan realized that with those forces gone, it would be advantageous to go on the offensive. U. S. Grant also wanted Sheridan to go on the offensive. He went to Monocacy Junction, met with Sheridan and listened to his plan of attack. Grant gave his okay and said that Sheridan should destroy and clean out the Southern forces.[11]

Five days' rations were issued. The sick and wounded, along with any extra equipment, were sent to Harpers Ferry. In the darkness of the early morning on September 19, the Vermont Brigade led Getty's division and the VI Corps out of camp. They traveled to the Winchester Turnpike. Dawn was just coming up when they reached and crossed the Opequon Creek. There, they made contact with the enemy. The Southern skirmishers fired on them, and the Vermonters returned their fire. Early advanced two divisions. It was only when the Vermont men came under heavy artillery fire that they were ordered back to the east back of the creek. Some were wounded.

Second Lieutenant Henry E. Bedell was wounded and left for dead. After months of great care by strangers, he recovered and would eventually return to his family.[12] That circumstance occurred a few times during the war.

Westfield Library, Vermont

**Lieutenant Henry E. Bedell
Company D, 11th Vermont**

Mary H. Joslyn, Orleans, Vermont

**Captain Charles E. Joslyn
Company A, 6th Vermont
Joslyn was promoted to captain
in August 1864**

After all their experience, the Vermonters didn't think the past engagement was a battle. It was of short duration and a minor altercation according to the men.[13]

The ranks of the Vermont regiments were low. Although officially Sheridan had over thirty thousand men starting the campaign, in reality the units had about one-third the numbers they should. Despite those statistics, Sheridan continued his offensive against the South. Gathering themselves together, the Vermonters with Getty's division marched along the right side of the Berrysville Pike going into Winchester. War was not new to that area. Having already seen much fighting, the town would see over seventy-five engagements and battles during the war. As the troops moved along, they took over positions that had been taken by the Union cavalry.

Under artillery fire the "Green Mountain Men" formed a line of battle on open ground to the left flank of the VI Corps. Their right flank rested on the Pike. Sheridan himself placed his troops. It gave the men encouragement to see their commander leading in the front line.

The XIX Corps delayed attacking because they couldn't reach their positions due to wagons and guns blocking the way. There was a traffic jam. The delay was costly. Early was able to strengthen his position. When the XIX Corps was finally in place, the order to attack was given just before noon. The battle lines were over three

miles in length. The sun shone brightly on the regimental flags as
they waved, a sight most would never forget.

The battle was fought in two stages. In the first assault, some
units did not advance and it was stalled. Other units were driven
back to the rear in total disorder. The Vermont Brigade's right flank
rested on the Berrysville Pike with the left flank of the 3rd Division
used to guide the brigade. That line of attack was almost impossible
to follow. Charging through a stand of small timber, the Vermonters came upon an open field. It sloped down to a swampy area and
then up again on a hill covered with small scrub trees. The men
threw themselves to the ground and waited for the 3rd Division to
initiate the attack. The 3rd couldn't advance. They were under heavy
fire from Rodes' division. Rodes was killed in that fighting.[14]

The Confederates were on the offensive! The XIX Corps was being driven to the rear. It could be said that if Early had more troops,
the battle would have been a major victory for the South. Upton's
brigade was rushed to relieve the 3rd Division. They made a mighty
charge that finally stopped the Confederate advance and drove them
back in total disorder. Upton was wounded in that fight, but more
devastatingly, Brigadier General David Russell was killed. When
Sheridan heard about his death, he was even more determined to
win as Russell had been a heroic division general of the VI Corps.

Under orders, the Vermont Brigade waited for the 3rd Brigade's
regiments, so they could come abreast of them in the advance. When
they didn't come up, their commander came over into the Vermont
lines and asked Colonel Warner if he and his Vermont units would
start the advance. Warner lined his brigade and ordered the attack
because L. A. Grant had taken a two-week furlough.[15] At the same
time, Major Walker took over command of the 11th Vermont. When
the Vermont soldiers started their assault, the 3rd Division also
finally started theirs. The line of attack came apart due to the lay of
the land. The Vermonters had charged downhill into the low swampy
area and were out of sight of the brigade on their right flank. The
men were in the headwaters of Abraham Creek and the going was
tough. The steep hill in front of them was even tougher. Marksmen
were firing directly into the ranks of the Vermonters, and many
soldiers were cut down. In sheer desperation, the men scrambled
up, grasping at small trees and bushes to help them to the top of
the hill. As they reached the top, they opened fire on the "johnny-
rebs". They continued to fire with accuracy and with the 3rd Division coming up, the Confederates fled. Those Southern soldiers were
men of Major General Stephen D. Ramseur's division and were all
veterans. The Vermonters continued their charge, storming over a
long line of the enemy's breastworks. Some of the riflemen in the

trenches fled but most surrendered even though they outnumbered the Vermont men. The brigade pursued for almost a mile. Then they came under heavy fire and, with no support on their flanks, took cover in a long ditch. The only flag of the brigade to reach the ditch was that of the 5th Vermont.[16]

A small squad of Union infantry finally came up on the left flank of the Vermonters. Under severe rifle fire, they also began to fall back and called to the Vermont soldiers to do the same. Being in an exposed position, with their flanks wide open, they fell back to the breastworks that the rest of the brigade was holding. The first stage of the offensive had ended.

Sheridan then started to straighten out his lines of battle. He paid special attention to the front lines which consisted of Ricketts' division of the VI Corps and part of the XIX Corps. They were in disarray and had taken a mauling in the fighting. More than three thousand troops had been driven from one part of the battlefield and they were brought up and put into line again.

In the meantime, Sheridan sent two small divisions of the VIII Corps, with cavalry, to the left flank of Early's forces. He realized that Early's lines were breaking up and falling back. He rode along in front of the VI and XIX Corps, yelling to the men to attack. Getty, seeing the advance of the VIII Corps, ordered his division to charge. Colonel Warner, leading with the Vermont Brigade, approached a large brick house on the turnpike, where they came under severe artillery fire from a battery to the left. The brigade dug in, using fence rails, trees, posts, and rocks; anything that would give cover. They returned fire, and received support from the 5th Maine battery. When the battery started to withdraw, Colonel Charles H. Tompkins, Chief of the VI Corps Artillery, ordered them to stay and continue firing.[17] The battle was at its peak and could go either way. Shells fell everywhere. Smoke filled the air, making it hard to breathe or see. The dead and wounded lay everywhere. The Union batteries kept firing charge after charge of canister, which was a big factor in enabling the Vermont forces to hold their lines.

At that critical time, the Union cavalry broke through and caused the enemy to scatter right in front of the Vermonters' positions. In one spontaneous rush, the "Green Mountain Men" leaped over their breastworks, charging the retreating Southern forces. Confusion was rampant. Rebels fled and many surrendered. They retreated, some through the city of Winchester.

The heroic Brigadier General Bryan Grimes, upon seeing his North Carolina regiments fleeing, went into a rage. He rode in among his men, striking out, right and left, trying to stop their fleeing, but to no avail.

The Union soldiers began to cheer so loud they could be heard over the artillery noise. Advancing in that victorious charge, the Vermont Brigade finally came to a halt just outside the city. They were right in the middle of a vineyard, full of ripe grapes. They ate that luscious fruit, and to men who had not eaten in quite a while, it was a just reward. As they ate, Sheridan rode up to them. The men from Vermont gave him cheer after cheer. It was a great tribute to him.

That was the first battle which the Vermont Brigade felt was a true and complete victory. A decisive battle had come at an important time of the Civil War. The people of the North were tired of hearing of defeat and high casualties. It would help with the election of Lincoln, as the victory gave credence to his determination to continue the war.

The victory at Winchester did not come cheap. Sheridan lost over four thousand men, killed, wounded, or missing. The Vermont Brigade had forty-eight killed, two hundred and twenty-four wounded, and nine men missing; all in one day.[18]

The brigade got very little rest and broke camp very early in the morning of September 20. By noon they had marched to within a mile of Strasburg. The men fell out by the roadside and then they were put out as skirmishers to feel out the enemy positions. It wasn't long before there was firing on both sides of the line.

The Vermont Brigade had met General Early's troops. Early had chosen a narrow part of the valley to fortify his position. His lines ran for three miles along the south side of a small stream called Tumbling Run. At one spot, in the center of the north side was Flint's Hill. That area had to be held; if not, Early's whole line would crumble. As the Union troops advanced, artillery fire increased and rifle fire from the Confederate side became more constant.

Sheridan knew that Flint's Hill had to be taken to ensure that Fisher's Hill would be conquered and held by the North. The Vermont Brigade was sent to the left of Flint's Hill where they dug in. It was difficult to move as shells flew over their heads. Three regiments from another brigade were sent up to take the hill in two attacks. They were repulsed. Then Warner, in charge of the 1st Brigade of Getty's division, was ordered to take the hill. In a gallant bayonet charge, they finally took the hill, with the Vermont Brigade in support. Not needed, the Vermont men advanced up to the crest of the hill, on the right flank of the 1st Brigade. There on the edge of a field they dug a line of trenches in the dark. From there Sheridan would direct his attack.

After Sheridan and his commanders looked over Early's positions, the Vermonters knew a major assault was going to take place. The general's plan was to send the VIII Corps around to the left flank of Early's lines. Next the cavalry was to ride to the rear and take the town of New Market. That would cut off any escape.

By late on the afternoon of September 22, Crook's VIII Corps had marched over hidden trails and mountain paths and began their attack. They completely surprised the Confederate forces. Sheridan then ordered the VI and XIX Corps to attack. The men of the Vermont Brigade leaped over their breastworks, with the 2nd Vermont out as advance skirmishers. They advanced to the banks of Tumbling Run. The shells overhead cut the branches of the trees. Splashing through a shallow pond and across a small branch of the stream, they made their way up to the top of the hill and to the Confederate positions. Most of the soldiers had taken cover from the Union artillery fire, and some had retired from the hill. The Southern division that had held that hill was a veteran one. They were fine soldiers and had seen much action, under command of Brigadier General John Pegram. The division was made up of troops from North Carolina and Virginia. Their regiments were down in numbers due to previous heavy campaigns and fighting. They were lucky to have one hundred and fifty to two hundred men on the firing line.[19] Also they were not well equipped. Rations were down to about nothing. When the Vermont men and the rest of Getty's division surged up the hill, those regiments were completely surprised. Over three hundred men were captured, along with four guns of the Southern batteries. The Vermonters captured a beautifully engraved flag staff and used it as their own. Then the Vermont Brigade took over Fisher's Hill. It was a complete victory. There was only one man killed from the Vermont Brigade, Corporal Thomas J. Miller of the 3rd Vermont, who was shot by a sharpshooter.[20]

There was only some minor mopping-up to do next. The 11th Vermont was sent to capture Confederate soldiers who had escaped. The rebels were thought to be cut off from their units. When the men from Vermont searched the area, however, they were gone.

If the Union cavalry had been successful in taking New Market, the retreat of the rest of Early's army would have been ensured. It really would have been a complete victory for Sheridan and the Union.[21]

The Union army lost only four hundred men, while the Confederate army lost over fourteen hundred.[22] Darkness saved the South from total disaster. If it had stayed lighter longer, their whole force would have been captured and Early might not have been able to fight in the next battle of Cedar Creek. General Early summed it up when he said that his entire force had retired in considerable confusion.

CHAPTER XVII

Victory at Cedar Creek

By this time in the war, the Union armies had adopted the policy of foraging for some of their food and supplies. Sheridan's army also lived off the land. The men of the Vermont Brigade were noted for their abilities to forage and scavenge along the line of march.

On the night of September 22, as the Vermonters pursued the fleeing Confederates, the way was lit by the burning wagons and supply trains of the retreating army. The next day at Woodstock, a supply train caught up to the VI Corps and the men received welcome food and supplies.

September 24, Sheridan's army advanced to Rude's Hill, overtaking the stragglers and wounded of Early's army. The men, checking the area, found many wounded in barns and in some of the homes. The "Johnnys" were pushed further back up the valley.

Sheridan was ready to go on the offensive again, but Early refused to fight because he felt his forces were too weak. He retired twenty miles down the valley to a place called Sparta. The marching was done in fine weather, with both armies keeping each other in sight. The infantry marched along the sides of the turnpike, while the supply wagons and artillery stayed on the road.

Sometime during the night, after the Vermonters made camp, Early and his troops sneaked away, leaving their campfires burning. Withdrawing five miles allowed Early to break contact with the Federals. Unknown to Sheridan, there Early's troops were reinforced by General Kershaw's crack infantry division, and a battalion of artillery.[1]

Sheridan and his men advanced to Harrisonburg. He was eighty or ninety miles from his supply base and thought Early wouldn't attack again soon. Therefore he decided to pull back his troops down the valley, nearer his base of supply. As the troops moved, they put the valley to the torch. Sheridan ordered his cavalry to burn and destroy everything except the houses themselves.

On October 6, 1864, L. A. Grant rejoined the Vermont Brigade as commander. The army was somewhere near New Market. By that time, the whole valley was in flames. Destruction and devastation were everywhere. Barns, storehouses and fields burned brightly. The Vermonters were unhappy to see that, as most of them were farmers, had worked the land and knew the labor and toil that went into making those farms productive.

It had started to snow and the weather was cold. The Vermont men were glad they were marching because that kept them warmer. When they reached Strasburg, Sheridan planned to send the VI Corps back to the lines around Petersburg. October 10, the men marched to Front Royal where they were supposed to take the train to Washington. That was impossible, because the railroads had been destroyed and were under repair. On October 13 they were ordered to march, by way of Ashby's Gap.

The officers of the VI Corps were fording the Shenandoah River, in midstream, when a messenger rode up to them with orders to return to Cedar Creek. Early's division had returned to the old position at Fisher's Hill. The next morning, before daylight, General Wright quick-marched his corps back, arriving at Cedar Creek in the late afternoon of October 14 after a grueling march.

On October 16, one hundred and thirty-four officers and men of the 6th Vermont were mustered out because their three years of service were up. That reduced the regiment to a battalion of six companies, under command of Major Sumner H. Lincoln.[2] The same day Sheridan left for Washington to confer with Secretary of War Stanton.

During Sheridan's absence, Major General Horatio G. Wright was left in command. The Union army settled into an easy routine and became somewhat lax. The Vermonters ground wheat and made flour for baking. Men were sent out to forage for all kinds of supplies; different meats and other food were confiscated. The men looked diligently for apple cider made by the people of the area. There was an air of complacency about the camp. Everyone was relaxed, even though the two armies were only five miles from each other.

Early planned to change that comfortable existence. He had drawn up an excellent plan of attack. He would send three divisions of infantry, under Major General John B. Gordon, around the left flank of the Union army. That flank was held by the small VIII Corps under Crook. The plan was also to attack through Strasburg, down the turnpike, hitting the center of the lines along Cedar Creek. In addition, he would send a small cavalry force to try to capture Sheridan at Belle Grove.[3] At dusk on October 18 Gordon's divisions started a stealthy march. The horses were left in the rear, and any gear that might make a noise was removed from the men. After a few hours they halted to rest. Finally they reached the Union's left flank. They waded across the rushing Shenandoah River at Bowman's and McIntyre's Fords. Holding rifles and ammunition over their heads, and keeping their balance in the cold, surging waters, Gordon's men crept up to the unsuspecting Federal forces.

The two small divisions of the VIII Corps were hit first. A heavy fog and the pre-dawn darkness helped the Confederates in the surprise assault. They stormed the Union breastworks with a frightening, high pitched, "Yip, Yip, Yip!" The breastworks had been built well. They were six to eight feet high and ten feet thick in most places. Every two hundred yards a strong fort had been built with artillery in it. In daylight, those positions would have been impossible to take. Wooden abatises made from pine trees had been put in front of the fortifications and yet the Southern brigades came pouring over them.

The men of the VIII Corps were sleeping. Many were killed before they knew what hit them. Some of the Union cannon were turned on the fleeing Union soldiers. Many men were captured, and the corps was knocked out in the first half hour of the attack. The battle of Cedar Creek was the last one the VIII Corps participated in as a unit.[4] Gordon's skill in directing the attack and the fighting ability of his battle-hardened veterans were the reasons. For some reason the attacking Confederates were not heard. The Union army paid a high price for their lack of vigilance.

Kershaw's brigades crossed Cedar Creek after capturing the Union pickets without firing a single shot.[5] Then they charged down the turnpike, and over the breastworks being held by the XIX Corps. The corps had only two divisions and was also taken by surprise. Some of the units of the XIX Corps put up a stiff fight, including Colonel Stephen Thomas' three-regiment brigade. After the full weight of the rebel attack hit their lines, most of the soldiers broke for the rear. Many of those men later reformed in their regiments behind the VI Corps and would eventually join in the last great attack of the Union army. Casualties were heavy, however, and the Confederates took many prisoners.

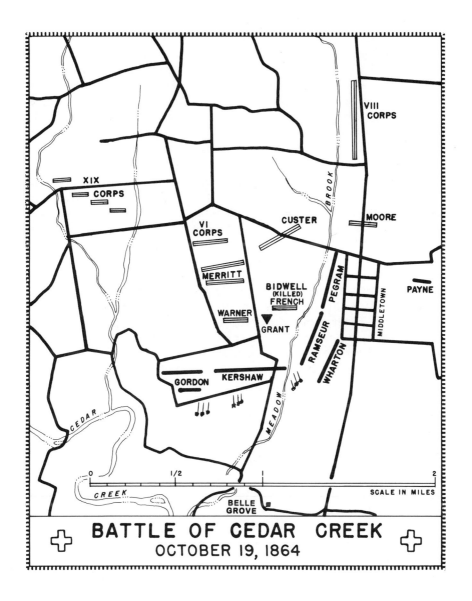

BATTLE OF CEDAR CREEK
OCTOBER 19, 1864

The VI Corps was situated to the right of the XIX, further along the creek. Brigadier General Frank Wheaton commanded the 1st Division, Brigadier General George W. Getty the 2nd; and Brigadier General James B. Ricketts the 3rd. Due to Sheridan's absence, Ricketts also commanded the entire VI Corps, because Wright was still in charge of all Union forces.[6]

The VI Corps had advance pickets near a back road on the right flank. Those pickets were commanded by Colonel George P. Foster of the 4th Vermont. Confederate Major General Thomas L. Rosser's cavalry surprised the pickets and Captain Lewis of the 11th Vermont, had twenty-six of his men taken prisoner. The rest of the pickets were able to hold the Southern cavalry for hours before they had to retreat back into their main lines.

The Union's 1st and 3rd Divisions moved to their left flank, rushing to stop the attacking Confederates. The fighting was fierce. Ricketts' 3rd Division formed on a hill just west of the pike, with Wheaton's division on his left flank, parallel to the road. By that time, Gordon's and Kershaw's forces had joined forces. Together their troops went into battle, hitting the Northern units hard. Ricketts' and Wheaton's divisions took the brunt of the savage fighting. Ricketts was shot from his horse and was carried from the field. The battle continued for over an hour, and although they fought a hard and bitter fight the Union forces were forced to fall to the rear. They even had to leave six cannon behind to the enemy, which were immediately turned on them as they fell back.

Altogether twenty-four guns were taken by the Southerners, putting their artillery units in command of over forty guns. That was a great advantage over Northern troops. The Confederate artillery, commanded by Colonel Thomas H. Carter, was well served at Cedar Creek.

Due to the wounding of Ricketts, Getty was given command of the VI Corps and in turn L. A. Grant took command of the 2nd Division. Colonel Amasa A. Tracy became the leader of the Vermont Brigade. Those three commanders were not only leaders but fighters as well. They would prove that in the next few hours of fighting.

Having come the longest distance to the area of battle, Getty's Second Division was just in time to cover the retirement of the 1st and 3rd Divisions. The 2nd Division was then the only unit holding the line of the Union army.[7] They took up positions along the side of a stream called Meadow Brook. Brigadier General Daniel D. Bidwell's brigade was on the left flank. At a right angle running along the crest of a hill were Colonel Tracy and the Vermont Brigade. Colonel Warner and the First Brigade were on the right flank of the Vermont Brigade.

L. A. Grant immediately advanced a strong skirmish line made up of the 5th and 6th Vermont and a battalion of the 11th Vermont. That was the first organized skirmish line formed and used at the battle of Cedar Creek.[8] They drove out a body of enemy troops that were firing into the lines. Heavy smoke and fog covered the battlefield, making it hard for the soldiers from Vermont to see as they fired. They fired volley after volley and were soon counter-attacked by Brigadier General John Pegram's division. Included in the South's offensive were a veteran North Carolina Brigade and a hardened Virginia Brigade.

The Union cavalry was holding the flanks, and doing a great job. Getty, realizing that the division was too far advanced, ordered L. A. Grant to move back to a better position. The brigades in one single line moved back in an orderly manner. Bidwell's brigade was on the left flank and the Vermont Brigade was on the right. Directly in front of the Vermont Brigade was an open field. As there was no cover, the men lay down just over the crest of a hill and awaited the attack. Pegram's and Ramseur's advancing brigades hit part of Warner's brigade and the Vermont regiments right in the center of the line. The Vermonters waited until the Rebels were less than a hundred feet in front before opening fire. Their firepower was devastating and it wasn't long before the Confederate regiments fell back in total disorder. They left many of their dead and wounded lying on the hillside. The South's artillery was brought into action and shelled the Union lines. For over a half hour the Vermonters took cover where they could find it. Staying just over the crest of the hill, the men were protected from the enemys shells.

Realizing that his attack was being repulsed and not effective, Early ordered Brigadier General Gabriel C. Wharton's Virginia division to the front, adding more strength for the next assault. Bidwell's brigade and the 6th and 11th Vermont regiments received the brunt of the next attack. Bidwell's unit was driven back a short distance by the advancing Confederates. L. A. Grant ordered the men of the 6th and 11th Vermont to face their position left, keeping the division lines intact. The Vermonters defended, rolling onto their back to reload. They poured heavy fire into the lines of the attacking soldiers.

The enemy's attack was almost a success, but for fate. As he was leading the 3rd Brigade, General Bidwell was hit by a shell fragment that tore open his chest. Soon after he fell from his horse his brigade began to fall apart. Lieutenant Colonel Winsor B. French of the 77th New York saw what was happening. The men had begun to go to the rear. Yelling as loud as he could, over the noise of battle, he shouted to them, "Don't run men, till the Vermonters do!"[9] They stopped, and threw back the Southern attack. Skirmishers from the Vermont Brigade were put forward, and the men waited for the next attack.

Bidwell died from his wounds shortly after, and he would be missed as a leader. He helped the VI Corps to become such a great fighting unit. Colonel W. B. French, then took command of his brigade.

Meanwhile, the 1st and 3rd Divisions of the VI Corps had withdrawn about a mile to the rear of the 2nd Division. The XIX Corps proceeded to organize a short distance to the rear of them. What was left of the VIII Corps was scattered down the pike past Newtown.

The Confederates began their next offensive on the flank of the 2nd Division. Colonel Warner realized his right flank wasn't covered and ordered his men to fall back. The Vermont Brigade and the 3rd Brigade were ordered to do likewise by L. A. Grant. They set up new positions a half mile back. Getty was in a better position to see, and again ordered the 2nd Division to retire to better positions as he thought they would have a greater advantage in the long run. In good order, but with a lot of grumbling, the Vermonters moved. The 2nd and 3rd Vermont were left in forward positions as skirmishers.

The Confederates stopped their assault for good reasons. Early's men were exhausted. They had been up all night and had marched hard. For the last five hours they had fought, driving the Union forces back down the Valley. The units were mixed up. The men had very little to eat and were looting the abandoned Union camps. The clothes they wore were worn and tattered.

On the Confederate armies' flanks, the Union cavalry was very strong. Early feared they would attack him at any time and started to muster his forces together again. He was pleased with the way the battle had gone so far. His forces had broken and driven two Union army corps from the field and the rest of them had retired before his victorious fighting units.

As Early was with his staff and officers, he looked down the Valley. He saw a small Union line drawn up to do battle. He casually made a comment that they probably were a Yankee rear guard and that they would soon go away. Gordon turned to Early and told him that the Union unit was the VI Corps and, with their reputation, they wouldn't go away unless they were driven away.[10]

The battle-hardened VI Corps awaited orders. Wright was bringing his battered army together. The XIX Corps reorganized its veteran regiments; the 114th, 160th, 161st and 116th New York. The 8th Vermont, 12th Connecticut, 26th Massachusetts, and the 14th New Hampshire were also assembled.[11] They were ready for battle. Time was running out for General Early and his army.

The Vermont Brigade, under command of Lieutenant Colonel Tracy, was put in the center of the 2nd Division's line. The battle line was set up with French's brigade on the left, from the pike and down the hill to Meadow Brook. Next came the Vermont Brigade. Then Warner's brigade was on the right flank of the Vermonters. The 1st and 3rd Divisions of the VI Corps were a half mile behind and to the rear of the 2nd Division. The XIX Corps reinforced the right flank. Union cavalry were on both flanks. The men from Vermont dug in, taking advantage of any cover they could, and then had a late breakfast.

The Vermonters realized that the Union army had been driven off the field of battle, and, although they had been ordered to retire, they remained eager to do battle and win for the Union. As they waited to go on the offensive, the Vermonters heard cheering coming from some distance down the pike. It sounded like men who were victorious. They couldn't believe their ears and couldn't figure out who was doing the cheering. Then they saw the answer. General Sheridan was riding up on his large black horse, "Rienzi." As the men cheered, he rode off the pike and down the lines of men. The first to greet him was Colonel Tracy. He exclaimed that they were very glad to see him. Sheridan, in turn, said he was glad to be there. He then asked what troops were there. Before the colonel could answer, men from the ranks shouted, "VI Corps, Vermont Brigade".[12] "All right, we're all right and we'll have our camps back by night," said Sheridan.[13] He then rode off down the line and the men's cheers became louder and louder.

Sheridan had ridden twenty miles from Winchester and along the way he had met with many of the soldiers who had retreated earlier, and he urged them to return to their units. As he approached the front lines, he saw that Getty's division was lined up and ready to fight. His mood turned to anger as he rode past the men that were still falling to the rear. "Turn about, you cowardly curs or I'll cut you down. I don't expect you to fight, but come and see the men who will!"[14] He then pointed to the VI Corps. That exclamation was a great tribute to the corps, coming from that fighting general.

Sheridan took over his command, putting his army into position. The XIX Corps was moved up to the right flank and given heavy artillery support. Just before noon, the Vermont Brigade was rushed to their rear, as an attack was upon the XIX Corps and Sheridan feared it might become a major battle. That didn't develop though, and the Vermonters were returned to their old positions. They were able to grab a few minutes of sleep.

At four o'clock in the afternoon Sheridan began his attack. French's brigade was to the left. The Vermont Brigade was between it and Warner's brigade on the right. They were on the extreme left flank of Sheridan's attacking infantry forces. Warner's troops proceeded into heavy woods, while the Vermont Brigade advanced through the low brush and over stone walls. French's men were forced to attack over an open field. The Confederates were hiding at the end of the field behind a stone wall and opened fire on the exposed soldiers. At that devastating volley French's brigade fell back. Warner's men were fighting in the wooded area and were out of sight. The Vermonters continued their advance until they halted in front of a house, a mill and several other buildings. They encountered many Confederate riflemen hiding there. The Confederates poured heavy fire into the Vermont lines. The Vermonters returned the rifle fire. Volley after volley was thrown at the enemy. Getty ordered French's retiring brigade to advance again, and they did so at a faster pace. When they came abreast of the Vermont Brigade, the "Green Mountain Men" charged over the wall and right into the buildings after the Rebels. The fighting was fierce. They swarmed into the area. The Confederate soldiers were finally forced to retire to their second line of defense, fighting all the way.

The rate of fire by the Vermont men slowed because they were running out of ammunition. They took ammunition from where they could find it, removing it from the dead and wounded. Rebel artillery had been moved in front of the Vermont Brigade. The enemy opened fire on them. It was so bad that it was impossible even to move the wounded from the field.

Early's army was starting to crumble. One brigade after another started to retreat. Warner's brigade was advancing on the right. They saw the Confederates starting to fall back. When the Vermont Brigade saw Warner attacking, they surged forward in another assault. They charged ahead, chasing the retreating troops. They stopped only long enough to refill their cartridge boxes from captured supplies. The retreat was becoming a rout. The divisions of Kershaw and Ramseur gave way. Those Southern officers tried to rally their troops. Ramseur rode out in front of his men, shouting and urging the men on. Suddenly, he was shot right off his prancing horse. There is little doubt that a Vermonter's bullet felled him. As he was being brought to the rear in a wagon, he was captured by a trooper of the 1st Vermont cavalry.[15]

Darkness was approaching and the Union cavalry attacked on the flanks of the retreating Confederates and shot and sabered the Rebel forces. They took many prisoners. They also retrieved many trophies of the battle. The Southerners eventually gave way under the heavy Union attack. For miles up the pike there were burning and overturned wagons. Soldiers surrendered by the hundreds.

The Vermont Brigade was the most advanced infantry unit of Sheridan's army. Even so, they received orders to return to camp as darkness was upon them and the cavalry was mopping up. Very little had changed in their camp area. Nothing had been touched. That was not the case when the VIII Corps got back to their camps, which had been torn apart. The Union dead had been stripped and lay naked. Many of the wounded had been treated the same way.[16] Throughout the night the men went out looking for wounded. Many were found by following their weak calls and groans of pain. Any prisoners who had been taken by the South had been sent to the rear immediately and on to prison camps, which was the only advantage for the South.[17]

The victory at Cedar Creek was a very important one for the North. The Union up to that time had not done well in that theater, and taking over the Shenandoah Valley put the Federals finally in control. The Valley had been the bread-basket for the South and its loss was devastating.

President Lincoln was well aware of the importance of winning the Valley campaign of 1864. In appreciation for deeds well done, he promoted Sheridan to major general. To show how much he thought of the officers who led the men, eight of the Vermont Brigade were breveted up in rank. Those promotions were given for gallant action in the line of duty. The following received that honor: George P. Foster, 4th Vermont, breveted to brigadier general; James W. Warner, 11th Vermont, breveted to brigadier general; Aldace F. Walker, 11th Vermont, breveted to lieutenant colonel; Enich E. Johnson, 2nd Vermont, breveted to lieutenant colonel; Horace W. Floyd, 3rd Vermont, breveted to full colonel; Elijah Wales, 2nd Vermont, breveted to major; James E. Eldredge, 11th Vermont, breveted to major; and Henry C. Baxter, 11th Vermont, breveted to captain.[18] Although those men were outstanding, others of the Vermont Brigade could have well been put on that list. General Sheridan also recommended General Getty for promotion.

Lieutenant Colonel Amasa A. Tracy of the 2nd Vermont thirty years later would receive the Medal of Honor for his leadership of the Vermont Brigade at Cedar Creek.[19]

The fighting at Cedar Creek took its toll on both sides. In helping the Union victory, the Vermont Brigade's losses were: fifty-nine killed, two hundred and fourteen wounded, and forty-one missing in action.[20] The one officer of the Vermont Brigade to be killed in action was Lieutenant Oscar R. Lee of the 11th Vermont.[21] The Union losses, altogether, were just under four thousand, and half of that number were from the VI Corps.[22]

Cedar Creek was the end of General Early and his Southern veteran army as a fighting force. The fighting men who wore the emblem of the Greek Cross could justly say that they had been one of the biggest factors causing Early's "sunset of his career".

The Vermont Brigade, along with the division, marched to Strasburg. Strong picket forces were put out toward Fisher's Hill. During the next two weeks the men from Vermont rested. They were quartered in people's homes, which was sheer comfort, and in extreme contrast to what they previously endured and what they were to encounter in time to come.

Of the soldiers in the Vermont Brigade who were captured during the battle of Cedar Creek, only two died in captivity. Most were paroled in about four months. That was a big change from what happened to the men who had been captured at Weldon Railroad. Most of those men died within six months of imprisonment at Andersonville and Millan, Georgia.

The campaign at the Shenandoah made Sheridan one of the most prominent officers in the Union army. It actually sky-rocketed his career. His reputation and leadership ability were duly noted. The general also noted the fighting abilities of the VI Corps and the Vermont Brigade.

CHAPTER XVIII

Above and Beyond

On November 9, 1864, the Vermont Brigade camped at Kernstown with the rest of the VI Corps. The railroad had been repaired between Harpers Ferry and Stevenson's Depot. Light duty, mounting guard and parading were the order of the day for that month.

Thanksgiving day came and barrels of turkeys, mince pie and other goodies were shipped from Vermont. The troops were reviewed by Sheridan on November 21 in the pouring rain. The Vermonters got nothing but wet, as Sheridan just quickly rode down the lines, with little or no reviewing. The review was written up in the New York papers, although the account was contrary to what really occurred, suggesting the review was done with grandeur.[1]

That inaccurate news reporting was common during the Civil War, which caused much dissension. It infuriated many noted generals, including General George E. Meade, General Alpheus S. Williams and General William T. Sherman. They wouldn't allow reporters into their camps.[2]

All that attention gave the whole VI Corps, including the Vermont Brigade, a slight feeling of superiority. They became a little cocky. A song was written about them. Verse four summed it up: "Come up with me, you nineteenth and eighth, Come up with me I say; Why do you lag so far behind? We have not lost the day. Come up upon this crest of hill, 'twill be a glorious sight; You won't get hurt; you needn't fire; But see that Sixth Corps fight!"[3]

By December the weather in the Valley was turning nasty, and the men of the 2nd Division were asking why they were being held in camp. The 1st and 3rd Divisions of the VI Corps had already gone to the lines and fortifications around Petersburg. There, U. S. Grant was mounting another attack against Lee's lines of supply and needed all the troops he could get. Sheridan wouldn't release the 2nd Division because he didn't know whether Early was going to attempt any more attacks.

On December 9 the Vermont Brigade finally started the march to Petersburg. Temperatures were below freezing, and the water in the soldiers' canteens turned to ice. As long as the men kept marching, they were able to keep from succumbing to the cold.

Reaching Stevenson's Depot at eleven o'clock in the morning, the Vermonters found no train waiting for them. They stacked arms and tried to keep warm. The delay made them impatient and led to trouble. A sutler, authorized by the government to sell food, drinks and supplies to the soldiers, started to sell his wares. The men decided to relieve him of his goods by force, especially the whiskey. Soldiers didn't like those sutlers. Colonel Foster came along just in time to save the man from the soldiers.[4] Foster probably would have allowed the men to have the whiskey if he had known what the train ride was going to be like.

The cars provided to transport Vermonters were coal cars, which were open with a foot high board around the sides. The floors were covered by coal dust, cinders and rock. After boarding, the men tried to find places to sit or lie down, attempting to keep warm. Although they hadn't been issued winter overcoats, they did have woolen blankets.

The train pulled out a little before 6:00 P.M. A cold northeast wind was blowing and as the train picked up speed the wind became unbearable. The soldiers hugged the floor trying to keep warm. When the train slowed on steep grades, the men would jump off and run alongside, anything to keep from freezing! Snow began to fall and soon the troops were covered with five to six inches of the white stuff. Between the snow, mud, coal dust and ash on the floor of the cars, the men from Vermont thought the night would never end. By morning the snow had turned to sleet and rain. At daylight the train stopped to take on coal and water. Many of the troops climbed down near the engine for heat.

The station master asked what the train was carrying. Someone replied that it was carrying soldiers. He commented he could see that, but he wanted to know what was in the open coal cars and was stunned to find out that soldiers were in them. It was impossible to see people because the snow completely covered them as they slept.

As the train passed through small towns, the inhabitants waved flags and handkerchiefs. The men didn't respond. They were too tired, cold and dirty and needless to say, felt poorly. The men were looking forward to arriving at the Soldiers Retreat Barracks in Washington. There they could wash up and eat. They figured they could dry their clothes as well because they knew that remaining wet was a sure way of getting sick.

Much to everyone's surprise the train did not stop and went right past the retreat, through the depot and past the capital.[5] Many congressmen and Washingtonians watched as the train moved through and out of the city. At the wharf the Vermont soldiers were boarded onto the transport *Massachusetts*. Two days later they landed at City Point.

Those hard fighting men felt they had been mistreated and couldn't understand the reason for not allowing them to stop and be taken care of. Only five months before they had helped save the capital. After that they had fought four big battles and destroyed the Confederate army in the Valley. Yet they had been treated like cattle, or as if they had some dreaded disease. It was very disappointing to the men. Much later they learned that the politicians in Washington thought those men of the VI Corps were a rough group who might do damage to the capital if let off the trains.

At City Point the brigade rejoined Getty's division. Moving by rail again, they went southeast of Petersburg and camped near the old battleground of the Weldon Railroad. They took over positions held by units of the II Corps. With that addition, the VI Corps held over two miles of the lines in front of Petersburg.

The Vermont Brigade held positions between Forts Tracy and Urmston about five and a half miles southwest of Petersburg.[6] Extra pickets were put out in order to watch the strongly fortified lines of the Confederates. Winter was upon them, and everyone realized that no heavy fighting would be done until warmer weather came. Therefore the Vermonters made their camps as comfortable as possible.

Since the defeats and repulses of the Federal forces in the spring and early summer of 1864, the Confederate army had turned Petersburg into a fortress. Two lines of entrenchment extended for miles. They were manned by first line troops and reserve units who were battle tested. The soldiers from Vermont didn't realize, although they could sense victory, that the oncoming campaign was to be their last.

CHAPTER XIX

Final Battle and Victory

Union forces built a tower more than one hundred and forty feet high so they could watch the movements of the Confederate units. The tower was to the left of the Vermont Brigade's position, near Fort Welch. Weather conditions were horrible. Frostbite was a constant concern. The men had to keep moving just to keep from freezing. They also had to keep alert because of snipers. The duty all along the Union lines was agonizing and hazardous to all the men.

Conditions were worse for the Southerners. Food and clothing were scarce. Desertion was rampant; in fact, one bitter cold night, one whole company from a Carolina regiment came over into the lines of the Vermonters.[1]

By March of 1865, hundreds of men were rejoining their regiments, most coming off a sick list. Three Vermont companies from the recently disbanded famed U.S. Sharpshooters regiments were reassigned to the 4th Vermont. Forty other men who had been exchanged also came back into the regiment. That spring the brigade had 2,446 men on the muster rolls.[2]

At the end of March the weather improved, and Grant ordered a movement to the left of the lines in order to gain control of the two remaining railroad lines which were supplying Lee's army. However, the Confederates struck first.

Early in the morning of March 25, Gordon's units attacked and captured Fort Stedman. Retaliating, the IX Corps counter-attacked, cut off the attacking troops and retook the fort after some heavy fighting.

Grant realized that Lee had weakened his lines to make that assault and so ordered his troops to attack. The Vermont Brigade was approximately seven miles from the fort. In order to find a weak spot in the Southern defenses, Wright ordered Seymour and the 3rd Division to attack early in the afternoon of the same day. That attack was repulsed.

Getty's 2nd Division was then ordered to make an assault. To the rear of the Vermont Brigade, the 3rd Vermont battery opened fire from Fort Fisher to soften up the enemy positions. Meanwhile Getty's troops were lining up for the attack. The Vermont Brigade was on the left flank of the line, divided into three columns. The first line had the 2nd and 6th Vermont in front. Two battalions of the 11th Vermont formed the second line. The third line was comprised of the 3rd, 4th, and 5th Vermont.[3]

Lee was a master at building strong fortifications, and the Union troops were aware of that. To make the attack stronger, Colonel J. Warren Keifer's 2nd Brigade from the 3rd Division was added to Getty's troops.

Very late in the afternoon of March 25 Wright gave the signal to attack. The Vermonters charged across open ground. Artillery shells flew past, landing to the rear of the men. The running men were lucky the enemy's aim was high. As the "Green Mountain Men" reached the Confederate lines and their well dug rifle pits, they gave a mighty cheer and charged over the breastworks. A short skirmish ensued. Fighting with great determination, the Vermonters captured the defenders. The 2nd Vermont, with a few companies from the 11th Vermont, advanced a quarter of a mile farther to a house later known as the "Jones House". Realizing that they had no support, they withdrew to their own lines. Colonel Tracy was credited with that wise move. Not long after the Vermonters pulled back, Confederate sharpshooters occupied the house which would have spelled trouble for the Vermont soldiers.

Soon after that Captain Ward B. Hurlbert took Companies D, F, and H of the 2nd Vermont and charged in a bold attack against that house. After a brief encounter the sharpshooters were driven out. The house was then burned and the 3rd Vermont battery was brought up to hold the position. General A. P. Hill tried to regain that position and made several attacks, but to no avail.

The Confederates lost over nine hundred men, five hundred and forty of them taken by Getty's division. Most of those captured were taken by the men of the Vermont Brigade. In all over one thousand Confederates were killed or wounded and three thousand were taken prisoner. Seven men of the Vermont Brigade were killed and thirty wounded.[4]

Early in the morning of March 27 the Confederates launched a surprise attack on the Vermonters. All of the Vermont regiments were engaged in that short but savage fight in the rifle pits. They fought hand-to-hand, stabbing and shooting in close quarters. The assault occurred just before daylight which made it hard to see. Twenty-two Vermont soldiers were wounded. Twenty-two from the 11th Vermont, and four from the 4th Vermont were taken prisoner during the fighting. Even with those losses, they held the rifle pits and drove the enemy back.

At a meeting of the high command, a plan was devised to cut Petersburg off completely from Lee's forces. Grant used the II and V Corps to accomplish it. The two units crossed Hatcher's Run and advanced northward. Lee sent his cavalry, under Major General William H. F. Lee, his second son, and an infantry division to stop the Union forces. Sheridan, in command of that endeavor, sent a dispatch to Grant, requesting that he be sent the VI Corps to help do the job. He said that he didn't want the V Corps. Grant informed him that the VI Corps was too far away. He also told Sheridan that Wright was ready to break the lines where they were, and that he was confident his men of the VI would succeed. Their reputation and fighting abilities were well known. Sheridan proceeded as ordered, and the V Corps with help from the cavalry won the battle of Five Forks. They did their job well.

The defeat at Five Forks was blamed on Pickett. It wasn't completely his fault but was due to the condition of the Army of Northern Virginia. Losses were staggering, desertions many, and supplies impossible to obtain.

The Northern armies were becoming stronger and stronger. Their soldiers could smell victory, as their enemy was becoming weaker. The Union army was ready for the great push and as the fight at Five Forks was being won, the troops readied for the assault on the Petersburg defenses.

Union artillery opened a heavy barrage of fire on the Rebel lines. All through the night the bombardment continued. The VI Corps was to make the first attack in a "V" formation, with the 2nd Division at the center point. Heading the division's charge was the Vermont Brigade. The 5th Vermont was first in the column, and had been selected personally by L. A. Grant as it was his old regiment. Then came the 2nd, 6th, 4th, and 3rd Vermont regiments, followed by the 1st and 2nd battalions of the 11th Vermont.[5] The plan was so complete that they sent artillerymen along so that they could fire any captured cannon. They also sent ax-men to clear any

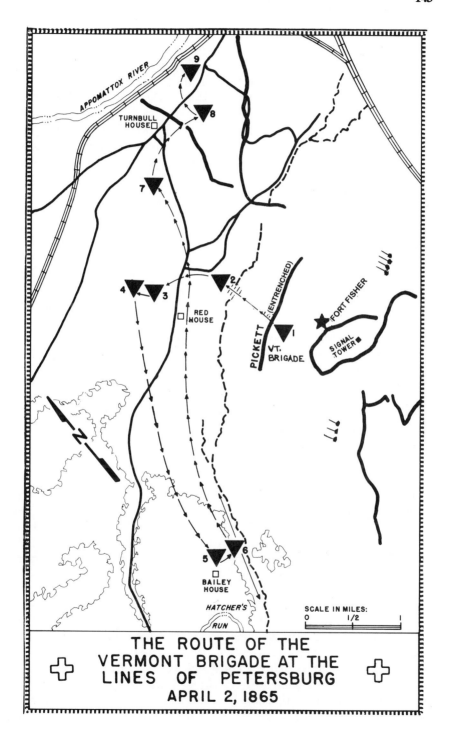

THE ROUTE OF THE
VERMONT BRIGADE AT THE
LINES OF PETERSBURG
APRIL 2, 1865

obstructions. The soldiers were ordered not to fire their rifles until they entered the Rebel entrenchments. The men carried no knapsacks and their rifles were not capped. Lined up by regiments, the Vermont Brigade was prepared for battle.

The weather was cold and raw as the men lay in an open area very early on the morning of April 2, 1865. By 2:00 A.M. the other brigades had positioned themselves. The men tried to be very quiet. As the units moved though, someone discharged his rifle by mistake. All hell broke loose! The Confederates returned fire. Some of the units still moving were hit pretty hard. The men in the open areas also took many casualties. L. A. Grant received a head wound and Colonel Tracy took over the command of the Vermont Brigade. Lieutenant Colonel Charles Mundee also led the Vermonters in this attack. The Confederates were firing blindly and were not aware of what troops they were firing upon. Because there was no return fire from the Union troops, the rifle fire stopped all along the lines. The assault was still on.

The concentration of the whole attack plan had been selected by L. A. Grant. He had noticed an opening in the fortifications where the Southerners would come out to cut wood. That small ravine seemed like a perfect place to enter the enemy lines. Generals Wright, Getty and Meade were brought down to view the area and gave their approval.[6]

By the time 4:00 A.M. rolled around, the men were numb with cold. Still no signal was given to start the attack. The IX Corps artillery was still bombarding the enemy lines. At 4:30 A.M. the 3rd Vermont artillery at Fort Fisher fired the gun, signaling the start of attack. Tracy ordered the Vermonters to go forward. The men got to their feet and advanced. The units the Vermonters were to fight against were battle-tested veterans, with their brigades reinforced to help hold the positions at all cost. The Mississippi Brigade under Brigadier General Joseph Davis and the Tennessee Brigade, under Brigadier General William McComb were the Vermonters' opposition.[7] The fortifications held by the Confederates were the strongest the Vermont Brigade had to attack the four years of war.

The plan of attack sent the Vermont Brigade in by regimental front. A few minutes later the other brigades started their advance from the right and left flanks of the Vermont Brigade. The soldiers charged and the only noise was the muffled sound of thousands of running feet, as they made their way toward the breastworks. Southern skirmishers, after firing a few quick shots at the "Green Mountain Men", scurried back to their lines. With no need for surprise the Vermonters cheered and advanced forward to the breastworks. Heavy rifle and artillery fire cut into their ranks. That slowed the

USAMHI

**Captain Charles G. Gould
5th Vermont Infantry**

attack, but, with encouragement from the officers, the men tore away the obstructions and ran through the ditches. They climbed over the fortifications, stabbing with the bayonet, shooting when possible and sometimes using their rifles as clubs, and finally drove the Confederates from their fortifications.

Captain Charles G. Gould of the 5th Vermont was the first man to enter the enemy trenches. As he jumped in, he was bayoneted through the cheek and back, but was strong enough to kill his attacker. While lying on the ground, he received a third wound in the back. Two days later, at the VI Corps hospital near City Point, Gould wrote to his parents in Vermont that he was fine, walking about and receiving good care. He assured them that his wounds were "very slight", when in reality, they were severe. The bayonet had sliced through his face and into his mouth and jaw. Also he had been sabered on the right side of his skull. Gould was eventually breveted to major for his gallantry at Petersburg. He survived his wounds and twenty-five years later was awarded the Medal of Honor.[8]

A few seconds after Gould entered the trenches, Lieutenant Robert Pratt and Color Sergeant Jackson Sargent, 5th Vermont, scrambled into the pits. Later Sargent was awarded the Medal of Honor for carrying the colors and leading the regiment.[9]

Bitter hand-to-hand fighting raged through the trenches. Sergeant Lester G. Hack, also of the 5th Vermont, came upon a squad of Confederate soldiers guarding their colors. He fired at them, wounded several and quickly demanded the surrender of the rest. He grabbed the 23rd Tennessee's battle flag and took several prisoners. For his heroism he was awarded the Medal of Honor on May 12, 1865.[10]

A short distance away, Major William J. Sperry of the 6th Vermont led his men against artillery positions. With determination and fervor, they drove the artillerymen away, and turned the guns

USAMHI.

**Brevet Lieutenant Colonel
William J. Sperry
6th Vermont Infantry**

on the fleeing soldiers. Twenty-seven years later he was given the Medal of Honor for that gallant leadership.[11]

Originally the Vermonters planned to stop and regroup after advancing through the first lines of the enemy. However, they were so caught up in the excitement of the battle that they continued to advance.

As the fighting slowed, Lieutenant Gardner C. Hawkins, Company E, 3rd Vermont, though wounded, staggered to his feet and led his men into the enemy's positions. He refused to be taken to the rear and continued to fight. Twenty-eight years later he was awarded the Medal of Honor.[12]

The officers finally were able to stop the advance of the Union forces and reorganize them. The Petersburg attack was no easy victory. The Confederates stalled the Federal attacks many times.

The Union forces broke through the first line of defense. Then the Vermont Brigade headed in a southern direction in the rear of the Confederate positions. They immediately turned their guns around and started firing hurried shots at the advancing men. Realizing that they were going to be trapped, the Southerners fled all along the line. The pursuit continued for over four miles. The Vermont soldiers didn't have to fire a shot as many "Johnnies" surrendered, while others escaped through the woods and swamps.

By that time in the battle, the Vermont units were near Hatcher's Run. There the brigade reformed next to a building known as the Bailey House. After a short rest, they again faced north and retraced the route to the Red House from where they had started.

The Vermonters performed many heroic deeds during that battle. Major Elijah Wales of the 2nd Vermont and several of his men captured an artillery piece and turned it on the enemy. Captain George G. Tilden, Company H, 11th Vermont, with a squad captured several pieces of artillery and seventy-three officers and men of the 42nd Mississippi. Both of those men were brevetted in rank for those actions.[13] Corporal Charles H. Dolloff of the 11th Vermont captured singlehandedly the battle flag of the 42nd Mississippi. In the same month he received the Medal of Honor for his deed.[14]

Lee made a stand at the junction of the Boydton and Cox Roads. General Wilcox's division and a battery of North Carolina artillery started an assault to retake their old positions. Lee himself directed that attack. Getty didn't wait for support but ordered his division to counter-attack at once. The Vermonters formed only one line, amid much confusion. They attacked and as they advanced they were hit with fire from a battery of four guns which were located in a garden of the Turnbull House, formerly Lee's headquarters. Colonel Floyd sent men from the 3rd Vermont to shoot the horses belonging to the artillery, which prevented them from pulling the guns away. Then the Vermont Brigade moved left and charged the guns. After fierce fighting, the Confederates raised the white flag of surrender. Union troops advancing on the left of the house didn't see the white flag and opened fire. The gunners fled, and the guns were taken by Floyd and the 3rd and 11th Vermont.

The Confederates retreated so rapidly that it was almost a rout. The Union forces were too strong and numerous. Fleeing through the woods the soldiers came to the Appomattox River. The river was so high that crossing it was not possible, though some tried and drowned. Others were captured.

Joseph Covais, Private Collection

Captain Charles C. Morey Company E, 2nd Vermont

Typifying the officers of the Vermont Brigade was Captain Charles C. Morey of Company E, 2nd Vermont. He had enlisted in April 1861 as a private and after three years of hard service, re-enlisted and was promoted to the rank of sergeant. A short time later he became first sergeant. In June of 1864, he was commissioned first lieutenant and served with Company C. He was wounded first on August 21, 1864, at a gallant fight at Charlestown, Virginia. During his four years of loyal service,

Massachusetts Commandery Military Order of the Loyal Legion and the USAMHI
Attack at Petersburg, April 2, 1865

Morey took part in twenty-seven battles as well as many smaller actions. At that last battle at Turnbull House he was wounded by "grape" shot and later died from his wounds.[15] His loss was a hard blow to the men of the 2nd Vermont.

After being under arms for more than eighteen hours, in action most of that time, the men of the Vermont Brigade were near exhaustion. Finally they camped near the Nottingham House. They had done their job, which was to attack, fight and drive the Confederate army from the field. The "mopping up" could be left to other units.

Many people, including historians, have had the impression that the Confederate troops defending Petersburg were second line units. The Vermont Brigade and others who fought with them knew that was not true. They knew their opponents were battle-hardened veterans, the best fighting units in the Army of Northern Virginia. For example, brigades led by Davis, McComb, Cooke, and McCrae were first rate units which had been worn down. Lee knew he must hold the line at Petersburg or all would be lost. Therefore he put his most trusted and best troops to defend Petersburg.

The price the Vermont Brigade paid for being in point position and being successful in the battle at Petersburg was high. On April 2, 1865, the brigade lost thirty-three men killed and one hundred and sixty-one wounded. Five men from the 5th Vermont were listed as missing. They had been captured but were returned to their regiment before the day was out.[16]

As the dawn came up on the morning of April 3, 1865, the Vermonters started on the march with the VI Corps, in the race to catch Lee retreating with his small, weary and hungry army. They marched along the road that ran on the south side of the Appomattox River. It was a dirty and tiring march. The road was a sea of mud, and they made only fourteen miles that day. That night they camped at Whipponock Creek, and the next day they reached Deep Creek. They had to stop as they had out-marched their supply wagons and had to acquire rations from the V Corps. After receiving them, the brigade marched another sixteen miles to Jetersville Station. On the 6th of April all three corps were put into line and advanced toward Amelia Courthouse with the hope of engaging Lee's small army in battle. They found no one there. Lee had marched his exhausted and starving troops all through the night.

Brigadier General George A. Custer and his cavalry cut the line of march. At Sailor's Creek the rear guard of Lee's army awaited a Union attack. Getty's 2nd Division was not engaged in that part of the battle. They had advanced in support of the 1st and 3rd Divisions but were not needed. Ewell's and Anderson's corps were badly defeated.

Ironically, at Sailor's Creek, in the last battle of the war, the small artillery brigade of the VI Corps was commanded by Captain Andrew Cowan. His battery had been with the Vermont Brigade at Lee's Mill, the brigade's very first battle. Now, with his veteran 1st New York artillery and 3rd New York light artillery, Cowan commanded the VI Corps brigade, pouring devastating fire power into the Confederate positions.[17] The VI Corps started in pursuit of Lee's dwindling army. Since Getty's division was leading the advance, the 2nd Vermont was at the point as skirmishers. On the west branch of Sailor's Creek they came into contact with units of Mahone's division who were rear guard for the fleeing army. Mahone's men opened fire but none of the Vermonters were hit. The return fire were the last shots fired by the VI Corps. The 2nd Vermont had that distinction.[18]

Some thought that the last shot may have been fired by Private Henry A. Horton. He became the last surviving soldier of the Vermont Brigade, who lived to the age of one hundred and one and died on July 1, 1948. He had been made corporal in 1865 and was in the last battle with the 2nd Vermont.[19]

The next day the Vermont Brigade eagerly marched to Farmville. They crossed the Appomattox River by pontoon bridge and went into camp on the north side, where Grant had his headquarters.

There was much confusion, and the wounded were everywhere. Wagon trains, supply carts, ambulances and prisoners moved through the streets. Union soldiers from all branches came and went. At night the bonfires and torches produced an eerie and frightening scene, especially to the people of the town.

The next morning the Vermont Brigade was detached from the VI Corps and sent to guard the large supply train which was bringing rations and other supplies for the troops.

General Robert E. Lee surrendered the Army of Northern Virginia to General Ulysses S. Grant on April 9, 1865. The generals met at the McLean House to sign the papers which meant that the war was over. When it ended, the Vermont Brigade was the only brigade which still had the same regiments and was with the same division with which they began in May of 1862.[20] The constant fighting and campaigns of the last year changed most of the other fine fighting units. Those units were worn out and it was fortunate for the Union that the war ended. On the day of the surrender the rosters of the six Vermont regiments showed a total of two thousand and fifteen present for duty.[21]

After the war ended, General George Gordon Meade, in a speech to the VI Corps, said that he didn't want to make any distinctions between the corps, but he did say that the decisive movement of the campaign that resulted in the surrender of the Army of Northern Virginia was the gallant and successful charge of the VI Corps on the morning of April 2, 1865.[22] The Vermont Brigade had led that charge. Meade had recognized that they had delivered the knockout punch to the South and the rest would be up to other units.

Grant stated in a letter to his wife, "altogether this has been one of the great victories of the war."[23] He was referring to the Battle of Petersburg. The commander of all Federal forces praised both the VI Corps and the Vermont Brigade.

The Vermont Brigade left Farmville and rejoined the VI Corps at Burksville Junction. The men were anxious to go home and couldn't understand why they were being held in Virginia. There was a diversity in the terms of surrender given by Grant to Lee and those given by Sherman to Johnston in North Carolina. Grant rushed down to Raleigh, North Carolina, with his terms given to Lee and told Sherman to give the changes to Johnston. He told him if Johnston refused those conditions, the war would resume. Grant then hurried back to Virginia secretly, and told Sheridan to take an army corps with cavalry south to be ready to fight Johnston if he didn't agree to the new terms. Sheridan picked the VI Corps to do the job. On April 23 the Vermonters marched south, averaging twenty-five miles a day. They covered more than one hundred miles in a little over four days. They even beat the Union cavalry.

The area around Danville, Virginia, had not been touched by the war. It was some of the prettiest country the Vermonters had seen in a long time. For the next four weeks, the men from Vermont guarded the railroad which ran between Greensboro and Richmond. That was boring duty and only done to keep the troops busy while waiting to see if Johnston accepted the terms. While there, Sergeant Carlton Green of Company E, 4th Vermont, was killed by an enraged Southern citizen; even though the war had been over for a month. He was the last soldier of the Vermont Brigade to be killed in the American Civil War.[24]

Finally the Vermont troops received word that they were going back to Washington to be disbanded and sent home. They left Danville on May 18, 1865, aboard railroad cars and arrived in Manchester, Virginia, on May 19. There they waited for four days to obtain further transportation to Washington. While waiting, many of the men went sight-seeing.

The reason for the delay in transportation was that the United States government was using the rails to transport Confederate soldiers back to points nearest their homes. Wright then decided to march his men back to Washington, much to the dismay of the troops. They thought they had finished marching.

On May 24, 1865, the last march of the Vermont Brigade began. Rain and mud did not dampen the spirits of the men. They were going home. Passing many of the battlefields they had fought on, and covering twelve miles a day, the men camped near Camp Griffin, Virginia on June 2, after ten days of undisciplined marching.

There on the outskirts of Washington on June 7 the Vermont regiments assembled together for their own Grand Review. Governor John G. Smith of Vermont and other officials attended. Adjutant Inspector General Peter T. Washburn said at the review that some of those regiments had taken part in nearly every battle the Army of the Potomac had fought.[25] The review was a huge success.

Earlier on May 23 and 24, the Army of the Potomac and Sherman's Western army had paraded in Washington, D.C. The VI Corps had not taken part in that review because they had been detached temporarily. So the VI Corps, including the Vermont Brigade, paraded on June 8.

In that final review, the 2nd Division was commanded by Brevet Major General Lewis A. Grant. Brevet Brigadier General George Foster was in command of the Vermont Brigade. The 2nd Vermont, led by Colonel Tracy, had two hundred fifty men marching. The 3rd

Vermont, under Brevet Colonel Floyd, had two hundred twenty men, the smallest unit. The 4th Vermont, under Colonel John E. Pratt, contained two hundred forty men. The 5th Vermont, led by Lieutenant Colonel Kennedy, could field an even three hundred soldiers. Lieutenant Colonel S. H. Lincoln commanded the 6th Vermont, three hundred eighty men strong. Lieutenant Colonel Hunsdon led two battalions of the 11th Vermont, with a total of nine hundred men. In that final grand review 2,290 men, survivors of many battles, marched past.[26]

It was the hottest day on record. Although the regimental flags were tattered and torn, the officers and men were at their best. All the men wore a sprig of evergreen in their hats, and their marching was superb. As it happened, the Vermont Brigade was the only unit to salute President Andrew Johnson properly.[27] Reporting the event afterward, the papers complimented the Vermont Brigade. Those who had watched the parade said that the Vermont Brigade was indeed the best.

The down side to that review was the heat which caused many men to fall from the lines of march due to heat stroke and exhaustion. Most of those staunch Vermonters stood up well. They had marched over two thousand miles in some of the worst conditions possible during the war, and that march was their last. Within a few short years many would die from the effects of that hard campaigning.

On June 28, 1865, the Vermont Brigade was officially disbanded. It had earned recognition for having one of the best records in the Union army, having been called upon many times to stop the enemy's advance. The brigade took part in over thirty major battles and over one hundred small skirmishes and never lost the colors.[28] When the generals asked for the Vermonters, they never failed, but the price had been high. The Vermont Brigade suffered the highest losses of all the brigades in the Union army.[29]

Many people did not know of the Vermont Brigade's success and great record because no officers or correspondents wrote about them. That was partly due to the men themselves, who did not talk about or discuss their deeds.

Little history of the Vermont Brigade was ever written. When the men of the brigade marched into history they wanted to forget the death and destruction that they had taken part in. It was enough for the men to say that they were a part of the Vermont Brigade. The men of Vermont would leave the talking to others, and would stand on the record of their Indomitable Brigade, the First Vermont Brigade!

EPILOGUE

Early in the summer of 1865 the Vermont Brigade marched into history, leaving behind an unbeatable record. Unfortunately, very little was ever recorded about those gallant regiments.

To clarify, when the term "Old Brigade" is used, it refers to the 2nd, 3rd, 4th, 5th, and 6th Vermont regiments.

The 11th Vermont was added in May 1864, and became part of the 1st Vermont Brigade.

The state of Vermont commissioned George G. Benedict to write a history of Vermont in the Civil War, but because of little or no funding and many postponements, it was not completed for twenty-one years. Benedict received little or no help from the officers and men of the Old Brigade. Some men had died, some moved away and others were reluctant to tell of the deeds of their regiments. The state was remiss in recording anything about the Vermont regiments, as they did not do it as soon as the war was over.

Lieutenant Colonel A. F. Walker of the 11th Vermont did write a small history entitled "The Vermont Brigade in the Shenandoah Valley" in 1869. To my knowledge, no histories were written about the Old Brigade.

In order to write the story of the Vermont Brigade, I have visited many towns and talked with people in the beautiful state of Vermont. I obtained much information from small town libraries, and personnel at the University of Vermont Library were helpful in gathering data.

Town clerks helped greatly. I was able to get information from the rosters of the soldiers who served in the Civil War.

The Vermont Historical Society in Montpelier and the State of Veterans Affairs Department, specifically the Department of Graves Registration, gave me courteous and much needed help.

I had several reasons for writing about the Vermont Brigade. As I studied the Civil War, I found that those men from Vermont were courageous and steadfast soldiers. I also noted that not much had ever been written about their deeds. In visiting the many battle-fields where the Vermonters fought, I was disappointed to find very few if any markers or monuments to those heroic men.

I found only one monument to the Vermont Brigade on a battle-field where they participated, and that was at Antietam. They took part in over twenty battles and dozens of smaller actions, yet received little recognition from historians of the Civil War.

Writing about the Vermont Brigade was a large but thoroughly enjoyable task. With hundreds of places to visit, I met and con-ferred with many people. That in itself was satisfying. Of the thou-sands of officers and men I read about and the information given by relatives of the men who served in the war, I fear I may have missed some of them and their stories.

One particularly interesting incident concerned the Medal of Honor recipient Gardner C. Hawkins. In the spring of 1992, Mrs. Iris Miller visited the Lindenwood Cemetery in Stoneham, Massa-chusetts, looking for the grave of her great uncle. Unable to find the grave, she enlisted the help of Superintendent Jerry Sullivan. Check-ing records, they located the grave site. The records revealed that Hawkins had been with the 3rd Vermont in the Civil War and also had received the Medal of Honor. However, the grave was completely unmarked.

With the help of members of the Veterans of Foreign Wars, Gardner Hawkins' grave was finally properly identified with the Medal of Honor plaque, after more than seventy-five years.

I sincerely hope this book, although perhaps not be as com-plete as it might be, will give some rightfully owed recognition to that Indomitable Brigade!

POSTSCRIPT

VERMONT ARMY NATIONAL GUARD
Headquarters, 86th Brigade, 42nd Infantry Division
Campbell Armory, RR #4, Box #1240
Montpelier, Vermont 05602-8904

March 7, 1994

Mr. George Parsons

Re: Vermont Brigade

Dear Mr. Parsons:

This is to thank you for undertaking to write the history of the Vermont Brigade. It is a history of which we are enormously proud.

The "old brigade," as it is known here, did not disband after the Civil War. Reduced to a regiment, it became known as the "First Vermont" in honor of those who answered President Lincoln's call in 1861.

The "First Vermont" has served in the Spanish-American War, chased Pancho Villa along the Mexican Border, and fought in both world wars. During World War II, the unit fought in the Philip-

155

pines and won a Presidential Unit Citation for gallantry in seizing the Ipo Dam. This critical dam, which the enemy planned to blow up, held back the reservoir which provided fresh water to the people of Manila.

Today, the "old brigade" is a tank battalion identified as the 1st Battalion, 172d Armor. I am sure you will not be surprised to learn that it is considered to be one of the finest tank battalions on the east coast. The unit's crest depicts the Greek Cross of the VI Corps and its motto is General Sedgwick's admonition on the way to Gettysburg, "Put the Vermonters Ahead."

The spirit of the Vermont Brigade has never died here. The men and women of this brave little state are proud to be citizen soldiers. They stand ready to follow in their ancestors' footsteps and do their duty. When the fighting is over, they will stack arms and, as they have always done, come home to the Green Mountains and wait yet again for the nation's call.

Bruce M. Lawlor
COL AR VTARNG
Former Commander
"First Vermont"

APPENDIX A

MEDAL OF HONOR RECIPIENTS
OF THE VERMONT BRIGADE

	REGT.	PLACE EARNED	ISSUED
Alex M. Beattie, Capt.	3rd Vt.	Cold Harbor	4/25/1894
Frank G. Butterfield, Lt.	6th Vt.	Banks Ford	5/04/1891
John W. Clark, Lt.	6th Vt.	Warrenton, Va.	8/17/1891
Dayton P. Clarke, Capt.	2nd Vt.	Spotsylvania	6/30/1892
Robert J. Coffey, Sgt.	4th Vt.	Banks Ford	5/13/1892
Charles W. Dolloff, Sgt.	11th Vt.	Petersburg	4/24/1865
James Drury, Sgt.	4th Vt.	Weldon Railroad	1/18/1893
Charles G. Gould, Capt.	5th Vt.	Petersburg	7/30/1890
Lewis A. Grant, Col.	5th Vt.	Banks Ford	5/11/1893
Lester G. Hack, Sgt.	5th Vt.	Petersburg	5/10/1865
Ephraim W. Harrington, Sgt.	2nd Vt.	Fredericksburg	1/13/1893
Garner C. Hawkins, Lt.	3rd Vt.	Petersburg	9/30/1893
Edward A. Holton, Sgt.	6th Vt.	Lee's Mill	7/09/1892
George W. Hooker, Lt.	4th Vt.	Crampton's Gap	9/17/1891
Willie Johnston, Drummer	3rd Vt.	Peninsula Campaign	9/16/1863
William W. Noyes, Pvt.	2nd Vt.	Spotsylvania	3/22/1892
Sam E. Pingree, Capt.	3rd Vt.	Lee's Mill	8/17/1891
Carlos Rich, Sgt.	4th Vt.	Wilderness	1/04/1895
Augustus Robbins, Lt.	2nd Vt.	Spotsylvania	3/24/1892
Jackson Sargent, Sgt.	5th Vt.	Petersburg	10/28/1891
Julian A. Scott, Drummer	3rd Vt.	Lee's Mill	2/10/1865
Thomas O. Seaver, Col.	3rd Vt.	Spotsylvania	4/08/1892
William J. Sperry, Maj.	6th Vt.	Petersburg	8/12/1892
Amasa A. Tracy, Lt. Col.	2nd Vt.	Cedar Creek	6/24/1892
Dan D. Wheeler, Lt.	4th Vt.	Banks Ford	3/24/1892

From: *America's Medal Of Honor Recipients*

157

APPENDIX B

OFFICERS OF THE VERMONT BRIGADE WHO WERE BREVETTED TO HIGHER RANK FOR GALLANT AND MERITORIOUS SERVICE

Captain George H. Amidon, 4th Vermont-to Bvt. Major
1st Lieutenant Charles H. Anson, 11th Vermont-to Bvt. Captain-Major
1st Lieutenant George A. Bailey, 11th Vermont-to Bvt. Captain
Captain Erastas G. Ballou, 2nd Vermont-to Bvt. Major
1st Lieutenant Henry C. Baxter, 11th Vermont-to Bvt. Captain
Colonel Asa P. Blunt, 6th Vermont-to Bvt. Brigadier General
Captain George W. Bonett, 3rd Vermont-to Bvt. Major
Major Eugene O. Cole, 5th Vermont-to Bvt. Lieutenant Colonel
Captain Adomisan N. Austin, 5th Vermont-to Bvt. Major
Captain James E. Eldridge, 11th Vermont-to Bvt. Major
Lieutenant Colonel Horace W. Floyd, 3rd Vermont-to Bvt. Colonel
Colonel George P. Foster, 4th Vermont-to Bvt. Brigadier General
Captain Charles G. Gould, 5th Vermont-to Bvt. Major
Brigadier General Lewis A. Grant, Comm. Vt. Brigade-to Bvt. Maj. General
Captain Ephraim W. Harrington, 2nd Vermont-to Bvt. Major
Lt. Colonel Amasa S. Tracy, 2nd Vermont-to Bvt. Colonel
Major Enoch E. Johnson, 2nd Vermont-to Bvt. Lt. Colonel
Captain Elijah Wales, 2nd Vermont-to Bvt. Major
Colonel Charles B. Stoughton, 4th Vermont-to Bvt. Brig. General
Captain George W. Hooker, 4th Vermont-to Bvt. Major and Lt. Colonel
Major William J. Sperry, 6th Vermont-to Bvt. Lt. Colonel
Captain Charles S. Shattuck, 6th Vermont-to Bvt. Major
Colonel James M. Warner, 11th Vermont-to Bvt. Brig. General

158

Major Aldace F. Walker, 11th Vermont-to Bvt. Lt. Colonel
1st Lieutenant John H. Macomber, 11th Vermont-to Bvt. Captain
Captain Alfred L. Carlton, 11th Vermont-to Bvt. Major
1st Lieutenant Henry J. Nichols, 11th Vermont-to Bvt. Captain
Captain George G. Tilden, 11th Vermont-to Bvt. Major
Captain Benjamin R. Jenne, 5th Vermont-to Bvt. Major
Captain Alfred H. Keith, 6th Vermont-to Bvt. Major
Brig. General George J. Stannard, to Bvt. Major General

From: *Vermont's Adjutant General's Records and Muster Rolls-Peck's edition, pp. 735-36.*

APPENDIX C

FIRST VERMONT BRIGADE ORGANIZATIONAL CHART

SIXTH ARMY CORPS

Brig. Gen. William F. Smith, ...	Oct. 15-24, 1861.
Brig. Gen. William T. H. Brooks	Oct. 24, 1861-Oct. 21, 1862
° Colonel Henry Whiting..............................	Oct. 21, 1862-Feb. 9, 1863
Brig. Gen. Lewis A. Grant	Feb. 9, 1863-June 21, 1865

SECOND VERMONT INF.
Colonel Henry Whiting°
Colonel James H. Walbridge°
Colonel Newton Stone*
Colonel John S. Tyler*
Colonel Amasa S. Tracy

THIRD VERMONT INF.
Colonel William F. Smith
Colonel Breed N. Hyde°
Colonel Thomas O. Seaver
Colonel Horace W. Floyd

FOURTH VERMONT INF.
Colonel Edwin H. Stoughton
Colonel Charles B. Stoughton+
Colonel George P. Foster

FIFTH VERMONT INF.
Colonel Henry Smalley°
Colonel Lewis A. Grant
Colonel John A. Lewis+
Colonel Ronald Kennedy

SIXTH VERMONT INF.

Colonel Nathan Lord Jr.°
Colonel Oscar L. Tuttle°
Colonel Elisha L. Barney*
Colonel Sumner H. Lincoln

ELEVENTH VERMONT, 1ST VT. HVY. ARTILLERY
Colonel James M. Warner
Lt. Col. Reuben Benton-1st Batt.°
Lt. Col. Geo. Chamberlin-2nd Batt.*
Lt. Col. Charles Hunsdon-3rd Batt.
Lt. Col. Aldace F. Walker-1st Batt.
Lt. Col. Darius Safford-2nd Batt.

LEGEND: * KILLED
+DISABLED
° RESIGNED

From: Vermont's Adjutant General's Records and Muster Rolls

160

Appendix D

REVISED ROSTER
OF
VERMONT VOLUNTEERS
1861-66
THEODORE S. PECK, ADJUTANT GENERAL

MONTPELIER, VT. 1892

Press Of The Watchman Publishing Co.

SECOND REGIMENT
(THREE YEARS)

Mustered into the service of the United States June 20, 1861. Original members, not veterans, mustered out of service June 29, 1864. Recruits for one year and recruits whose term of service would expire previous to October 1, 1865, mustered out of service June 19, 1865. Remaining officers and men mustered out of service July 15, 1865.

Field and Staff

Name and Rank	Residence	Date of Commis'n.	Date of Issue	Remarks
Colonels				
Henry Whiting	St. Clair, Mich.	June 6, '61	June 6, '61	Resgd. Feb. 9, '63.
James H. Walbridge	Bennington	Feb. 9, '63	Feb. 23, '63	Capt. Co. A; Prom. Maj. May 21, '62; do. Lieut.-Col., Jan. 8, '63; Resgd. April 1, '63.
Newton Stone	Bennington	Apr. 2, '64	Apr. 21, '64	1st Lieut. Co. A; Prom. Capt. Co. I Jan. 22, '62; do. Maj. Jan. 8, '63; do. Lieut.-Col. Feb. 9, '63; killed in action May 5, '64.
John S. Tyler	Brattleboro	May 6, '64	May 30, '64	1st Lieut. Co. C.; Prom. Capt. Co. C. Jan. 23, '62; do. Maj. Feb 9, '62; do. Lieut. Col. Apr. 2, '64; died May 23, '64 of wds. recd. in action May 5, '64.
Amasa S. Tracy	Middlebury	June 7, '65	June 17, '65	1st Lieut. Co. K.; Prom. Capt. Co. H. Jan. 24, '62; do. Maj. Apr. 2, '62; do. Lieut.-Col. June 17, '64; Bvt. Col. Apr. 2, '65, for gallantry at Petersburg, Va., Apr. 2, '65; Wd. May 3, '63, and Oct. 19, '64. Must. out as Lieut.-Col. July 15, '65.

Lieut. Colonels				
George J. Stannard	St. Albans	June 6, '61	June 6, '61	Prom. Col. 9th Vt. May 21, '62.
Charles H. Joyce	Northfield	May 21, '62	May 21, '62	Maj.; Resgd. Jan. 6, '63.
Newton Stone	Bennington	Feb. 9, '63	Feb. 23, '63	See Colonel.
John S. Tyler	Brattleboro	Apr. 2, '64	Apr. 21, '64	See Colonel.
Amasa S. Tracy	Middlebury	June 17, '64	June 20, '64	See Colonel.
Enoch E. Johnson	Castleton	June 7, '65	June 17, '65	2d Lieut. Co. B.; Prom. 1st Lieut, Co. B. Sept 2, '61; do. Capt. Co. I, Jan. 25, '62; do. Maj. June 17, '64; Brev. Lieut. Col. Oct. 19, '64 for gallantry in all the actions since Cold Harbor, and especially Cedar Creek; Must. out as Maj. July 15, '65.
Majors				
Charles H. Joyce	Northfield	June 6, '61	June 6, '61	See Lieut. Col.
James H. Walbridge	Bennington	May 21, '62	May 21, '62	See Colonel.
Newton Stone	Bennington	Jan. 8, '63	Jan. 20, '63	See Colonel.
John S. Tyler	Brattleboro	Feb. 9, '63	Feb. 23, '63	See Colonel.
Amasa S. Tracy	Middlebury	Apr. 2, '64	Apr. 21, '64	See Colonel.
Enoch E. Johnson	Castleton	June 17, '64	June 20, '64	See Lieut.-Col.
Erastus G. Ballou	Boston, Mass.	June 6, '65	June 17, '65	1st Sergt. Co. I.; Prom. Sergt. Maj. Oct. 14, '61; do. 1st Lieut. Co. I Jan. 27, '62; do. Capt. Co. K, Aug. 4, '62; Bvt. Maj. Aug 1, 63, for gallantry in the Wilderness, and subsequent engagements; Wd., May 3, '63, July 10, '63, May 5, '64 and Apr. 2, '65; Must. out Capt. Co. K, July 15, '65.
Adjutants				
Guilford S. Ladd	Bennington	June 11, '61	June 11, '61	Resgd. July 17, '62.
Francis M. Edgerton	Poultney	Aug. 4, '62	Aug. 16, '62	Sergt. Co. B; Prom. 2d Lieut. Co. F, Jan. 25, '62; Must. out June 29, 63.

(Continued)

SECOND REGIMENT   **Field and Staff** *(Continued)*

Name and Rank	Residence	Date of Commis'n	Date of Issue	Remarks
Orman P. Ray	Essex	Dec. 24, '64	Jan. 31, '65	Priv. Co. G; Prom. Sergt.-Maj. Nov. 1, '64; Must. out June 19, '65
Quartermasters				
Perley P. Pitkin	Montpelier	June 6, '61	June 6, '61	Prom. Capt. and A. Q. M., U.S. Vols. Feb. 19, '62; Lieut-Col. Q. M. Aug. 2, '64; Resgd. Nov 7, '64.
Lauriston L. Stone	Stowe	Apr. 3, '62	Apr. 3, '62	Com.-Sergt.; Prom. Q. M. Sergt. Jan. 16, '62; taken pris. Oct. 26, 6_; Par. Dec. 10, '64; Must. out Apr. 16, 65.
Surgeons				
Newton H. Ballou	Burlington	June 11, '61	June 11, '61	Resgd. Dec. 18, '62.
William J. Sawin	Chicopee Falls, Mass.	Dec. 18, '62	Dec. 27, '62	Tr. from 10th Mass. Regt. as Priv. to Co. E, 3d Vt. Vols.; Prom. Asst.-Surg. 2d Regt. June 21, '62; Wd. and taken pris. June 29, '62; Par. July 22, '62; Must. out June 29, '64.
Melvin J. Hyde	Isle La Mott	Aug. 1, '64	Aug. 23, '64	Asst. Surg; Must. out July 15, '65.
Asst. Surgeons				
—— W. Carpenter	Burlington	June 11, '61	June 11, '61	Prom. Surg. 9th Regt. Vt. Vols. June 21, '63.
William J. Sawin	Chicopee Falls, Mass.	June 21, '62	June 21, '62	See Surgeon.
Augustus A. Atwood	Sharon	Sept. 22, '62	Oct. 7, '62	Resgd. June 25, '63.
William A. Noyes	Tunbridge	Apr. 14, '63	Apr. 14, '63	Resgd. May 27, '63.
Melvin J. Hyde	Isle La Mott	Sept. 12, '63	Sept. 13, '63	See Surgeon.
Edwin R. Brush	Cambridge	Oct. 15, '63	Oct. 27, '63	Drafted; Priv. Co. H; Must. out July 15, '65.
Chaplains				
Claudius B. Smith	Brandon	June 6, '61	June; 6, '61	Resgd. July 8, '62.
Tirell W. Dayton	Middlebury	Aug. 18, '62	Aug. 18, '62	Resgd. Jan. 6, '63; Comnd. again as Chap. Mch. 10, '63 and Oct. 9, '63; comns. not accepted.

Non-Commissioned Staff

Name and Rank	Residence	Date of Enlistment	Date of Muster	Remarks
Sergeant-Majors				
William Guinan	Montpelier	June 6, '61	June 20, '61	Disch. Sept. 21, '61, for wds. recd. July 21, '61.
Erastus G. Ballou	Boston, Mass.	May 7, '61	June 20, '61	See Major.
Cadbury W. Hight	Burlington	May 20, '61	June 20, '61	See 2d Lieut. Co. C.
Henry H. Prouty	Brattleboro	May 1, '61	June 20, '61	See Capt. Co. B.
—— Ufford	Fairfax	May 18, '61	June 20, '61	Corp. Co. H; Prom. Sergt; do. Sergt.-Maj. Dec. 1, '63; Re-en. Dec. 21, '63; killed in action May 5, '64
Henry Stiles	Peru	Oct. 16, '61	Oct. 31, '61	Priv. Co. A; Prom. Corp. June 30, '62; do. Sergt. Sept. 24, '63; do. Sergt.-Maj. May 7, '64; Must. out Oct. 31, '64.
Orman P. Ray	Essex	Aug. 30, '62	Sept. 15, '62	See Adjt.
Russell Fisk	Bennington	Dec. 1, '63	Jan. 7, '64	See 2d Lieut. Co. K.
Q. M. Sergts.				
William J. Cain	Rutland	June 6, '61	June 20, '61	Disch. Jan. 12, '62, for disability.
Lauriston L. Stone	Stowe	June 6, '61	June 20, '61	See. Regt. Q. M.
H. Fifield	Poultney	May 1, '61	May 17, '61	June 20, '61 See 1st Lieut. Co. B.
Dennis C. Dunham	Tunbridge	May 1, '61	June 20, '61	See. Capt. Co. E.
—— Fassett	Jericho	Feb. 26, '62	Apr. 12, '62	See 1st Lieut. Co. E.
Wilbur Fisk	Tunbridge	Sept. 5, '61	Sept. 7, '61	Priv. Co. E; Re-en. Dec. 21, '63; Prom. Q. M.-Sergt. July 1, '65; Must. out July 15, '65.
Com. Sergts.				
Lauriston L. Stone	Stowe	June 6, '61	June 20, '61	See Regtl. Q. M.
—— G. Guyett	Montpelier	May 7, '61	June 30, '61	Priv. Co. F; Prom. Com.-Sergt.; Re-en. Dec. 21, '63; Must. out July 15, '61.

(Continued)

SECOND REGIMENT Non-Commissioned Staff *(Continued)*

Name and Rank	Residence	Date of Enlistment	Date of Muster	Remarks
Augustus J. Robbins	Grafton	May 7, '61	June 20, '61	See 2d Lieut. Co. B.
Hospital Stewards				
Z. Stearns	Burlington	June 6, '61	June 20, '61	Disch. Dec. 10, '61, for disability.
William Aubry	Burlington	June 1, '62	June 20, '61	Disch. Jan. 15, '63, for disability.
John W. Sherry	Lowell	June 1, '61	July 16, '61	Priv. Co. B. 3d Vt.; Tr. to Co. H, 2d Vt. Feb. 1, '63; Prom. Hosp. Stew, Feb. 1, '63; Must. out June 29, '64.
Dudley C. Merriam	Westford	May 7, '61	June 20, '61	Priv. Co. G; Re-en. Dec. 21, '63; Prom. Corp.; Red. March 5, '64; Prom. Hosp. Stew. Aug. 1, '64; Must. out July 15, '65.
Prin. Musicians				
Charles E. Remick	Hardwick	June 6, '61	June 20, '61	Disch. Oct. 28, '62, by order of W. D.
James E. Stone	Northfield	June 6, '61	June 20, '61	See 2d Lieut. Co. I.
David Tho's. Sharpley	Burlington	May 7, '61	June 20, '61	Musician Co. G; Re-en. Jan. 31, '64; Prom. Prin. Musician April 7, '64; Must. out July 15, '65.

THIRD REGIMENT
(THREE YEARS)

Mustered into the service of the United States, July 16, 1861. Original members, not veterans, mustered out of service July 27, 1864. Veterans and recruits consolidated into six companies, July 25, 1864, but their record is completed in their original company. Recruits for one year and recruits whose term of service would expire previous to October 1, 1865, mustered out of service June 19, 1865. Remainder of regiment mustered out of service July 11, 1865.

Field and Staff

Name and Rank	Residence	Date of Commis'n	Date of Issue	Remarks
Colonels				
William F. Smith	U.S. Army	Apr. 27, '61	Apr. 27, '61	Prom. Brig.-Gen. U.S. Vols. Aug. 13, '61; do. Maj. Gen. July 4, '62; Resgd. from Vol. service Nov. 4, '65; (See list of U.S. Reg. Army officers.)
Breed N. Hyde	Hyde Park	Aug. 13, '61	Aug. 13, '61	Lieut.-Col.; Resgd. Jan. 15, '63.
Thomas O. Seaver	Pomfret	Jan. 15, '63	Feb. 2, '63	Capt. Co. F; Prom. Maj. Aug. 13, '61; do, Lieut.-Col. Sept. 27, '62; Must. out July 27, '64.
Horace W. Floyd	Springfield	June 4, '65	June 17, '65	2d Lieut. Co. A; Prom. 1st Lieut. Co. F, Aug. 13, '61; Tr. to Co. A Dec. 1, '61; Prom. Capt. Co. C. Sept. 22, '62; do. Maj. Aug. 4, '64; do. Lieut.-Col. Oct. 18, '64; Bvt. Col. Oct. 19, '64, for gallantry before Richmond, Va., and in the Shenandoah Valley; Wd. June 21, '64; Must. out as Lieut.-Col. July 11, '65.
Lieut. Colonels				
Breed N. Hyde	Hyde Park	June 6, '61	June 6, '61	See Colonel.
Wheelock G. Veazey	Springfield	Aug. 13, '61	Aug. 13, '61	Capt. Co. A; Prom. Maj. Aug. 10, '61; do. Col. 16th Vt. Sept. 27, '62.
Thomas O. Seaver	Pomfret	Sept. 27, '62	Oct. 4, '62	See Colonel.
Samuel E. Pingree	Hartford	Jan. 15, '63	Feb. 2, '63	1st Lieut. Co. F; Prom. Capt Co. F, Aug. 13, '61; do. Maj. Sept. 27, '62; Wd. Apr. 16, '62; Must. out July 27, '64.
Horace W. Floyd	Springfield	Oct. 18, '64	Nov. 4, '64	See Colonel.

(Continued)

THIRD REGIMENT Field and Staff *(Continued)*

Name and Rank	Residence	Date of Commis'n	Date of Issue	Remarks
William H. Hubbard	Lyndon	June 4, '65	June 17, '65	Sergt. Co. G; Prom. 2nd Lieut. Co. I, Jan. 15, '63; do. 1st Lieut. Co. D. Nov. 1, '63; do. Capt. Co. I, June 26, '64; do. Maj. Apr. 19, '65; Wd. Oct. 19, '64; Must. out as Maj. July 11, '65.
Majors				
Walter W. Cochran	Rockingham	July 12, '61	July 12, '61	Resgd. Aug. 10, '61.
Wheelock G. Veazey	Springfield	Aug. 10, '61	Aug. 10, '61	See Lieutenant-Colonel.
Thomas O. Seaver	Pomfret	Aug. 13, '61	Aug. 13, '61	See Colonel.
Samuel E. Pingree	Hartford	Sept. 27, '62	Oct. 6, '62	See Lieutenant-Colonel.
Thomas Nelson	Ryegate	Jan. 15, '63	Feb. 2, '63	Capt. Co. I; Wd. June 29, '62; Must. out July 27, '64.
Horace W. Floyd	Springfield	Aug. 4, '64	Aug. 23, '64	See Colonel.
John F. Cook	Hardwick	Oct. 18, '64	Nov. 4, '64	Priv. Co. I; Prom. Sergt. June 1, '62; do. 2d Lieut. Co. I, Oct. 13, '62; do. 1st Lieut. Co. E, Jan. 15, '63; do. Capt. Co. E. Nov. 1, '63; Wd. May 12, '64; Disch. Apr. 8, '65.
William H. Hubbard	Lyndon	Apr. 19, '65	May 3, '65	See Lieutenant-Colonel.
Alonzo H. Newt	St. Johnsbury	June 4, '65	June 17, '65	Corp. Co. C; Prom. Sergt.; do Sergt-Maj. Oct. 18, '62; do. 2d Lieut. Co. K, Jan. 15, '63; do. 1st Lieut. Co. C, Nov. 1, '63; do. Capt. Co. B, June 26, '64; Must. out as Capt. Co. B, July 11, '65.
Adjutants				
Asa P. Blunt	St. Johnsbury	June 6, '61	June 6, '61	Prom. Lieut.-Col. 6th Vt. Sept. 25, '61.
Waterman F. Corey	Fairfield	Sept. 1, '61	Sept. 1, '61	See Capt. Co. H.
Edward Mattocks	Lyndon	Sept. 22, '62	Oct. 13, '62	Priv. Co. B; Prom. Sergt.-Maj. Jan. 4, '62; cashiered and dismissed the service Apr. 12, '64.

Name	Residence			Remarks
Abel Morrill	Cabot	Apr. 18, '64	May 5, '64	Corp. Co. E; Prom. 2d Lieut. Co. K, Sept. 22, '62; do. 1st Lieut. Co. K, Jan. 15, '63; killed in action May 6, '64.
Hubbard H. Phillips	Springfield	June 26, '64	July 10, '64	(Commission not accepted); See 1st Lieut. Co. H.
Quartermasters				
Austin H. Hall	Waterford	Oct. 18, '64	Nov. 4, '64	1st Lieut. Co. I; Must. out July 11, '65.
Redfield Proctor	Cavendish	June 19, '61	June 19, '61	Prom. Maj. 5th Vt. Sept. 25, '61.
Frederick Crain	Springfield	Aug. 10, '61	Aug. 10, '61	1st Lieut. Co. A; Prom. Capt. and A. Q. M. U.S. Vols. May 18, '64; do. Maj. Q. M. May 22, '65; Must. out Feb. 8, '66. (See U.S. Reg. Army officers.)
George F. Brown	Lyndon	Oct. 18, '64	Jan. 30, '65	Priv. Co. G; Prom. Sergt.-Maj. Nov. 14, '63; Re-en. Jan. 20, '64; Prom. 1st Lieut. Co. C June 26, '64; Must. out July 11, '65.
Surgeons				
Henry Janes	Waterbury	June 24, '61	June 24, '61	Prom. Surg. U.S. Army Mch. 26, '63; Bvt. Lieut.-Col. U.S. Vols. Mch. 13, '65, for faithful and meritorious service during the war; Must. out Jan. 4, '66.
David M. Goodwin	Cabot	Apr. 29, '63	May 7, '63	Asst.-Surg.; Must. out July 27, '64.
John J. Meigs	Hyde Park	Oct. 1, '64	Oct. 24, '64	Asst.-Surg. 11th Vt.; Must. out July 8, '65.
Asst. Surgeons				
David M. Goodwin	Cabot	June 20, '61	June 20, '61	See Surgeon.
Henry F. Smith	Castleton	Sept. 15, '62	Sept. 17, '62	Disch. Apr. 21, '64.
Henry C. Newell	St. Johnsbury	Oct. 2, '63	Oct. 2, '63	Drafted; Resgd. May 20, '65.
Chaplains				
Moses P. Parmalee		June 10, '61	June 10, '61	Resgd. Dec. 18, '61.
Daniel A. Mack	Royalton	Jan. 11, '62	Jan. 11, '62	Must. out July 27, '64; Comnd. again Mch. 30, '65; Must. out July 11, '65.

THIRD REGIMENT

Non-Commissioned Staff

Name and Rank	Residence	Date of Enlistment	Date of Muster	Remarks
Sergeant-Majors				
Leo Hyde	Hyde Park	June 24, '61	July 16, '61	See Capt. Co. A.
Edward Mattocks	Lyndon	Sept. 17, '61		See Adjutant.
William H. Bowker	Colchester	July 10, '61	July 16, '61	See 1st Lieut. Co. E.
George F. Brown	Lyndon	June 1, '61	July 16, '61	See Quartermaster.
Orsamus B. Robinson	Weathersfield	June 1, '61	July 16, '61	See 1st Lieut. Co. B.
Abram J. Locke	Cavendish	Oct. 14, '61	Oct. 29, '61	See 2d Lieut. Co. K.
Alonzo H. Newt	St. Johnsbury	June 1, '61	July 16, '61	See Major.
Q. M.-Sergts.				
John W. Ramsey	Newbury	June 1, '61	July 16, '61	See 2d Lieut. Co. C.
Frank E. Rew	Hartford	June 1, '61	July 16, '61	See 1st Lieut. Co. B.
George J. Quimby	Lyndon	June 10, '61	July 16, '61	Corp. Co. G; Re-en. Jan. 20, '64; Prom. Q. M.-Sergt. Feb. 28, '63; Must. out July 11, '65.
Com.-Sergts.				
Henry L. Mathews	Barnet	June 1, '61	July 16, '61	Died July 1, '62 of disease.
John R. Seaver	Cavendish	June 1, '61	July 16, '61	See 2d Lieut. Co. A.
Arring't'n C. Wakefield	Rockingham	June 1, '61	July 16, '61	See 1st Lieut. Co. C.
Geo. E. Farrington	Springfield	Aug. 13, '62	Sept. 30, '62	Priv. Co. A; Prom. Corp. Nov. 7, '63; do. Sergt. June 1, '64; do. Com.-Sergt. Mch. 25, '65; Must. out June 19, '65.
George A. Brown	Hardwick	June 1, '61	July 16, '61	Priv. Co. C; Re-en. Dec. 21, '63; Prom. Corp.; do. Sergt. Oct. 17, '64; do. Com.-Sergt. June 20, '65; Must. out July 11, '65.
Hospital Steward				
William L. Jackson	St. Johnsbury	June 1, '61	July 16, '61	Must. out July 27, '64.

Princ. Musicians				
Seymour O. Cook	Springfield	June 1, '61	July 16, '61	Disch. June 18, '62 for disab.
Henry H. Crossman	St. Johnsbury	June 1, '61	July 16, '61	Disch. July 17, '62, for disab.
Richard D. Bagley	Craftsbury	July 9, '61	July 16, '61	Muscn. Co. G; Re-en. Dec. 21, '63, and Tr. to Co. I; Prom. Prin. Muscn. Mch. 12, '64; Must. out July 11, '65.
Moses O. Bagley	Craftsbury	July 5, '61	July 16, '61	Muscn. Co. I; Re-en. Dec. 21, '63; Prom. Prin. Muscn. July 15, '64; Must. out July 11, '65.

FOURTH REGIMENT
(THREE YEARS)

Mustered into the service of the United States, September 21, 1861. Original members, not veterans, mustered out of service September 30, 1864. First, Second and Third Companies of Sharp Shooters transferred to Fourth Regiment, February 25, 1865, but their names do not appear in this organization, their record having been completed in their original companies. Veterans, recruits, and men transferred from the Sharp Shooters consolidated into eight companies February 25, 1865. Recruits for one year and recruits whose term of service would expire previous to October 1, 1865, mustered out of service June 19, 1865. Remainder of regiment mustered out of service July 13, 1865.

Field and Staff

Name and Rank	Residence	Date of Commis'n.	Date of Issue	Remarks
Colonels				
Edwin H. Stoughton	Rockingham	Aug. 1, '61	Aug. 1, '61	Prom. Brig.-Gen. U.S. Vols. Nov. 5, '62; appointment expired Mch. 4, '63.

(Continued)

FOURTH REGIMENT Field and Staff *(Continued)*

Name and Rank	Residence	Date of Commis'n.	Date of Issue	Remarks
Charles B. Stoughton	Rockingham	Nov. 5, '62	Nov. 5, '62	Adjt.; Prom. Maj. Feb. 25, '62; do. Lieut.-Col. July 17, '62; Wd. July 10, '63; Bvt. Brig.-Gen. U.S. Vols. Mch. 13, '65 for gallant and meritorious service during the war; Resgd. Feb. 2, '64.
George P. Foster	Walden	Feb. 3, '64	Mch. 22, '64	Capt. Co. G; Prom. Maj. July 18, '62; do. Lieut.-Col. Nov. 5, '62; Bvt. Brig. Gen. Aug 1, '64, for gallant and meritorious service before Richmond and in the Shenandoah Valley; Wd. May 5, '64; Must. out July 13, '65.
Lieut.-Colonels				
Harry N. Worthen	Bradford	Aug. 15, '61	Aug. 15, '61	Resgd. July 17, '62.
Charles B. Stoughton	Rockingham	July 17, '62	Aug. 16, '62	See Colonel.
George P. Foster	Walden	Nov. 5, '62	Nov. 5, '62	See Colonel.
Stephen M. Pingree	Stockbridge	Apr. 30, '64	May 9, '64	1st Lieut. Co. E; Prom. Capt. Co. K Apr. 21, '62; do. Maj. Nov. 5, '62; Must. out Sept. 30, '64.
John E. Pratt	Bennington	Mch. 14, '65	Mch. 20, '65	Capt. Co. A; Prom. Maj. Apr. 30, '64; taken pris. June 23, '64; Par. Mch. 1, '65; Must. out July 13, '65.
Majors				
John Curtis Tyler	Brattleboro	Sept. 14, '61	Sept. 14, '61	Resgd. Jan. 17, '62.
Charles B. Stoughton	Rockingham	Feb. 25, '62	Feb. 25, '62	See Colonel.
George P. Foster	Walden	July 18, '62	Aug. 16, '62	See Colonel.
Stephen M. Pingree	Stockbridge	Nov. 5, '62	Jan. 24, '63	See Lieutenant-Colonel.
John E. Pratt	Bennington	Apr. 30, '64	May 9, '64	See Lieutenant-Colonel.

Name	Residence			Remarks
Charles W. Boutin	Windham	June 4, '65	June 17, '65	1st Lieut. Co. K; Prom. Capt. Co. D, Dec. 14, '62; taken pris. June 23, '64; Par. Mch. 1, '65; Must. out as Capt. Co. D, July 13, '65.
Adjutants				
Charles B. Stoughton	Rockingham	Aug. 1, '61	Aug. 1, '61	See Colonel.
John Faxon	Rockingham	Jan. 19, '62	Jan. 19, '62	Sergt.-Maj.; Prom. 2d Lieut. Co. B, Dec. 18, '61; Resgd. July 16, '62.
George B. French	Cavendish	July 17, '62	Aug. 16, '62	1st Lieut Co. C; Wd. May 5, '64; Must. out Sept. 30, '64.
James Gallagher	Brookfield	May 8, '65	May 20, '65	Corp. Co. B; Re-en. Apr. 24, '64; Prom. Sergt. May 1, '62; do. Sergt.-Maj. Apr. 1, '63; do. 2d Lieut. Co. F, Apr. 19, '64; do. 1st Lieut. Co. A, June 5, '64; taken pris. June 23, '64; Par. Mch. 1, '65; Must. out July 13, '65.
Quartermasters				
John H. Cushman	Bennington	Aug. 10, '61	Aug. 10, '61	Resgd. Jan. 24, '63.
Henry T. Cushman	Bennington	Jan. 29, '63	Sept. 7, '63	Q. M.-Sergt.; Must. out Sept. 30, '64.
Henry W. Spafford	Bennington	Nov. 6, '64	Dec. 6, '64	Priv. Co. A; Prom. Com.-Sergt. May 28, '62; Must. out Sept. 30, '64; enlisted again Oct. 25, '64, as R. Q. M.; taken pris. Oct. 11, '63; Par. Mch. 21, '64; Must. out July 13, '65.
Surgeons				
Samuel J. Allen	Hartford	Aug. 15, '61	Aug. 15, '61	Must. out Sept. 30, '64.
Edward M. Curtis	Burlington	Oct. 24, '64	Oct. 26, '64	Hosp. Stew.; Prom. Asst.-Surg. 6th Vt. Jan. 29, '63; Must. out July 13, '65.
Asst.-Surgeons				
Willard A. Child	Pittsford	Aug. 15, '61	Aug. 15, '61	Prom. Surg. 10th Vt. Aug. 6, '62.
Edwin Phillips	Tinmouth	Aug. 6, '62	Aug. 6, '62	Priv. Co. G 6th Vt.; Prom. Surg. 6th Vt. Oct. 28, '63.
Armentus B. Bixby	Londonderry	Oct. 6, '62	Oct. 6, '62	Must. out Sept. 30, '64.

(Continued)

FOURTH REGIMENT Field and Staff *(Continued)*

Name and Rank	Residence	Date of Commis'n	Date of Issue	Remarks
Chaplains				
Salem M. Plimpton	West Haven, Conn.	Sept. 8, '61	Sept. 18, '61	Resgd. Sept. 1, '62.
John L. Roberts	Chelsea	Sept. 25, '62	Sept. 25, '62	Resgd. May 9, '63; Comnd. again July 3, '63; Must. out July 13, '65.

Non-Commissioned Staff

Name and Rank	Residence	Date of Enlistment	Date of Muster	Remarks
Sergeant-Majors				
John Faxon	Rockingham	Sept. 14, '61	Sept. 21, '61	See Adjutant.
George W. Hooker	Londonderry	Sept. 6, '61	Sept. 21, '61	See 1st Lieut. Co. E.
Charles A. Reed	Ludlow	Aug. 19, '61	Sept. 21, '61	See 1st Lieut. Co. F.
James Gallagher	Brookfield	Aug. 22, '61	Sept. 21, '61	See Adjutant.
Frank Hastings	Burlington	Feb. 20, '62	Apr. 12, '62	(Real name William A. Cameron). See 2d Lieut. Co. B.
Charles C. Chapin	Westminster	Sept. 5, '61	Sept. 21, '61	See 2d Lieut. Co. C.
Q. M.-Sergts.				
Edwin A. Wilcox	Westminster	Aug. 14, '61	Sept. 21, '61	Red. and assigned to Co. D Mch. 1, '62.
Henry T. Cushman	Bennington	Mch. 1, '62	Mch. 1, '62	See Quartermaster.
Charles W. Cade	Hardwick	Aug. 23, '61	Sept. 21, '61	Priv. Co. H; Prom. Q. M.-Sergt. Jan. 29, '63; Must. out Sept. 30, '64.
John Wheeler	Substitute	July 31, '63	July 31, '63	See Drum-Major.
Nathan A. Smith	Shaftsbury	Sept. 2, '61	Sept. 21, '61	See 2d Lieut. Co. F.
Joseph C. Waterson	Chelsea	Feb. 12, '62	Apr. 12, '62	See 2d Lieut. Co. B.

Com.-Sergts.				
George N. Harvey	Barnet	Aug. 14, '61	Sept. 21, '61	See 2d Lieut. Co. G.
Henry W. Spafford	Bennington	Sept. 4, '61	Sept. 21, '61	See Quartermaster.
Russell T. Chamberlin	Montpelier	Sept. 5, '61	Sept. 21, '61	See 1st Lieut. Co. A.
Martin J. Bixby	Reading	Aug. 15, '62	Sept. 30, '62	Priv. Co. C; Prom. Com.-Sergt. May 1, '65; Wd. Aug. 21, '64; Must. out June 19, '65.
Willard C. Brown	Pittsford	Oct. 22, '61	Nov. 9, '61	Priv. Co. G; Tr. from Co. E, 2d U.S.S.S. Feb. 25, '65, as Sergt.; Prom. Com.-Sergt. June 24, '65; Must. out July 13, '65.
Hospital Steward				
Edward M. Curtis	Burlington	Aug. 27, '61	Sept. 21, '61	See Surgeon.
Charles S. Brooks	West Fairlee	Aug. 26, '61	Sept. 21, '61	Priv. Co. B; Prom. Hosp. Stew.___, '62; Disch. Dec. 31, '63, for promotion in U.S.C.T.
Marshall P. Felch	Piermont, N.H.	Aug. 29, '61	Sept. 21, '61	Priv. Co. H; Re-en. Feb. 15, '64; Prom. Hosp. Stew. Jan. 14, '64; Must. out July 13, '65.
Prin. Musicians				
Samuel L. Thompson	Cavendish	Sept. 18, '61	Sept. 21, '61	Disch. May 3, '62 for disab.
Augustus Dow	Northfield	Sept. 6, '61	Sept. 21, '61	Muscn. Co. K; Prom. Prin. Muscn. Mch, 1, '62; Disch. Oct. 15, '62, for disab.
Henry E. Mosler	Bethel	Oct. 1, '61	Nov. 9, '61	Priv. Co. G; Tr. from Co. E 2d U.S.S.S. Feb. 25, '65; Prom. Prin. Muscn. May 1, '65; Must. out July 13, '65.
Drum-Major				
John Wheeler	Brattleboro	Aug. 24, '61	Sept. 21, '61	Sergt. Co. F; Prom. Drum Major May 1, '62; Dishon Disch. July 26, '62 by sentence of G. C. M.; enlisted again in Co. F July 31, '63, as Sub. for Clark Pierce, Wardsboro; Prom. Q. M.-Sergt. Sept. 21, '64; Red. Feb. 3, '65; Tr. to Co. A, Feb. 25, '65; Dcs. Mch. 2, '65.

FIFTH REGIMENT
(THREE YEARS)

Mustered into the service of the United States September 16, 1861. Original members, not veterans, mustered out of service September 15, 1864. Recruits for one year, and recruits whose term of service would expire previous to October 1, 1865, mustered out of service June 19, 1865. Remainder of regiment mustered out of service June 29, 1865.

Field and Staff

Name and Rank	Residence	Date of Commis'n.	Date of Issue	Remarks
Colonels				
Henry A. Smalley	1st Lieut. 2d Art. U.S.A.	July 30, '61	Sept. 16, '61	Leave of absence from Regular Army revoked Sept. 10, '62; Prom. Capt. 2d U.S. Art. Aug. 1, '63; Resgd. Mch. 8, '65.
Lewis A. Grant	Rockingham	Sept. 16, '62	Sept. 16, '62	Major; Prom. Lieut.-Col. Sept. 25, '61; do. Brig.-Gen. U.S. Vols., Apr. 27, '64; Bvt.-Maj. Gen. Oct. 19, '64, for gallant and meritorious service; Wd. Dec. 14, '62; Must. out Aug. 24, '65.
John R. Lewis	Burlington	May 6, '64	May 24, '64	Capt. Co. I; Prom. Maj. July 15, '61; do. Lieut.-Col. Oct. 6, '62; Wd. May 5, '64; Tr. to V. R. C. as Col. Sept. 4, '64; Bvt. Brig.-Gen. Mch. 13, '65, for gallant service in battle of Wilderness; Disch. June 12, '67.
Ronald A. Kennedy	Concord	June 9, '65	June 28, '65	Capt. Co. K, 3d Vt.; Prom. Lieut.-Col. 5th Vt. Feb. 20, '65; Must. out as Lieut.-Col. June 29, '65.
Lieut.-Colonels				
Nathan Lord, Jr.	Montpelier	Sept. 16, '61	Sept. 16, '61	Prom. Col. 6th Vt. Sept. 16, '61.

Lewis A. Grant	Rockingham	Sept. 25, '61	Sept. 25, '61	See Colonel.
John R. Lewis	Burlington	Oct. 6, '62	Oct. 15, '62	See Colonel.
Charles P. Dudley	Manchester	May 6, '64	May 30, '64	Capt. Co. E; Prom. Maj. Oct. 6, '62; died May 21, '64 of wds. recd. May 10, '64.
Addison Brown, Jr.	Brattleboro	Sept. 18, '64	Sept. 28, '64	Capt. Co. F, 4th Vt.; Disch. Dec. 9, '64 for disab.
Ronald A. Kennedy	Concord	Feb. 20, '65	Mch. 13, '65	See Colonel.
Eugene O. Cole	Bennington	June 9, '65	June 28, '65	Major; Bvt. Lieut.-Col. Apr. 2, '65, for gallantry at Petersburg; Must. out as Maj. June 29, '65.
Majors				
Lewis A. Grant	Rockingham	Aug. 15, '61	Aug. 15, '61	See Colonel.
Redfield Proctor	Cavendish	Sept. 25, '61	Sept. 25, '61	Q. M. 3d Vt.; Resgd. July 11, '62.
John R. Lewis	Burlington	July 15, '62	July 31, '62	See Colonel.
Charles P. Dudley	Manchester	Oct. 6, '62	Oct. 15, '62	See Lieut.-Colonel.
Eugene O. Cole	Bennington	Dec. 26, '64	Jan. 30, '65	See Lieut.-Colonel.
Thomas Kavaney	Burlington	June 9, '65	June 28, '65	Priv. Co. I; (real name Isaac Moss); Prom. Corp.; do. Q. M.-Sergt. May 1, '63; do. Capt. Co. A, Aug. 5, '64; Wd. Oct. 19, '64; Must. out as Capt. Co. A, June 29, '65.
Adjutants				
Edward M. Brown	Montpelier	Aug. 24, '61	Aug. 24, '61	Prom. Lieut.-Col. 8th Vt. Jan. 8, '62.
Cornelius H. Forbes	Brandon	Jan. 8, '62	Oct. 5, '63	1st Lieut. Co. H; Must. out Sept. 15, '64.
Charles F. Leonard	Brattleboro	Oct. 20, '64	Oct. 21, '64	Must. out June 29, '65.
Quartermasters				
Aldis O. Brainerd	St. Albans	Aug. 24, '61	Aug. 24, '61	Resgd. May 28, '62.
Isaac L. Eells	Middlebury	May 16, '64	July 12, '64	Corp. Co. F; Prom. Sergt; do. Com.-Sergt. May 1, '63; Re-en. Dec. 15, '63; Prom. 2d Lieut. Co. A (and acting R. Q. M.) Apr. 5, '64; Must. out June 29, '65.

(Continued)

FIFTH REGIMENT Field and Staff *(Continued)*

Name and Rank	Residence	Date of Commis'n.	Date of Issue	Remarks
Surgeons				
William P. Russell	Middlebury	Aug. 15, '61	Aug. 15, '61	Wd. and taken pris. June 29, '62; Par. July 17, '62; Disch. Oct. 11, '62 for disab.
Philander D. Bradford	Northfield	Dec. 3, '62	Dec. 3, '62	Resgd. Mch. 1, '63.
Alwyn H. Chesmore	Huntington	Mch. 1, '63	Mch. 17, '63	Asst.-Surg.; Must. out Sept. 15, '64.
Cyrus H. Allen	Thetford	Oct. 1, '64	Oct. 24, '64	Asst.-Surg. 8th Vt.; Must. out June 29, '65.
Asst.-Surgeons				
Henry C. Shaw	Waitsfield	Aug. 15, '61	Aug. 15, '61	Died Sept. 7, '62, of disease.
Arthur F. Burdick	Underhill	Sept. 23, '62	Sept. 29, '62	Resgd. May 26, '63.
Alwyn H. Chesmore	Huntington	Sept. 25, '62	Sept. 25, '62	See Surgeon.
Henry C. Atwood	Salisbury	May 6, '63	May 7, '63	Resgd. June 25, '63.
Daniel C. Colburn	Burlington	Aug. 18, '63	Aug. 18, '63	Must. out June 29, '65.
Chaplains				
Volney M. Simons	Swanton	Aug. 24, '61	Aug. 24, '61	Resgd. Mch. —, '62.
Charles S. Hale	Brandon	May 24, '62	May 24, '62	Resgd. May 25, '63; Re-appointed Aug. 8, '63; Must. out Sept. 15, '64.
John D. Cargill	Richmond	Sept. 29, '64	Nov. 4, '64	Corp. Co. K; Prom. Sergt.; Re-en. Dec. 15, '63; Wd. June 5, '63; Must. out June 29, '65.

Non-Commissioned Staff

Name and Rank	Residence	Date of Enlistment	Date of Muster	Remarks
Sergeant-Majors				
Charles C. Spaulding	Montpelier	Sept. 16, '61	Sept. 16, '61	See 1st Lieut. Co. D.

Name	Town			Remarks
C. Henry Benton	Johnson	Aug. 29, '61	Sept. 16, '61	See 1st Lieut. Co. D.
Orrin L. Spencer	Salisbury	Aug. 20, '61	Sept. 16, '61	See 1st Lieut. Co. G.
Willard G. Davenport	Brandon	Aug. 23, '61	Sept. 16, '61	See 1st Lieut. Co. H.
William H. Newton	Leicester	July 16, '63	July 16, '63	See Priv. Co. E.
Charles V. Cool	Sudbury	Aug. 28, '61	Sept. 16, '61	See 1st Lieut. Co. B.
Theodore Willett	Burlington	Aug. 23, '61	Sept. 16, '61	Priv. Co. I; Re-en. Dec. 15, '63; Prom. Sergt.-Maj. May 4, '65; Must. out June 29, '65.
Q. M.-Sergts.				
Adoniram N. Austin	Colchester	Sept. 9, '61	Sept. 16, '61	See 1st Lieut. Co. F.
Orvis H. Sweet	Burlington	Mch. 28, '62	Apr. 12, '62	See 1st Lieut. Co. A.
Isaac Farnsworth	St. Albans	Sept. 14, '61	Sept. 16, '61	See 2d Lieut. Co. A.
Thomas Kavaney	Burlington	Oct. 27, '62	Oct. 27, '62	See Major.
Nathaniel A. Bucklin	Sudbury	Sept. 4, '61	Sept. 16, '61	See 1st Lieut. Co. I.
Com.-Sergts.				
George R. Hall	Rutland	Sept. 14, '61	Sept. 16, '61	See 1st Lieut. Co. I.
Miner E. Fish	Sheldon	Sept. 9, '61	Sept. 16, '61	See Capt. Co. D.
Benjamin Peake	Swanton	Sept. 17, '61	Oct. 31, '61	See Priv. Co. C.
Isaac L. Eells	Middlebury	Aug. 27, '61	Sept. 16, '61	See Quartermaster.
Edwin H. Trick	Burlington	Sept. 9, '61	Sept. 16, '61	See 2d Lieut. Co. C.
Prin. Musicians				
Asa R. Burleson	Burlington	Sept. 16, '61	Sept. 16, '61	Disch. Apr. 11, '62.
John W. Taylor	Middlebury	Sept. 7, '61	Sept. 16, '61	Muscn. Co. B; Re-en. Dec. 15, '63; Prom. Prin. Muscn. May 1, '64; Red. and assigned to Co. A; Prom. Prin. Muscn. again Sept. 14, '64; Must. out June 29, '65.
Martin V. Williams	Tinmouth	Dec. 31, '63		Priv. Co. B; Prom. Prin. Muscn. May 3, '64; Must. out June 29, '65.
Hospital Steward				
Silas C. Isham	Burlington	Aug. 21, '62	Sept. 15, '62	Priv. Co. I; Prom. Hosp. Stew. Mch. 1, '63; Must. out June 19, '65.

SIXTH REGIMENT
(THREE YEARS)

Mustered into the service of the United States, October 15, 1861. Original members, not veterans, mustered out of service October 28, 1864. Veterans and recruits consolidated into six companies, October 16, 1864, but their record is completed in their original companies. Recruits for one year and recruits whose term of service would expire previous to October 1, 1865, mustered out of service June 26, 1865. Remainder of regiment mustered out of service June 26, 1865.

Field and Staff

Name and Rank	Residene	Date of Commis'n.	Date of Issue	Remarks
Colonels				
Nathan Lord, Jr.	Montpelier	Sept. 16, '61	Oct. 17, '61	Lieut. Col. 5th Vt.; Resgd. Dec. 18, '62.
Oscar S. Tuttle	Cavendish	Dec. 18, '62	Dec. 27, '62	Major; Prom. Lieut. Col. Sept. 19, '62; Resgd. Mch. 18, '63.
Elisha L. Barney	Swanton	Mch. 18, '63	Mch. 26, '63	Capt. Co. K; Prom. Maj. Oct. 15, '62; do. Lieut.-Col. Dec. 18, '62; Wd. Sept. 14, '62; died May 10, '64, of wds. recd. May 5, '64.
Sumner H. Lincoln	Hartford	June 4, '65	June 17, '65	Corp. Co. B; Prom. Adjut. Feb. 3, '63; do. Maj. Oct. 21, '64; do. Lieut.-Col. Jan. 7, '65; Wd. May 5, '64, and Sept. 19, '64; Must. out as Lieut.-Col. June 26, '65.
Lieut.-Colonels				
Asa P. Blunt	St. Johnsbury	Sept. 25, '61	Oct. 14, '61	Adjt. 3d Vt.; Prom. Col. 12th Vt., Sept. 19, '62.
Oscar S. Tuttle	Cavendish	Sept. 19, '62	Oct. 6, '62	See Colonel.
Elisha L. Barney	Swanton	Dec. 18, '62	Dec. 27, '62	See Colonel.
Oscar A. Hale	Troy	Mch. 18, '63	Apr. 1, '63	Capt. Co. D; Prom. Maj. Jan 12, '63; Wd. Aug. 21, '64; Must. out Oct. 28, '64.

Name	Town	Date	Date	Remarks
Frank G. Butterfield	Rockingham	Oct. 21, '64		2nd Lieut. Co. A; Prom. 1st Lieut. Co. C Aug. 21, '62; do. Capt. Co. I Apr. 21, '64; Wd. Aug. 21, '64; Resgd. on account of wds. and Must. out as Capt. Co. I, Oct. 28, '64.
Sumner H. Lincoln	Hartford	Jan. 7, '65	Jan. 30, '65	See Colonel.
William J. Sperry	Cavendish	June 4, '65	June 17, '65	Sergt. Co. E; Prom. 2d Lieut. Co. E Aug. 21, '62; do. 1st Lieut. Co.E Mch. 3, '63; do. Capt. Co. C Aug. 8, '64; do. Maj. Jan. 7, '65; Bvt. Lieut.-Col. Apr. 2, '65, for gallantry in the assault on Petersburg; Must. out as Maj. June 26, 65.
Majors				
Oscar L. Tuttle	Cavendish	Sept. 25, '61	Oct. 15, '61	See Colonel.
Elisha L. Barney	Swanton	Oct. 15, '62	Oct. 24, '62	See Colonel.
Oscar A. Hale	Troy	Jan. 12, '63	Jan. 23, '63	See Lieutenant-Colonel.
Richard B. Crandall	Berlin	Mch. 18, '63	Apr. 1, '63	Adjt.; Prom. Capt. Co. K, Nov. 1, '62; killed in action June 7, '64.
Carlos W. Dwinell	Glover	June 27, '64	July 10, '64	2d Lieut. Co. D; Prom. 1st Lieut. Co. D, Jan. 11, '62; do. Adjt. Nov. 1, '62; do. Capt. Co. C, Jan. 12, '63; Wd. May 5, '64; died Aug. 24, '64, of wds. recd. Aug. 21, '64.
Sumner H. Lincoln	Hartford	Oct. 21, '64	Oct. 26, '64	See Colonel.
William J. Sperry	Cavendish	Jan. 7, '65	Jan. 30, '65	See Lieutenant-Colonel.
Edwin R. Kinney	Burlington	June 4, '65	June 17, '65	2d Lieut. Co. I; Prom. 1st Lieut. Co. I, Jan. 18, '62; do. Capt. Co. G, June 5, '63; Wd. Apr. 16, '62 and Oct. 19, '64; Must. out as Capt., Co. G, June 26, '65.
Adjutants				
Richard B. Crandall	Berlin	Oct. 10, '61	Oct. 15, '61	See Major.
Carlos W. Dwinell	Glover	Nov. 1, '62	Jan. 14, '63	See Major.
Sumner H. Lincoln	Hartford	Feb. 3, '63	Feb. 13, '63	See Colonel.

(Continued)

SIXTH REGIMENT **Field and Staff** *(Continued)*

Name and Rank	Residence	Date of Commis'n.	Date of Issue	Remarks
Hiram S. English	Woodstock	Nov. 12, '64	Dec. 15, '64	Priv. Co. C; Prom. Corp. Jan. 1, '63; do. Sergt. May 20, '64; do. 1st Lieut. Co. C Oct. 29, '64; Wd. May 4, '63; Must. out June 19, '65.
Henry Martin	Williamstown	June 23, '65	June 28, '65	Priv. Co. G; Sub. for Benjamin O. Flint, Williamstown; Prom. Corp. Sept. 23, '64; do. Sergt. June 20, '65; Must. out as Sergt. Co. G June 26, '65.
Quartermasters				
John W. Clark	Montpelier	Sept. 28, '61	Oct. 14, '61	Prom. Capt. and A. Q. M. U. S. Vols., Apr. 7, '64; Resgd. Dec. 6, '64.
Charles J. S. Randall	Bristol	Oct. 29, '64	Nov. 10, '64	Priv. Co. A; Prom. Q. M.-Sergt. Aug. 25, '62; do. 2d Lieut. Co. A, Nov. 1, '62; do. 1st Lieut. Co. A, May 15, '64; Must. out June 26, '65.
Surgeons				
R. C. M. Woodward	St. Albans	Oct. 10, '61	Oct. 14, '61	Disch. Oct. 29, '61 for disab.
Charles M. Chandler	Montpelier	Oct. 29, '61	Nov. 18, '61	Asst.-Surg.; Resgd. Oct. 7, '63.
Edwin Phillips	Tinmouth	Oct. 28, '63	Oct. 28, '63	Priv. Co. G; Prom. Asst.-Surg. 4th Vt., Aug. 4, '62; Must. out June 26, '65.
Asst. Surgeons				
Charles M. Chandler	Montpelier	Oct. 10, '61	Oct. 14, '61	See Surgeon.
Lyman M. Tuttle	Vernon	Nov. 7, '61	Nov. 18, '61	Resgd. Dec. 26, '62.
Edward M. Curtis	Burlington	Jan. 29, '63	Feb. 2, '63	Hosp.-Stew. 4th Vt.; Prom. Surg. 4th Vt. Oct. 24, '64.
Cornelius A. Chapin	Williston	July 8, '63	July 8, '63	Died Sept. 14, '63 of disease.
Chaplains				
Edward P. Stone	Berlin	Oct. 10, '61	Oct. 14, '61	Resgd. Aug. 27, '63.
Alonzo Webster	Windsor	Oct. 3, '63	Oct. 3, '63	Must. out Oct. 28, '64.
Harvey Webster	Randolph	Nov. 13, '64	Dec. 17, '64	Must. out June 26, '65.

Non-Commissioned Staff

Name and Rank	Residence	Date of Enlistment	Date of Muster	Remarks
Sergeant-Majors				
Benoni B. Fullam	Ludlow	Oct. 15, '61	Oct. 15, '61	See 1st Lieut. Co. G.
Bradford S. Murphy	Swanton	Sept. 25, '61	Oct. 15, '61	See 1st Lieut. Co. K.
William W. Carey	Cavendish	Sept. 26, '61	Oct. 15, '61	See 1st Lieut. Co. F.
Eri L. Ditty	Roxbury	Aug. 14, '61	Oct. 15, '61	See 1st Lieut. Co. H.
Edgar E. Herrick	Milton	Sept. 24, '61	Oct. 15, '61	See 2d Lieut. Co. I.
Barney Cannon	Mt. Holly	Sept. 30, '61	Oct. 15, '61	Priv. Co. C; Re-en. Dec. 15, '63; Prom. Corp.; do. Sergt. Oct. __, '64; do. Sergt.-Maj. May 12, '65; Must. out June 26, '65.
Com.-Sergts.				
George H. Hatch	Montpelier	Oct. 15, '61	Oct. 15, '61	See 1st Lieut. Co. H.
Patrick H. Murphy	Roxbury	Aug. 14, '61	Oct. 15, '61	See Capt. Co. G.
Sylvester Banister	Warren	Oct. 14, '61	Oct. 15, '61	Priv. Co. A; Re-en. Dec. 15, '63; Prom. Com.-Sergt. Oct. 15, '64; Must. out June 26, '65.
Q. M. Sergts.				
Frederick Swift	Middlebury	Oct. 15, '61	Oct. 15, '61	Died July 17, '62 of disease.
George W. Burleson	Franklin	Sept. 30, '61	Oct. 15, '61	See Capt. Co. C.
Henry C. Pomeroy	Franklin	Dec. 5, '63	Dec. 23, '63	Priv. Co. K; Prom. Corp.; do. Sergt. Oct. 16, '64; do. Q. M.-Sergt. Jan. 1, '65; Must. out June 26, '65.
Charles J. S. Randall	Bristol	Oct. 14, '61	Oct. 15, '61	See Quartermaster.
Hospital Steward				
John B. Crandall	Berlin	Oct. 15, '61	Oct. 15, '61	Prom. Asst.-Surg. 13th Vt., Oct. 7, '62.
Elijah L. Cushman	Lincoln	Sept. 30, '61	Oct. 15, '61	Priv. Co. A; Prom. Hosp.-Stew. Oct. 15, '62; Must. out Oct. 28, '64.

(Continued)

SIXTH REGIMENT Non-Commissioned Staff *(Continued)*

Name and Rank	Residence	Date of Enlistment	Date of Muster	Remarks
Ira Phillips, Jr.	Rutland	Dec. 10, '63	Jan. 5, '64	Priv. Co. I; Prom. Hosp.-Stew. Jan. 1, '65; Must. out June 26, '65.
Prin. Musicians				
William H. Gilchrist	Barnet	Oct. 15, '61	Oct. 15, '61	Disch. Nov. 6, '62.
James F. Stiles	Woodstock	Oct. 15, '61	Oct. 15, '61	Disch. May 14, '62 for disab.
Albert L. Thompson	Highgate	Jan. 5, '64	Jan. 21, '64	Priv. Co. K; Prom. Prin. Muscn. Mch. 1, '64; taken pris. Aug. 13, '64; Par. Mch. 10, '65; Red. and assigned to Co. K, Apr. 25, '65; Prom. Prin. Muscn. again June 20, '65; Must. out June 26, '65.
Michael P. Eagan	Moretown	July 17, '62	Sept. 15, '62	Priv. Co. G; Muscn.; Prom. Prin. Muscn. Nov. 1, '64; Must. out June 19, '65.

ELEVENTH REGIMENT
(FIRST REGIMENT HEAVY ARTILLERY)
(THREE YEARS)

Mustered into the service of the United States September 1, 1862. Original members, recruits for one year, and recruits whose term of service would expire previous to October 1, 1865, mustered out of service June 24, 1865. Remaining officers and men consolidated into battalion of four companies June 24, 1865, but their record is completed in their original company. Battalion mustered out of service August, 25, 1865.

Field and Staff

Name and Rank	Residence	Date of Commis'n.	Date of Issue	Remarks
Colonels				
James M. Warner	1st Lieut. U.S.A.	Aug. 15, '62	Aug. 27, '62	Bvt. Brig.-Gen. Aug. 1, '64, for gallantry at Spotsylvania Court House, Winchester, Fishers' Hill and Cedar Creek; Wd. May 18, '64; Prom. Brig.-Gen. U.S. Vols. May 8, '65; Must. out of Vol. service Jan. 15, 66.
Charles Hunsdon	Shoreham	May 23, '65	June 2, '65	Capt. Co. B; Prom. Maj. Nov. 2, '63; do. Lieut.-Col. Sept. 2, '64; Must. out June 24, '65.
Lieut.-Colonels				
Reuben C. Benton	Hyde Park	Aug. 26, '62	Aug. 27, '62	Capt. Co. D, 5th Vt.; Resgd. June 21, '64.
Geo. F. Chamberlin	St. Johnsbury	June 28, '64	July 11, '64	Capt. Co. A; Prom. Maj. Aug. 26, '62; died Aug. 22, '64 of wds. recd. Aug. 21, '64.
Charles Hunsdon	Shoreham	Sept. 2, '64	Oct. 3, '64	See Colonel.
Aldace F. Walker	Middlebury	May 23, '65	June 2, '65	1st Lieut. Co. B; Prom. Capt. Co. C Nov. 30, '62; Tr. to Co. D, July 11, '63; Prom. Maj. June 28, '64; Brev.-Lieut. Col. Oct. 19, '64, for gallantry in the Shenandoah Valley; Must. out June 24, '65.
Darius J. Safford	Morristown	July 10, '65	July 26, '65	1st Lieut. Co. D; Prom. Capt. Co. I July 11, '63; do. Maj. May 23, '65; taken pris. June 23, '64; escaped; Wd. Sept. 19, '64; Must. out Aug. 25, '65.
Majors				
Geo. E. Chamberlin	St. Johnsbury	Aug. 26, '62	Aug. 27, '62	See Lieutenant-Colonel.
Charles Hunsdon	Shoreham	Nov. 2, '63	Nov. 20, '63	See Colonel.

(Continued)

ELEVENTH REGIMENT Field and Staff *(Continued)*

Name and Rank	Residence	Date of Commis'n.	Date of Issue	Remarks
Charles K. Fleming	Rockingham	Jan. 21, '64	Mch. 15, '65	1st Lieut. Co. G; Prom. Capt. Co. M Oct. 7, '63; taken pris. June 23, '64; Par. Feb. 28, '65; Hon. Disch. May 15, '65.
Aldace F. Walker	Middlebury	June 28, '64	July 11, '64	See Lieutenant-Colonel.
Charles Buxton	Rockingham	Sept. 2, '64	Oct. 3, '64	Capt. Co. G; killed in action Sept. 19, '64.
George D. Sowles	Alburgh	Oct. 16, '64	Jan. 30, '65	Capt. Co. K; Wd. June 1, '64; Must. out June 24, '65.
Robinson Templeton	Worcester	May 23, '65	June 2, '65	Capt. Co. I; Must. out June 24, '65.
Darius J. Safford	Morristown	May 23, '65	June 2, '65	See Lieutenant-Colonel.
Henry R. Chase	Guilford	July 10, '65	July 26, '65	1st Sergt. Co. E; Prom. 2d Lieut. Co. E, Sept. 6, '62; do. 1st Lieut. Co. E, Aug. 11, '63; do. Capt. Co. M, Dec. 2, '64; Tr. to Co. A, June 24, '65; taken pris. June 23, '64; Par. Mch. 1, '65; Must. out Aug. 25, '65.
Adjutant				
Hunt W. Burrows	Vernon	Aug. 22, '62	Aug. 29, '62	See Capt. Co. M.
Quartermaster				
Alfred L. Carlton	Montpelier	Aug. 14, '62	Sept. 3, '62	See 2d Lieut. Co. C.
Surgeons				
Chas. W. B. Kidder	Vergennes	Aug. 18, '62	Sept. 3, '62	Resgd. Sept. 10, '63.
Castanus B. Park, Jr.	Grafton	Oct. 3, '63	Oct. 3, '63	Must. out June 24, '65.
Asst.-Surgeons				
Edward O. Porter	Cornwall	Aug. 19, '62	Sept. 3, '62	Resgd. Jan. 16, '65.
John J. Meigs	Hyde Park	Aug. 11, '62	Aug. 11, '62	Prom. Surg. 3d Vt., Oct. 1, '64.
Charles W. Bourne	Pawlet	Nov. 15, '64	Nov. 19, '64	Priv. Co. C; Prom. Hosp. Stew. Dec. 22, '62; Must. out June 24, '65.

Name and Rank	Residence	Date of Enlistment	Date of Muster	Remarks
Joseph L. Harrington	Weston	Mch. 4, '65	Mch. 17, '65	Priv. Co. I, 4th Vt.; Tr. to Co. F 4th Vt., Feb. 25, '65; Must. out Aug. 25, '65.
Chaplains				
William E. Bogart	Weybridge	Aug. 18, '62	Aug. 18, '62	Resgd. Nov. 29, '62.
Arthur Little	Ludlow	Mch. 20, '63	Apr. 1, '63	Must. out June 24, '65.

Non-Commissioned Staff

Name and Rank	Residence	Date of Enlistment	Date of Muster	Remarks
Sergeant-Majors				
Ranceler Wright	Vernon	July 21, '62	Sept. 1, '62	See 1st Lieut. Co. F.
Sylvester Soper	Burlington	Sept. 21, '62	Sept. 25, '62	See Priv. Co. B.
Dustan S. Walbridge	St. Johnsbury	Aug. 7, '62	Sept. 1, '62	See 2d Lieut. Co. A.
Charles G. Gould	Windham	Aug. 13, '62	Sept. 1, '62	See 2d Lieut. Co. F.
Hollis D. Morrill	St. Johnsbury	Aug. 28, '63	Oct. 7, '63	See 1st Lieut. Co. D.
Charles L. Benson	Worcester	July 14, '62	Sept. 1, '62	See 2d Lieut. Co. I.
Burton Works	Waterford	Oct. 30, '63	Oct. 30, '63	Priv. Co. A; Prom. Sergt.-Maj. June 27, '65; Must. out Aug. 25, '65.
Q. M.-Sergeants				
Charles H. Anson	Montpelier	Aug. 30, '62	Sept. 1, '62	See 1st Lieut. Co. E.
Charles L. Benson	Worcester	July 14, '62	Sept. 1, '62	See 2d Lieut. Co. I.
Frank Anson	Halifax	Jan. 5, '64	Jan. 5, '64	See 1st Lieut. Co. A.
Andrew J. Dunton	Dorset	Dec. 2, '63	Dec. 17, '63	Priv. Co. G; Tr. to Co. A, June 24, '65; Prom. Corp. June 27, '65; do. Q. M.-Sergt., July 20, '65; Must. out Aug. 25, '65.
Com.-Sergeants				
Charles W. Clark	Montpelier	Sept. 1, '62	Sept. 1, '62	See 1st Lieut. Co. G.
Edward L. Foster	Calais	Aug. 2, '62	Sept. 1, '62	See 1st Lieut. Co. I

(Continued)

ELEVENTH REGIMENT Non-Commissioned Staff *(Continued)*

Name and Rank	Residence	Date of Enlistment	Date of Muster	Remarks
Judson A. Lewis	Poultney	Aug. 11, '62	Sept. 1, '62	See 1st Lieut. Co. C.
Watson S. Eaton	Grafton	Aug. 9, '62	Sept. 1, '62	See 2d Lieut. Co. G.
Frank Anson	Halifax	Jan. 5, '64	Jan. 5, '64	See 1st Lieut. Co. A.
Samuel B. Jones	Halifax	Feb. 26, '64	Feb. 26, '64	See 2d Lieut. Co. D.
Chandlerr Watts, 2d	Stowe	Aug. 7, '62	Sept. 1, '62	Priv. Co. E; Prom. Corp. Aug. 2, '63; do. Sergt. Jan. 1, '65; do. Com. Sergt. June 12, '65; Must. out June 24, '65.
John M. Safford	Cambridge	Jan. 5, '64	Jan. 5, '64	Priv. Co. L; Prom. Corp. Mch. 25, '65; Tr. to Co. C June 24, '65; Prom. Sergt. July 15, '65; do. Com.-Sergt. Aug. 1, '65; Must. out Aug. 25, '65.
Drum Major				
George S. Blake	Rockingham	Aug. 28, '62	Sept. 1, '62	Disch. Jan. 9, '63, for disab.
Prin. Musicians				
George Colton	Irasburgh	Aug. 8, '62	Sept. 1, '62	See 2d Lieut. Co. I.
John J. Crandall	Brattleboro	Aug. 4, '62	Sept. 1, '62	Priv. Co. E; Prom. Prin. Muscn. Jan. 17, '64; Must. out June 24, '65.
Hospital Stewards				
Daniel G. Field	Montpelier	Aug. 18, '62	Sept. 1, '62	Disch. Dec. 22, '62.
Charles W. Bourne	Pawlet	Aug. 12, '62	Sept. 1, '62	See Asst.-Surgeon.
Lorenzo W. Hubbard	Lyndon	Sept. 1, '63	Oct. 7, '63	Corp. Co. M; Prom. Sergt. Nov. 29, '63; Red. Sept. 11, '64; Prom. Hosp. Stew. Jan. 1, '65; Must. out Aug. 25, '65.

APPENDIX E

STATISTICS OF MEN FROM REGIMENTS OF THE VERMONT BRIGADE

K.I.A. or DIED FROM WOUNDS

2nd VT.	224
3rd VT.	206
4th VT.	162
5th VT.	213
6th VT.	203
1st VT.H.A.	164
TOTAL	1172

DIED FROM DISEASE OR WHILE IN PRISON

2nd VT.	175
3rd VT.	165
4th VT.	162
5th VT.	125
6th VT.	182
1st VT.H.A.	412
TOTAL	1372

In regiments of the "Old Brigade" (2nd, 3rd, 4th, 5th, 6th Vt.), more men were killed in action than died of disease.

NUMBER OF SUBSTITUTES TO THE REGIMENTS

2nd VT.	181
3rd VT.	276
4th VT.	108
5th VT.	52
6th VT.	84
1st VT.H.A.	12
TOTAL	674

Note: In the "Old Brigade" of the substitutions, 219 deserted.

189

DRAFTED INTO THE VERMONT BRIGADE

2ND VT. 43
3rd VT. 60
4th VT. 85
5th VT. 9
6th VT. 84
1st VT.H.A. 0
TOTAL 281

Note: Most of those men were drafted into the brigade in the summer of 1863, and most had an excellent record.

NUMBER OF DESERTERS

2nd VT. 170
3rd VT. 261
4th VT. 111
5th VT. 98
6th VT. 66
1st VT.H.A. 124
TOTAL 830

Fifty men later returned to their regiments.
Thirty-seven men were reported missing, or were in unmarked graves.

From: *Vermont Adjutant General's Records and Muster Rolls*

ENDNOTES

INTRODUCTION

1. Benedict, George G., *Vermont In The Civil War*, vol. 1 (Burlington, Vermont: Free Press Assoc., 1886), 618.
2. Fox, William F. Lt. Col., *Regimental Losses In The Civil War*, (Dayton, Ohio: Morningside Bookshop, 1985), 116.
3. Ibid., 150.

CHAPTER I

1. Benedict, *Vermont In The Civil War*, vol. 1, 62.
2. Ibid.
3. Ibid., 66.
4. *America's Medal Of Honor Recipients, Complete Official Citations* (Golden Valley, Minnesota: Highland Publishers, 1980), 791.
5. Benedict, *Vermont In The Civil War*, vol. 1, 65.
6. Ibid., 66.
7. Warner, Ezra J., *Generals In Gray, Lives Of The Confederate Commanders* (Baton Rouge and London: Louisiana State University Press, 1959), 250.
8. Benedict, *Vermont In The Civil War*, vol. 1, 618.
9. Warner, Ezra J., *Generals In Blue, Lives Of The Union Commanders* (Baton Rouge and London: Louisiana State University Press, 1964), 298.
10. Ibid., 430.
11. Benedict, *Vermont In The Civil War*, vol. 1, 69.
12. Ibid.
13. Ibid., 71.
14. Warner, *Generals In Blue*, 404.
15. Benedict, *Vermont In The Civil War*, vol. 1, 76.
16. Ibid., 77.
17. Ibid., 77.

18. Warner, *Generals In Gray*, 151.
19. Warner, *Generals In Blue*, 493.
20. Benedict, *Vermont In The Civil War*, vol. 1, 81.
21. Ibid., 83.

CHAPTER II

1. Benedict, *Vermont In The Civil War*, vol. 1, 236.
2. Warner, *Generals In Blue*, 462.
3. Boatner, Mark M., III, *Civil War Dictionary*, Revised, (New York: David McKay Company,1988), 869-870.
4. Fox, *Regimental Losses In The Civil War*, 116.
5. Benedict, *Vermont In The Civil War*, vol. 1, 618.
6. Ibid., 126.
7. Fox, *Regimental Losses In The Civil War*, 148.
8. *Peck's Adjutant General's Report*, Revised, (Montpelier, Vermont: Press of the Watchman Publishing Co., 1892), 108-141.
9. Benedict, *Vermont In The Civil War*, vol. 1, 180.
10. Fox, *Regimental Losses In The Civil War*, 150.
11. Ibid.
12. Benedict, *Vermont In The Civil War*, vol. 1, 204.
13. Ibid., 208.
14. *Peck's Adjutant General's Report*, Revised, 181-212.
15. Fox, *Regimental Losses In The Civil War*, 161.
16. *Peck's Adjutant General's Report*, Revised, 27-213; 409-455.
17. Warner, *Generals In Blue*, 47.
18. Benedict, *Vermont In The Civil War*, vol. 1, 237.
19. *Peck's Adjutant General's Report*, Revised, 158.
20. Benedict, *Vermont In The Civil War*, vol. 1, 277.

CHAPTER III

1. Warner, *Generals In Gray*, 182.
2. Benedict, *Vermont In The Civil War*, vol. 1, 245.
3. Stevens, George T., *Three Years In The Sixth Corps* (Albany, New York: S. R. Gray, 1866), 34.
4. Benedict, *Vermont In The Civil War*, vol. 1, 246.
5. Warner, *Generals In Gray*, 207.
6. Swinton, William, *Campaigns Of The Army Of The Potomac* (Secaucus, New Jersey: The Blue and Gray Press, 1988), 102.
7. Benedict, *Vermont In The Civil War*, vol. 1, 248.
8. Ibid., 249.
9. Schiller, Herbert M., ed., *Autobiography Of Major General William F. Smith, 1861-1864* (Dayton, Ohio: Morningside Press, 1990), 11.
10. *Battles And Leaders Of The Civil War*, vol. 2, (Secaucus, New Jersey: Castle, 1887), 200.
11. Benedict, *Vermont In The Civil War*, vol. 1, 255.
12. Glover, Waldo F., *Abraham Lincoln And The Sleeping Sentinel Of Vermont* (Montpelier: Vermont Historical Society, 1936), 43.
13. *Peck's Adjutant General's Report*, Revised, 3rd Vt., 83.
14. Crute , Joseph H., Jr., *Units Of The Confederate States Army* (Midlthian, Virginia, Derwent Books, 1987), 222.
15. Benedict, *Vermont In The Civil War*, vol. 1, 257.
16. *Peck's Adjutant General's Report*, Revised, 3rd Vt., 83.

17. Benedict, *Vermont In The Civil War,* vol. 1, 139.
18. *America's Medal Of Honor Recipients,* 895.
19. Stevens, *Three Years In The Sixth Corps,* 42.
20. Benedict, *Vermont In The Civil War,* vol. 1, 214.
21. *America's Medal Of Honor Recipients,* 802 & 871.
22. Warner, *Generals In Blue,* 480.
23. Benedict, *Vermont In The Civil War,* vol. 1, 265.
24. Ibid., 269.
25. *Battles And Leaders Of The Civil War,* vol. 2, 200.
26. Tucker, Glen, *Hancock The Superb,* (Dayton, Ohio: Morningside, Reprint, 1990), 88.

CHAPTER IV

1. Benedict, *Vermont In The Civil War,* vol. 1, 277.
2. *Battles And Leaders Of The Civil War,* vol. 2, 315.
3. Ibid.
4. Child, William, M.D., *History Of The 5th New Hampshire Volunteers* (Bristol, New Hampshire: R. W. Musgrove, Printer, 1893), 63-65.
5. Benedict, *Vermont In The Civil War,* vol. 1, 287.
6. Schiller, ed. *Autobiography Of Major General William F. Smith, 1861-1864,* 42 & 43.
7. Benedict, *Vermont In The Civil War,* vol. 1, 291.
8. Allan, William, *The Army Of Northern Virginia In 1862* (Dayton, Ohio: Morningside Bookshop, 1984), 103.
9. Fox, *Regimental Losses In The Civil War,* 150.
10. Benedict, *Vermont In The Civil War,* vol. 1, 297.
11. Warner, *Generals In Blue,* 47.
12. Allan, *The Army Of Northern Virginia In 1862,* 103.
13. *Battles And Leaders Of The Civil War,* vol. 2, 316.
14. Stevens, *Three Years In The Sixth Corps,* 103.
15. *Battles And Leaders Of The Civil War,* vol. 2, 378.
16. Scrymser, James A., Capt., *The Rally Of The Vermont Brigade* (Vermont Historical Society, No date), 31-33.
17. *America's Medal Of Honor Recipients,* 845.
18. Hyde, Thomas W., *Following The Greek Cross or, Memories Of The Sixth Army Corps* (Cambridge, Boston and New York: Houghton, Mifflin and Company, The Riverside Press, 1894), 73.
19. *Battles And Leaders Of The Civil War,* vol. 2, 381.
20. Stevens, *Three Years In The Sixth Corps,* 109.
21. Benedict, *Vermont In The Civil War,* vol. 1, 309.
22. Warner, *Generals In Gray,* 152.
23. *America's Medal Of Honor Recipients,* 814.

CHAPTER V

1. Warner, *Generals In Blue,* 377.
2. Sears, Stephen W., *Landscape Turned Red, The Battle Of Antietam* (New York: Warner Books, Inc., 1983), 118.
   Battles And Leaders Of The Civil War, vol. 2, 598.
3. Sears, *Landscape Turned Red, The Battle Of Antietam,* 161.
4. *America's Medal Of Honor Recipients,* 80.
5. *Battles And Leaders Of The Civil War,* vol. 2, 594 (Gun taken first by 95th Penn., reported by regimental historian and the same reported by Gen. W. B. Franklin.)
   Benedict, *Vermont In The Civil War,* vol. 1, 323.

6. Winslow, Richard Elliott, III, *General John Sedgwick, The Story Of A Union Commander,* (San Francisco: Presido Press, 1982), 46-47.
7. *Battles And Leaders Of The Civil War,* vol. 2, 603.
   Powell, William H., *The Fifth Army Corps, Army Of The Potomac,* (Dayton, Ohio: Morningside Bookshop, 1984), 283 & 306.
8. Macartney, Edward C., *Grant And His Generals* (New York: The McBride Company, 1953), 188-222.
9. Hyde, W., *Following The Greek Cross,* 104.
10. *America's Medal Of Honor Recipients,* 808.
11. Benedict, *Vermont In The Civil War,* vol. 1, 330.
12. Siegel, Alan A., *For The Glory Of The Union, Myth, Reality, And The Media In Civil War New Jersey* (New Jersey, London, Toronto: Fairleigh Dickinson University Press, 1939), 128.
13. Warner, *Generals In Blue,* 47.
14. *Battles And Leaders Of The Civil War,* vol. 3, 107.
15. Benedict, *Vermont In The Civil War,* vol. 1, 329.

CHAPTER VI

1. *Battles And Leaders Of The Civil War,* vol. 3, 122.
2. Benedict, *Vermont In The Civil War,* vol. 1, 343.
3. Fox, *Regimental Losses In The Civil War,* 566.
4. *Peck's Adjutant General's Report,* Revised, 3rd Vt.,70.
5. Benedict, *Vermont In The Civil War,* vol. 1, 165.
6. Ibid., 345.
7. Warner, *Generals In Blue,* 235.
8. Winslow, *General John Sedgwick, The Story Of A Union Commander,* 47.
9. *America's Medal Of Honor Recipients,* 781.
10. Benedict, *Vermont In The Civil War,* vol. 1, 353.
11. Dickert, D. Augustus, *History Of Kershaw's Brigade* (Dayton, Ohio: Morningside Bookshop, 1988), 205.

CHAPTER VII

1. Benedict, *Vermont In The Civil War,* vol. 1, 354.
2. Stevens, *Three Years In The Sixth Corps,* 194-195.
3. Siegel, *For The Glory Of The Union, Myth, Reality And The Media In Civil War New Jersey,* 165.
4. *America's Medal Of Honor Recipients,* 791.
5. Benedict, *Vermont In The Civil War,* vol. 1, 366.
6. Hyde, Thomas W., *Following The Greek Cross,* 128.
7. *Peck's Adjutant General's Report,* Revised, 147.
8. Baquet, Camille, *History Of The First Brigade, New Jersey Volunteers* (Published by the State of New Jersey, 1910), 82.
9. Benedict, *Vermont In The Civil War,* vol. 1, 368.
10. *Battles And Leaders Of The Civil War,* vol. 3, 235-236.
11. Hyde, *Following The Greek Cross,* 130-131.
12. Benedict, *Vermont In The Civil War,* vol. 1, 368.
13. *America's Medal Of Honor Recipients,* 730.
14. Siegel, *For The Glory Of The Union, Myth, Reality And The Media In Civil War New Jersey,*169.
15. *O.R., L. A. Grant's Report of the Battle of May 4, 1864,* vol. XXXVII, (Washington Government Printing Off., 1884), 605.
16. *America's Medal Of Honor Recipients,* 935.
17. Ibid., 741.

18. *O.R., L. A.* Grant's *Report of the Battle of May 4, 1864,* vol. XXXVII, 605.
19. *America's Medal Of Honor Recipients,* 749.
20. Ibid., 781.
21. Benedict, *Vermont In The Civil War,* vol. 1, 373.
22. Barker, Harold R., *History Of The Rhode Island Combat Units In The Civil War,* (Alfred H. Gurney, ed., 1964), 149.
23. Benedict, *Vermont In The Civil War,* vol. 1, 375.

CHAPTER VIII

1. Winslow, *General John Sedgwick, The Story Of A Union Commander,* 86.
2. Dowdey, Clifford, *Death Of A Nation* (New York: Alfred A. Knopf, 1958), 31.
3. Siegel, *For The Glory Of The Union, Myth, Reality, And The Media In Civil War New Jersey,* 185.
4. *O.R., Report of Col. L. A. Grant 5th Vt. No. 230,* vol. XXXIX, (Washington Government Printing Off., 1883), 676-677.
5. Benedict, *Vermont In The Civil War,* vol. 1, 381.
6. *Peck's Adjutant General's Report,* Revised, 6th Vt., 178-179.
7. *Anti-Rebel, The Civil War Letters Of Wilbur Fisk* (Croton-on-Hudson, New York: Emil Rosenblatt, 1983), 105-106.
8. Benedict, *Vermont In The Civil War,* vol. 1, 383.
9. *Anti-Rebel, The Civil War Letters Of Wilbur Fisk,* 112-114.
10. Benedict, *Vermont In The Civil War,* vol. 1, 385.
11. Coffin, Charles C., *Four Years Of Fighting* (Boston: Arno Press, Reprint, 1970), 286.
12. Bates, Samuel P., *History And Muster Rolls Of The 93rd Pennsylvania,* (Reprint, 1993), 288.
13. Benedict, *Vermont In The Civil War,* vol. 1, 193-194.
14. *Peck's Adjutant General's Report,* 1892, 4th Vt., 108.
15. Benedict, *Vermont In The Civil War,* vol. 1, 394.
16. *Battles And Leaders Of The Civil War,* vol.4, 81-82.

CHAPTER IX

1. Winslow, *General John Sedgwick, The Story Of A Union Commander,* 113.
2. Benedict, *Vermont In The Civil War,* vol.1, 397.
3. Stevens, *Three Years In The Sixth Corps,* 276.
4. Benedict, *Vermont In The Civil War,* vol. 1, 144.
5. *Anti-Rebel, The Civil War Letters Of Wilbur Fisk,* 154.
6. Benedict, *Vermont In The Civil War,* vol. 2, 294.
7. *Battles And Leaders Of The Civil War,* vol. 3, 436.
8. *Report Of The Adjutant & Inspector General, 1865* (Montpelier: Walton's Steam Printing, Est., 1865), 17.
9. Higginson, Thomas W., *Massachusetts In The Army and Navy, 1865,* vol. 1(Boston: Wright and Porter Co., 1896), 36.

CHAPTER X

1. Report of Maine Commissioners, Executive Comm., *Maine At Gettysburg* (Portland, Maine: The Lakeside Press, 7th Maine, 1898), 458.
2. Warner, *Generals In Blue,* 417.
3. Boatner, *Civil War Dictionary,* Revised, 75.
4. Fox, *Regimental Losses In The Civil War,* 531.
5. *Peck's Adjutant General's Report,* Revised, 2nd Vt., 34; 5th Vt., 149.
6. Benedict, *Vermont In The Civil War,* vol. 1, 407.

7. *Peck's Adjutant General's Report,* Revised, 2nd & 6th Vt., 27-213.
8. Ibid., 142.
9. Fox, *Regimental Losses In The Civil War,* 116.
10. *Peck's Adjutant General's Report,* Revised, 2nd & 6th Vt., 27-213; 11th Vt., 409-455.

CHAPTER XI

1. Boatner, *Civil War Dictionary,* 919, 923-925.
2. Fox, *Regimental Losses In The Civil War,* 66 & 72.
3. *Battles And Leaders Of The Civil War,* vol. 4, 93.
4. Trudeau, Noah A., *Bloody Roads South* (New York: Fawcett Columbine, 1989), 321.
5. Catton, Bruce, *Civil War, A Stillness At Appomattox* (New York: Fairfax Press, 1984), 503.
6. *Battles And Leaders Of The Civil War,* vol. 4, 180.
7. *Peck's Adjutant General's Report,* Revised,128.
8. *Anti-Rebel, The Civil War Letters of Wilbur Fisk,* 215.
9. *Peck's Adjutant General's Report,* Revised, 30.
10. Fox, *Regimental Losses In The Civil War,* 149.
11. *America's Medal Of Honor Recipients,* 882.
12. Hunt, Roger D. & Jack R. Brown, *Brevet Brigadier Generals In Blue* (Gaithersburg, Maryland: Old Soldier Books, Inc., 1990), 356.
13. *Peck's Adjutant General's Report,* Revised, 181.
14. Ibid., 183.
15. Scott, Robert G., *Into The Wilderness With The Army Of The Potomac* (Bloomington: Indiana University Press, 1957), 82-83.
16. Schaff, Morris, *The Battle Of The Wilderness* (Cambridge, Massachusetts: Houghton, Mifflin Co., The Riverside Press, 1910), 198.
17. Scott, *Into The Wilderness With The Army Of The Potomac,* 112.
18. Benedict, *Vermont In The Civil War,* vol. 1, 431.
19. Powell, William H. Lt. Col. 11th Inf. *The Fifth Army Corps* (Dayton, Ohio: Morningside Bookshop, 1984), 629.
20. Smith, John D., *The History Of The Nineteenth Regiment Of Maine Volunteer Infantry, 1862–1865,* (Minnesota: Great Western Printing Co., 1909), 143.
21. Longstreet, James, *From Manassas To Appomattox* (Secaucus, New Jersey: The Blue and Grey Press, 1988), 564.
22. Naisawald, L. VanLoan, *Grape And Canister* (New York: Oxford University Press, 1960), 473.
23. Matter, William D., *If It Takes All Summer, The Battle of Spotsylvania* (London and Chapel Hill: University of N.C. Press, 1988), 12.
24. Fox, *Regimental Losses In The Civil War,* 147-151.

CHAPTER XII

1. Dowdey, Clifford, *Lee's Last Campaign, The Story Of Lee And His Men Against Grant,1864* (Wilmington, North Carolina: Broadfoot Publ. Co., 1988), 181.
2. Catton, Bruce, *Grant Takes Command* (Boston and Toronto: Little, Brown, and Co., 1968), 215.
3. *O.R., Report of Col. L. A. Grant, No. 230,* vol. XXX, ch. XLVIII, (Government Printing Off., 1884), 702.
4. Benedict, *Vermont In The Civil War,* vol. 1, 439.
5. Winslow, *General John Sedgwick, The Story Of A Union Commander,* 174.
6. Stevens, *Three Years In The Sixth Corps,* 330.
7. *O.R., Report of Col. L. A. Grant,* vol. XXX, ch. XLVIII, (Government Printing Office, 1884), 67.

8. Ibid., 668.
9. *America's Medal Of Honor Recipients,* 895.
10. Coffin, *Four Years of Fighting,* 325.
11. *Personal Memoirs Of U. S. Grant,* vol. 2, (New York: The Century Co, 1903), 135.
12. *America's Medal Of Honor Recipients,* 861.
13. Ibid., 739.
14. Hemenway, Abby, *Vermont Historical Gazetteer,* vol. 3, (No date), 657.
15. Benedict, *Vermont in The Civil War,* vol. 2, 351.
16. *Report Of The Adjutant & Inspector General Of The State Of Vermont, Oct. 1, 1864–Oct. 1, 1865* (Montpelier, Vermont: Walton's Steam Printing Estbl., 1865) 92-95.

CHAPTER XIII

1. *Peck's Adjutant General's Report,* Revised, 82.
2. Fox, *Regimental Losses In The Civil War,* 100.
3. Warner, *Generals In Blue,* 343.
4. Benedict, *Vermont In The Civil War,* vol. 2, 300.
5. Fox, *Regimental Losses In The Civil War,* 146-148.
6. *Battles And Leaders Of The Civil War,* vol. 4, 217.
7. *America's Medal Of Honor Recipients,* 709.
8. *Anti-Rebel, The Civil War Letters Of Wilbur Fisk,* 229.
9. Trudeau, *Bloody Roads South,* 302-306.
10. *O.R., Report Of C. A. Dana, Assistant Secretary of War,* vol. XXX, chap. XLVIII, (Government Printing Office, 1884), 94.
11. *Personal Memoirs Of U. S. Grant,* vol. 2, 171-172.
12. Catton, Bruce, *Civil War, A Stillness At Appomattox,* 581.

CHAPTER XIV

1. Walker, Francis A., *Second Army Corps* (New York: Charles Scribner's Sons, 1887), 544-546.
2. Benedict, *Vermont In The Civil War,* vol.2, 358.
3. *Battles And Leaders Of The Civil War,* vol. 4, 183.
4. Benedict, *Vermont In The Civil War* , vol. 2, 362-363.
5. Ibid, 366.
6. *America's Medal Of Honor Recipients,* 760.
7. *Peck's Adjutant General's Report,* Revised, 752-765.
8. Lyman, Theodore, *With Grant And Meade,* (Lincoln, Nebraska and London: University of Nebraska Press, 1994), 173-174.
9. Trudeau, Noah A., *The Last Citadel* (Boston: Little, Brown and Company, 1991), 81.
10. Catton, *Bruce, Grant Takes Command,* (Boston: Little, Brown and Company, 1968), 371-372.

CHAPTER XV

1. Benedict, *Vermont In The Civil War,* vol. 2, 372.
2. Boatner, *Civil War Dictionary,* 418-419, 761.
3. Catton, *Civil War, A Stillness At Appomattox,* 614.
4. *Anti-Rebel, The Civil War Letters Of Wilbur Fisk,* 238.
5. Benedict, *Vermont In The Civil War,* vol. 1, 486.

6. Stevens, *Three Years In The Sixth Corps*, 372-373.
7. Walker, Aldace F., *Vermont In The Shenandoah Valley, 1864* (Burlington, Vermont: The Free Press Assoc., 1869), 31.
8. Catton, *Civil War, A Stillness At Appomattox*, 614-615.
9. *Battles And Leaders Of The Civil War*, vol. 4, 498.
10. Benedict, *Vermont In The Civil War*, vol. 1, 490.
11. *Peck's Adjutant General's Report*, Revised, 70.
12. Russell, Charles W., ed., *Gray Ghost, The Memoirs Of Colonel John S. Mosby* (New York: Bantam Books, 1992), 211-215.
13. Warner, *Generals In Blue*, 195-196.
14. Benedict, *Vermont in The Civil War*, vol. 2, 373.
15. Catton, *Grant Takes Command*, 250-251.
16. Benedict, *Vermont In The Civil War*, vol. 1, 494-495.
17. Boatner, *Civil War Dictionary*, 329-330.

CHAPTER XVI

1. *Battles And Leaders Of the Civil War*, vol. 4, 530-531.
2. Catton, *Grant Takes Command*, 360.
3. Baquet, *History Of The First Brigade, New Jersey Volunteers*, 152.
4. Benedict, *Vermont In The Civil War*, vol. 1, 504.
5. Walker, *Vermont In The Shenandoah Valley, 1864*, 67-68.
6. Benedict, *Vermont In The Civil War*, vol. 2, 374.
7. Benedict, *Vermont In The Civil War*, vol. 1, 507.
8. Ibid., 508.
9. Walker, *Vermont In The Shenandoah Valley, 1864*, 67.
10. *Anti-Rebel, The Civil War Letters Of Wilbur Fisk*, 253.
11. *Personal Memoirs Of U. S. Grant*, vol. 2, 206.
12. Walker, *Vermont In The Shenandoah Valley, 1864*, 78-88.
13. Benedict, *Vermont In The Civil War*, vol. 1, 511.
14. Warner, *Generals In Gray*, 263.
15. Benedict, *Vermont In The Civil War*, vol. 1, 512-513.
16. Ibid., 520.
17. Hunt & Brown, *Brevet Brigadier Generals In Blue*, 620.
18. *O.R., Report Of Col. L. A. Grant*, Series 1, vol. XLIII, part 1, chpt. LV, 113.
19. *Battles And Leaders Of The Civil War*, vol. 4, 532.
20. *O.R., Report Of Col. L. A. Grant*, Series 1, vol. XLIII, part 1, chpt. LV, 208.
21. *Battles And Leaders Of The Civil War*, vol. 4, 510.
22. *O.R., Report Of Col. L. A. Grant*, Series 1, vol. XLIII, part 1, chpt. LV, 192.

CHAPTER XVII

1. Dickert, *History of Kershaw's Brigade*, 436.
2. *Report Of The Adjutant & Inspector General of The State Of Vermont, 1864–65*, 47.
3. Lewis, Thomas A., *The Guns Of Cedar Creek* (New York: Dell Publishing Group, Inc., 1988), 179.
4. Fox, *Regimental Losses In The Civil War*, 81-82.
5. Wert, Jeffry D., *From Winchester to Cedar Creek* (Carlisle, Pa: South Mountain Press, Inc., 1987), 179.
6. Stevens, *Three Years In The Sixth Corps*, 418.
7. Stackpole, Edward J., *Sheridan In The Shenandoah, Jubal Early's Nemesis*, (Harrisburg, Pennsylvania: The Stackpole Co., 1946), 312.
8. Benedict, *Vermont In The Civil War*, vol. 1, 550.
9. Walker, *The Vermont Brigade In The Shenandoah Valley*, 143.

10. Catton, *Civil War, A Stillness at Appomattox,* 641-42.
11. *O.R., Report of Col. L. A. Grant,* Series 1, vol. XLIII, part 1, chpt. LV, 159.
12. Walker, *The Vermont Brigade In The Shenandoah Valley,* 148.
13. Benedict, *Vermont In The Civil War,* vol. 1, 557.
14. Catton, *Civil War, A Stillness at Appomattox,* 643-644.
15. Benedict, *Vermont In The Civil War,* vol. 2, 669.
16. Benedict, *Vermont In The Civil War,* vol. 1, 561.
17. Stackpole, *Sheridan In The Shenandoah,* 340.
18. *Peck's Adjutant General's Report,* Revised, 735-736.
19. *America's Medal Of Honor Recipients,* 924.
20. *Report of The Vermont Adjutant & Inspector General of the State of Vermont, 1864–65,* 31.
21. Benedict, *Vermont In The Civil War,* vol. 2, 384.
22. Stackpole, *Sheridan In The Shenandoah,* 407.

CHAPTER XVIII

1. *Anti-Rebel, The Civil War Letters Of Wilbur Fisk,* 285-86.
2. Trudeau, *Bloody Roads South,* 310.
3. Benedict, *Vermont In The Civil War,* vol. 1, 563.
4. *Anti-Rebel, The Civil War Letters Of Wilbur Fisk,* 288.
5. Ibid., 291-292.
6. Benedict, *Vermont In The Civil War,* vol. 1, 570.

CHAPTER XIX

1. Hyde, *Following The Greek Cross,* 240.
2. Benedict, *Vermont In The Civil War,* vol. 1, 572.
3. Ibid., 576-577.
4. Ibid., 578.
5. *Report of the Adjutant & Inspector General of the State of Vermont, 1864-65,* 34.
6. Grant, L. A., *The Old Vermont Brigade At Petersburg* (Minnesota: St. Paul Book and Stationery Co., Vermont Historical Society, 1887),18.
7. *Battles And Leaders Of The Civil War,* vol. 4, 752-753.
8. *America's Medal Of Honor Recipients,* 780.
9. Ibid., 891.
10. Ibid., 784-785.
11. Ibid., 907.
12. Ibid., 794.
13. *Peck's Adjutant General's Report,* Revised, vol. 1, 736.
14. *America's Medal Of Honor Recipients,* 757.
15. *Anti-Rebel, The Civil War Letters Of Wilbur Fisk,* 322.
16. *Report of the Adjutant & Inspector General of the State of Vermont, 1864–65,* 40.
17. Naisawald, *Grape And Canister,* 532-533.
18. *Report of the Adjutant & Inspector General of the State of Vermont, 1864–65,* 41.
19. Hoar, J. S., *New England's Last Civil War Veterans* (Arlington, Texas: Seacliff Press, 1976), 144-147.
20. Boatner, *Civil War Dictionary,* 869-870.
21. Benedict, *Vermont In The Civil War,* vol. 1, 581-582.
22. Ibid., 600.
23. Ibid., 599-600.

24. *Peck's Adjutant General's Report,* Revised, 124.
25. *Report of the Adjutant & Inspector General of the State of Vermont, 1864-65,* 42.
26. Mark, Penrose G., *History of the 93rd Regiment Pennsylvania Veteran Volunteers* (Butternut & Blue, Reprint, 1993), 338.
27. Benedict, *Vermont In The Civil War,* vol. 1, 614.
28. Ibid.
29. Fox, *Regimental Losses In The Civil War,* 116.

BIBLIOGRAPHY

Abbot, John C. *The History Of The Civil War In America.* Springfield, Mass.: Gurdon Bill, Publisher, 1866.

Allan, A. M., LL.D. *The Army Of Northern Virginia In 1862.* Dayton, Ohio: Press Of Morningside Bookshop, 1984.

Benedict, G. G. *Vermont In The Civil War.* vols. 1 & 2, Burlington, Vt.: The Free Press Association, 1886.

Beyer, W. F. and O. F. Keydel. *Deeds Of Valor.* Stamford, Conn.: Republished, Longmeadow Press, 1993.

Boatner, Mark M. III. *The Civil War Dictionary.* Revised edition, 1988. New York: David McKay Company, Inc., 1959.

Catton, Bruce. *Civil War.* Three Volumes In One. New York: The Fairfax Press, 1984.

———. *Grant Takes Command.* Boston, Toronto: Little Brown and Company, 1968.

Coffin, Charles C. *Four Years Of Fighting.* Boston: Arno & *New York Times,* 1866, Reprint 1970.

Crute, Joseph H.,Jr. *Units Of The Confederate States Army.* Midlothian, Va., Derwent Books, 1987.

Dowdey, Clifford. *Lee's Last Campaign.* Wilmington, N.C.: Broadfoot Publishing Company, 1988.

———. *The Seven Days.* Wilmington, N.C. Broadfoot Publishing Company, 1988.

Glover, Waldo F. *Abraham Lincoln and The Sleeping Sentinel of Vermont.* Vermont: Vermont Historical Society, 1936.

201

Hoar, Jay S. *New England's Last Civil War Veterans.* Arlington, Tex.: Seacliff Press, 1976.

Hunt, Roger D. and Jack R. Brown. *Brevet Brigadier Generals In Blue.* Gaithersburg, Md.: Olde Soldiers Books, Inc., 1990.

Hyde, Thomas W. *Following The Greek Cross.* Boston and New York: Houghton and Mifflin & Company, The Riverside Press, 1894.

Krick, Robert K. *Lee's Colonels.* 3rd revised edition. Dayton, Ohio: Morningside, 1991.

Lewis, Thomas A. *Guns Of Cedar Creek.* New York: Bantam Doubleday Dell Publishing Group, Inc., 1988.

Livermore, Thomas L. *Numbers And Losses In The Civil War In America, 1861–65.* Dayton, Ohio: Morningside, 1986.

Longstreet, James. *From Manassas To Appomattox.* New Jersey: Blue and Gray Press, no date.

Matter, William D. *If It Takes All Summer.* Chapel Hill, N.C.: The University of North Carolina Press, 1988.

Mcartney, Clarence E. *Grant And His Generals.* New York: The McBride Company, 1953.

Rosenblatt, Emil. *Anti-Rebel: The Civil War Letters Of Wilbur Fisk.* New York: Croton-On-Hudson, 1983.

Russell, Charles N., ed. *Gray Ghost, Memoirs Of Col. John S. Mosby.* New York, London: Bantam Books, 1992.

Schaff, Morris. *The Battle Of The Wilderness.* Boston and New York: Houghton Mifflin Company, 1910. (No Editor), *Personal Memoirs of U. S. Grant.* Vol. 1 & 2, New York: The Century Company, 1903.

Scott, Robert G. *Into The Wilderness with the Army Of The Potomac.* Bloomington, Ind.: Indiana University Press, 1957.

Sears, Stephen N. *Landscape Turned Red: The Battle Of Antietam.* New York: Warner Books, 1983.

Schiller, Herbert M., ed. *Autobiography Of Major General William F. Smith, 1861–1864.* Dayton, Ohio: 1990.

Stackpole, Edward J. *Sheridan In The Shenandoah.* Harrisburg, Pa.: The Stackpole Company, no date.

Steere, Edward. *The Wilderness Campaign.* Mechanicsburg, Pa.: Stackpole Books, 1988.

Stevens, George T. *Three Years In The Sixth Corps.* Albany, N.Y.: S. R. Gray Publisher, 1866.

Swinton, William. *Campaigns Of The Army Of The Potomac.* New Jersey: The Blue & Grey Press, 1988.

Trudeau, Noah A. *Bloody Roads South.* New York: Fawsett Columbine, 1989.

———. *The Last Citadel.* Boston, Toronto, London: Little Brown and Company, no date.

Tucker, Glenn. *Hancock The Superb.* Dayton, Ohio: 1990.

Walker, Aldace F. *Vermont Brigade In The Shenandoah Valley*. Burlington, Vt.: The Free Press Association, 1869.

Warner, Ezra J. *Generals In Blue*. Baton Rouge, La.: Louisiana State University Press, 1964.

————. *Generals In Gray*. Baton Rouge, La.: Louisiana State University Press, 1959.

Wert, Jeffry D. *From Winchester to Cedar Creek*. Carlisle, Pa.: South Mountain Press, Inc., 1987.

Winslow, Richard E. III. *General John Sedgwick*. Novato, Calif.: Presido Press, 1982.

OFFICIAL RECORDS AND UNIT HISTORIES

America's Medal Of Honor Recipients. (no author or editor noted) Golden Valley, Minn.: Highland Publishers, 1980.

Baquet, Camille. *History Of The First New Jersey Volunteers, From 1861 to 1865*. Trenton, N.J.: State of New Jersey, 1910.

Barker, Harold R. *History Of The Rhode Island Combat Units in The Civil War*. Edited by Alfred H. Gurney, 1964.

Caldwell, J. F. J. *The History Of a Brigade Of South Carolinians*. Dayton, Ohio: Morningside Press, 1984.

Casler, John O. *Four Years In The Stonewall Brigade*. Dayton, Ohio: Morningside Bookshop, 1982.

Child, William, M.D. *A History of The Fifth New Hampshire Regiment in the Civil War, 1861–1865*. Bristol, N.H.: R. W. Musgrove (Printer), 1893.

Collier, Capt. Calvin L. *"They'll Do To Tie To", The Story Of The Third Regiment, Arkansas Infantry, C.S.A.* Jacksonville, Ark.: Eagle Press, 1959.

Curtis, Newton, M. *From Bull Run To Chancellorsville: The Story of the Sixteenth New York*. New York and London: G. P. Putnam's Sons, The Knickerbocker Press, 1906.

Dickert, D., Augustus. *History Of Kershaw's Brigade*. Dayton, Ohio: Morningside Bookshop, 1988.

Evans, Gen. Clement A., ed. *Confederate Military History*. Vols. III, IV, XI. Secaucus, NJ: Blue and Gray Press, no date noted.

Flemming, Francis P. *Memoir of Capt. C. Seton Fleming*. Jacksonville, Fl.: Times-Union Publishing House, 1881.

Fox, William P. *Regimental Losses In The American Civil War*. Dayton, Ohio: Morningside Bookshop, 1985.

Grant, L. A. Bvt. Maj. Gen. *The Old Vermont Brigade At Petersburg*. (Paper written and read at a mtg.) Vermont Historical Society, St. Paul Book And Stationary Co., 1887.

Hemenway, Abby. *Vermont Historical Gazeteer*. Vol. 3, no date.

Higginson, Thomas W. *Massachusetts In The Army And Navy, During The War Of 1861-65.* Boston: Wright & Potter Printing Co., State Printers, 1896.

Imholte, John Q. *The First Volunteers, History of First Minnesota Volunteer Regiment, 1861-1865.* Minn. MI: Ross & Haines, Inc., 1963.

Johnson, Robert U. and Clarence C. Buel, Editors. *Battles And Leaders Of The Civil War.* Vols. 1–4. New York: Castle, 1887.

Krick, Robert E. L. *40th Virginia Infantry.* 1st Edition. Lynchburg, Va: H. E. Howard Inc., 1985.

Mark, Penrose G., Capt. Co. D. *A History of the 93rd Pennsylvania, Vet. Vols.* Harrisburg, Pa.: Aughinbaugh Press, 1911; Reprint, Baltimore, Md.: Butternut and Blue, 1993.

Mills, George H. *History Of The 16th North Carolina Regiment.* Rutherfordton, N.C.: Edmonston Publishing, Inc., no date.

Naisawald, L. VanLoan. *Grape And Canister.* New York: Oxford University Press, 1960.

Newell, Capt. Joseph K. *"Ours". Annals of 10th Regiment, Massachusetts Volunteers, In The Rebellion.* Springfield, Mass.: C. A. Nichols & Co., 1875.

Official Records of the Union And Confederate Armies. Vol. XXXIX, Washington: Government Printing Office, 1883.

Peck. *Peck's Adjutant General's Report,* Revised, *Names And Locations Of Graves of Vermont Soldiers Buried in National Cemeteries.* Montpelier, Vt.:, Press Of The Watchman Publishing Co., Publishers and Printers, 1892.

Powell, William H. *The Fifth Army Corps* (The Army Of The Potomac). Dayton, Ohio: Morningside Bookshop, 1984.

Report Of The Adjutant & Inspector General Of the State Of Vermont, From Oct. 1, 1864 to Oct. 1, 1865. Montpelier, Vt.: Walton's Steam Printing, Est. 1865.

Report Of The Maine Commissioners. *Maine At Gettysburg.* Portland Maine: Lakeside Press, 1898.

Rhodes, Robert H. *All For The Union, A History Of The 2nd Rhode Island Infantry.* Lincoln, R. I.: Andrew Mowbray Incorporated, no date.

Robertson, James I. *4th Virginia Infantry.* 1st Edition. Lynchburg, Va.: H. E. Howard Inc., 1982.

Scrymesir, James A. (Capt. on Gen. Smith's Staff). Article, *The Rally Of The Vermont Brigade.* Vermont Historical Society, no date.

Siegal, Alan A. *For The Glory Of The Union: Myth, Reality, and the Media, in Civil War, 26th New Jersey.* New Jersey, Canada, England: Associated University Press, 1939.

Smith, John D. *The History Of The Nineteenth Regiment of Maine Volunteer Infantry, 1862–1865.* Minneapolis, Minn.: The Great Western Printing Company, 1909.

U.S. War Department. *The War of The Rebellion, A Compilation Of The Official Records of the Union And Confederate Armies.* Series I, Part I, vols. XI, XLIII; Series I, 3 parts, vol. XXXVI. Washington: Government Printing Office, 1884.

Walker, Francis A. *History Of The Second Army Corps.* New York: Charles Scribner's Sons, 1887.

Wellman, Manly W. *Rebel Boast.* New York: Henry Holt and Company, no date.

WORKS CITED

Official Records:
    War of the Rebellion, vol. XI, series I.
Official Records:
    War of the Rebellion, vol. XXXVI, parts 1, 2, 3.
Official Records:
    War of the Rebellion, vol. XLIII, series I, part I.
Adjutant General's Report. State of Vermont '64-65
America's Medal of Honor Recipients .... Highland Publishers
Anti-Rebel, Letters of Wilbur Fisk .... Emil Rosenblatt
Civil War Dictionary .... Boatner
Deeds Of Valor .... W. F. Beyer & O. F. Keydel
Following The Greek Cross .... T. Hyde
Battles And Leaders Of The Civil War .... Castle
Four Years Of Fighting .... Coffin
The Battle Of The Wilderness .... Morris Schaff
From Winchester To Cedar Creek .... Jeffry D. Wert
General John Sedgwick .... R. E. Winslow
Personal Memoirs of U. S. Grant .... U. S. Grant, vols.1, 2
Generals In Blue .... Warner
Generals In Gray .... Warner
If It Takes All Summer .... W. D. Matter
Into The Wilderness With The Army Of The Potomac ...... R. G. Scott
Lee's Last Campaign .... C. Dowdey
Massachusetts In The Army And The Navy, 1861–65 ..... T. W. Higginson
New England's Last Civil War Veterans .... J. S. Hoar
Numbers And Losses .... T. L. Livermore
Regimental Losses In The Civil War .... William L. Fox
Vermont Brigade In The Shenandoah Valley .... A. F. Walker
Three Years In The Sixth Corps .... Stevens
Units Of The Confederate States Army .... Crute
Vermont In The Civil War, Vols. 1, 2 .... G. G. Benedict
The Last Citadel .... Noah A. Trudeau
Bloody Roads South .... Noah A. Trudeau

Guns Of Cedar Creek	Thomas A. Lewis
The Seven Days	C. Dowdey
Sheridan In The Shenandoah	E. J. Stackpole
Confederate Military History, 3 vols.:	
Virginia, North Carolina, Florida	C. A. Evans
Army Of The Potomac	William Swinton
Army Of Northern Virginia	William Alan
Lee's Colonels	Robert K. Krick
History Of The Civil War, Publ. 1866	John C. Abbott

UNIT HISTORIES—NORTH

All For The Union 2nd Rhode Island Infantry	R. H. Rhodes
Annals Of The 10th Massachusetts Volunteers	J. K. Newell
For The Glory Of The Union 26th New Jersey	A. A. Siegal
Grape And Canister	L.VanLoan Naisawald
History Of The 5th New Hampshire Volunteers	W. Child, M.D.
History Of The 1st New Jersey Brigade	C. Baquet
History Of The 2nd Army Corps	F. A. Walker
History Of The 19th Maine	J. D. Smith
From Bull Run To Chancellorsville, 16th N.Y.	N. M. Curtis
History Of The 1st Minnesota	J. Q. Imholte

INDEX